About the Aut.

A former Sheffield steel worker and trade union convenor, Mick Drewry graduated from Sheffield Hallam University in 1997. He worked as a volunteer and then paid worker for a local community group before moving to Barnsley Council as a Community Development Worker in 2002. He took early retirement in 2010. *Insurrection* is his fourth publication and third as author.

Also by the author:

The Complete Hillsborough By Her People (Ed), 2006

Inundation – The History, The Times And The People Of The Great Sheffield Flood Of 1864, 2014

Intimidation – The History, The Times And The People Of The Sheffield Outrages, 2017

For Carwyn and Lemuel

Mick Drewry

INSURRECTION
THE HISTORY, THE TIMES AND THE PEOPLE OF THE SHEFFIELD RIOTS AND RISINGS OF THE 18TH AND 19TH CENTURIES

AUSTIN MACAULEY PUBLISHERS™
LONDON · CAMBRIDGE · NEW YORK · SHARJAH

A CIP catalogue record for this title is available from the British Library.

ISBN 9781398453685 (Paperback)
ISBN 9781398453692 (ePub e-book)

www.austinmacauley.com

First Published 2022
Austin Macauley Publishers Ltd®
1 Canada Square
Canary Wharf
London
E14 5AA

Acknowledgements

My most grateful thanks to the following people who have helped me in various ways and means to produce this book:

Claire Anderson, of The Salvation Army, for her contributions to the chapter on the Salvation Army Riot and for providing the photograph of early Sheffield Salvationists.

Ron Clayton, friend and fellow Sheffield historian, for snippets of information that add detail to the narrative; many small pieces of the jigsaw that completes the big picture.

Kathryn Hewson, my daughter and proof-reader.

Chris Hobbs, for permission to use sources provided on his excellent website on Sheffield history and for providing supplementary contemporary press cuttings.

Steven Kay, fellow Sheffield author, for reprinting John Wilson's original work on the lyrics to Joseph Mather's songs (a book every Sheffielder should read) and his blessing for my use and reproduction of relevant songs.

Malcolm Nunn, friend and archivist at Bradfield Parish Council, for providing the picture of Birley meadows overlooking Wardsend Cemetery and photograph of the Watch-House at Bradfield.

Sarah Jane Palmer, artist, for her kind permission to reproduce her caricature of Joseph Mather.

David Templeman, for providing the map of the Sheffield race course.

Joan Unwin at the Company of Cutlers in Hallamshire, for permission to use portraits from the galleries of the Cutlers' Hall.

Table Of Contents

Preface

I touched on the riots that had taken place in Sheffield during the 18th and early to mid-19th centuries in my last book, on the Sheffield Outrages. My research then gave me the idea of the subject for this, my third book, and the inspiration for a title that would complete a trilogy of *Ins*: *Inundation*, on the Great Sheffield Flood; *Intimidation*, on the Sheffield Outrages; and now, *Insurrection*, on the Sheffield Riots and Risings.

To consider the Sheffield riots as being insurrectionary may be a little strong. They may have been violent uprisings but for the most part, with the exception of the Pentrich and Chartist uprisings, they were not against constituted authority but in protest of the conditions that the constituted authority was allowing to prevail, yet inevitably those who took part in the Sheffield riots would find themselves up against the full force of that authority. On the other hand, the Irish Riot was specifically against the Sheffield Borough Police.

Whilst perhaps not as significant or as important a part of Sheffield's history as the Flood or the Outrages in terms of consequence, social transformation and heritage, the singular incidents of riot and civil unrest in Sheffield collectively presents a picture of reaction to life in Sheffield for the lower classes that was unequal, unjust or downright unfair.

It is a picture that highlights social depravation, inequality, corruption and all too often an abuse of power that was unacceptable in the eyes of the people at the time and could only be addressed by the one means at their disposal known to effect change: to take to the streets, to protest and to riot. Like the Flood and the Outrages, the civic authorities would rather forget occurrences of social unrest and consign them to the margins of history and the depths of the archives.

Certainly, they are not deemed appropriate for civic celebration or commemoration by those who govern us today. But they must not be forgotten and once more, I am motivated to write so as to remind people how things used to be and that the democratic rights, social standards and the freedom that we enjoy today were hard won by people who came before us, many paying the ultimate price.

I have a personal association with Wardsend Cemetery, the subject of one of the riots that I cover. As a young lad living on Bradfield Road, Owlerton, in the late 1950s and early 1960s, the cemetery was something of a playground, not that gravestones and monuments were ideal recreational surroundings.

My playmates and I, would briefly marvel at some of the monuments but our attention was mainly focused on the plentiful supply of blackberries and the passing steam locomotives belching smoke and steam as we stood above them on one of the two bridges that then spanned the railway line; there is now just one.

The area above the 1901 extension of the cemetery was the best grass-slide around and gangs of us would make our way there in the summer months, clutching the obligatory pieces of cardboard cadged from the local shopkeepers, on which we would sit and race down the hillside that overlooked the cooling towers and chimney stacks of the Neepsend power station.

We spent many days playing on the 'medders' (Birley Meadows), as they were known, but we made sure we went home before it got dark. Then, around forty years later, between 1998 and 2002, I worked for the Hillsborough Community Development Trust, first as a volunteer, later as a paid worker, then manager of the organisation.

During this time, the Trust held a ten-year lease for Wardsend Cemetery and it was one of its prime projects. The cemetery had been neglected since the Church abandoned it and was terribly overgrown. Despite a number of determined attempts using volunteers and at one time, a team of workers from a training agency, the Trust was never able to get on top of nature's invasions.

During my time with the Trust, a sub-group was established to take the project forward: the Friends of Wardsend Cemetery Group.[1] Sadly, the Hillsborough Community Development Trust has since dissolved but the Wardsend Cemetery Group has gone from strength to strength and has made great strides in making the cemetery accessible. This has enabled people to view the wealth of history written in stone with organised walks and talks to hear the stories, myths and legends associated with Wardsend Cemetery. The power of invention in the minds of my young playmates would have never conceived what had actually happened there in 1862.

---

[1] www.wardsendcemetery.wordpress.com

As for the other riots and the insurrectionary plots that I have covered in this book, I had heard of some but knew very little about them, others I was totally unaware of until coming across them whilst researching *Inundation* and *Intimidation*; I have also uncarthed more stories of riot during my research for this book which I consider worthy of inclusion.

I have no doubt other local historians and genealogists have also encountered them in their research but I hope to have covered even the most notable of them in more detail than ever before, and that in bringing them together in one volume, they will make a fascinating read for anyone interested in Sheffield and its history.

I have also uncovered and included some interesting bits of information about Sheffield and its people during these times, including some notable characters. I have included an extensive bibliography of the books, reports, directories, etc., from which I have drawn the information to construct each chapter. As with my previous books, I have also included a good number of references to help the reader to expand their interest beyond the central narrative and to take their own journey through what is a fascinating period of Sheffield's history.

A BIT OF OLD SHEFFIELD.

Robert Hubbard's confectionery shop, 37 Pinstone Street, at its junction with Norfolk Street c1879.

Introduction

I have described much of the life and times of Sheffield people through much of the 19th century in my previous books which, covering the Sheffield Flood and the Sheffield Outrages, give a fair idea of the grim existence for the ranks of the working class during that period of the town's history.

Indeed, the prevailing social conditions in poor housing, lack of sanitation, adulterated food, poor health and little health-care, hazardous working practises and conditions, and the polluted environment that existed in the 19th century affected all, even the very wealthy at times, such as with the cholera epidemic of 1832.

As the subject of this book takes us back to the first half of the 18th century, I have focussed on the history, the times, the people and the development of Sheffield predominantly through the 18th century and into the early 19th century; the period when most of the notable riots occurred.

The transformation of Britain brought about by the Industrial Revolution produced diverse fortunes across the land with the greatest impact on the emerging industrial cities and towns, particularly in the north. New technology brought greater wealth and power for the industrial capitalists but increased the misery and deprivation of the poor and the lower working class.

There were also mixed blessings for the relatively well-paid skilled workers. The boost to the economy brought more jobs but whatever influence the workers had on production in many industries was gradually eroded as mechanised industry, driven by the steam engine, gave even greater political power to the industrial capitalists, who maximised their profits by keeping wages down.

This transformation had the biggest impact on the great industrial centres and the ports from where the increasing diversity and quantity of manufactured goods were exported and where raw materials were imported, and of course, for the dispossessed and displaced rural labourers who were required to move into the towns and cities to make a basic living.

Sheffield, in the early 18th century, was partially insulated from this increasing pace of change by its isolated geographical location and somewhat protected from much of the impact felt elsewhere by the specialisation of its staple industries; predominately, the cutlery and metal trades, and the almost unique culture of the Sheffield workers.

Whereas great factories were replacing cottage industries in Lancashire and the rest of the West Riding, the modus operandi of the Sheffield artisans in their small workshops and smithies remained relatively unchanged throughout the 18th century and well into the 19th century.

Despite this somewhat unique situation, Sheffield still saw an unprecedented transformation in its size and its appearance through these times, engendered by the increase in national trade, the division of labour in the production of its goods, inward migration and its very own inventions.

Sheffield, through the 18th and 19th centuries, is a fascinating journey that begins with a small, haphazard township and ends with a world-renowned industrial town soon to become one of the country's major cities. However, the one aspect of life in Sheffield that is consistent throughout the period is the prevalence of poverty and deprivation, especially in times of economic depression.

The history of the Sheffield riots brings to light some interesting characters: some good guys, some bad guys, some whose skills, talents and knowledge were brought to the fore and impacted upon the economic development of the town, and others whose literary talents blossomed through the turbulent times that they lived including one of Sheffield's notabilities, James Montgomery, who suffered persecution at the hands of a reactionary state.

The title of this book is a little tongue in cheek as, of all the riots covered, just three could be considered as actually being against the constituted authorities. Such were the Enclosure riots of 1791; the activities of the Sheffield plotters allied with the Pentrich Rising of 1817, whose scheme was thwarted before it got off the ground; and the Chartist uprising of 1840.

The Irish Riot of 1855 was certainly an attack on agents of the State, the police, and for one rookie watchman, a fatal one. There were numerous other riots and disturbances in Sheffield throughout the 18th and 19th centuries but their objectives were not to overthrow the government, nor were they against the State *per se*. The objective of most of the riots was purely to bring about change to address the suffering of the people, especially in times of real hardship, when even many of those in work could not earn enough to live on.

They were not planned or organised but were spontaneous reactions to the prevailing social and economic conditions. However, the government, which was made up of the aristocracy, the gentry and land-owners and with no representation from the lower classes, was indifferent to these conditions. This indifference, and often contempt, did engender hostility towards the powerful and the wealthy.

The Food Riots occurred at times of food shortages and when the price of provisions rose to levels that the poor could not afford. Similarly, the prohibitive price of coal, a commodity essential to keep warm in winter and to fire the smithies all year round, was at times, another reason for stirring the wrath of the townsfolk, particularly as the coal-owners continued to amass ever-greater wealth. In conjunction with what was already an austere and miserable existence for the poor and the lower working classes, such exacerbations understandably led to discontent and to protest.

Mindful of the revolutions across Europe that had occurred during the late 18th and early 19th centuries, the government was determined to outflank any such moves in Britain and was prepared for seditious rising despite the likelihood of a repetition of such revolutionary uprisings in Britain being remote.

Military barracks were built in the perceived radical areas, which included Sheffield, and spies and *agent provocateurs* were sent out to infiltrate the potential rebels. Nonetheless, whilst defence of the realm against revolt was paramount within government circles, there were also moves to reform the political system which was undeniably corrupt and undemocratic, exemplified by the numerous Enclosure Acts; the Enclosure Act in respect of Sheffield was the catalyst for riot in 1791, for which one young protester was sentenced to death and hanged.

The Reform Act of 1832 gave Sheffield its first members of parliament but despite this seemingly progressive move towards democracy, the first parliamentary election in the town resulted in riot and the deaths of five of its townsfolk at the hands of the military. Ironically, whilst the military was frequently called out to put down a riot, it was soldiers who, inadvertently, triggered one of the most infamous riots in the annals of Sheffield's history that resulted in the deaths of another two of its townsmen: the Norfolk Street Riot of 1795.

Personal disputes can sometimes escalate to public disorder, often minor scuffles in the street that neighbours get embroiled in, but few reach the pages of the press or attract the interest of historians. Yet the dispute between a humble silversmith and a succession of challengers beginning with a dubious local surgeon and culminating in the Earl Fitzwilliam over a land inheritance claim took my interest. As a result, I felt that the Oldale riots at Millhouses were worthy of inclusion in this compilation.

Religious intolerance and suspicion of any new religion has been the source of many a conflict across the world since God was invented and Sheffield had its fair share of public disturbances in this vein. The first such occurrence during the 18th century was due to the introduction of Methodism in the 1740s when converts were persecuted and newly-provided Methodist chapels were destroyed by the mob.

Later in the 19th century, the arrival of the Salvationists and opposition towards the Mormons also created a stir and further riots ensued. Moral sensitivities also played a part in two of the other riots that occurred in 19th century Sheffield following rumours of body-snatching to supply the medical school which enraged the townsfolk.

They responded by attacking the medical school and the homes of those considered responsible. The thought of resurrection men trading in the bodies of their deceased loved ones to supply the dissection table resulted in mob violence in 1835 and again in 1862.

Whilst the predisposition of the Sheffield people to riot during the period covered is evident from the following narrative, such events do not substantiate the notion of Sheffield being the hotbed of radicalism that was perceived by the governments of the day. Nevertheless, the State was prepared to suppress any potential move towards political revolution.

Such preparedness, and the over-zealousness of the local magistrates, only served to make matters worse. What the authorities failed to recognise, were the root causes of the riots: hunger, inequality and injustice. Sheffield in the 18th and 19th centuries had its fair share of all of these and its people responded in their customary way; to take to the streets in protest and to riot.

In addition to the narrative and standard conclusion, I also offer the reader a polemic by way of an epilogue, where I draw some parallels with the period in question and Britain of today.

The Riot Act

'Our Sovereign Lord the King chargeth and commandeth all persons being assembled immediately to disperse themselves, and peaceably to depart to their habitations or to their lawful business, upon the pains contained in the Act made in the first year of King George for preventing tumultuous and riotous assemblies.
God Save the King.'

Becoming law on 20 July 1715, the Riot Act was introduced in the face of widespread rioting after the accession of King George I. Under the Act, any unlawful assembly of twelve or more persons must disperse within one hour of the above proclamation being read out by a magistrate. Any persons present after the adjudged time are guilty of a capital felony and may be dispersed by use of force.

The magistrate would call upon the military to enforce the dispersal and the commanding officer could, and often did, order his soldiers to fire upon those that remained. The Riot Act was repealed in 1967. The legal definition of a riot is an act of collective violence by three or more people in pursuit of a common purpose.

East Prospect of Sheffield print published in 1745. Frontispiece of Bradbury, Frederick, *A History of Old Sheffield Plate*, Macmillan and Co. Limited, 1912

Eighteenth and Nineteenth Century Sheffield

'In 1750, Sheffield was a rookery of squalid houses at the foot of a wild moorland.'[2]

'Sheffield: noisy, smoky, loathsome but surrounded on all sides by some of the most enchanting countryside to be found on this planet.'[3]

The most striking feature of 18th century Sheffield, is the physical development of the town from the century's beginning, with a pre-industrial economy, to its end, when the Industrial Revolution had brought unprecedented social and economic changes.

At the start of the century, Sheffield's feudal past is easily recognised with the layout of its streets and houses that still traced the ancient footpaths. Sheffield Castle had been demolished in 1648 following the Civil War, perhaps within living memory for a few locals.

Houses, almost half (45%) with a smithy attached,[4] and shops were dotted about with no form of symmetry to the layout of the town as there had been little regulation of buildings. The town was small, consisting of just twenty-nine streets in 1700,[5] although another source states thirty-five streets, lanes and passages.[6] This may have been deduced from the first map of Sheffield produced by Ralph Gosling in 1736.

---

[2] Fletcher, J.S., *The Making of Modern Yorkshire 1750-1914,* George Allen & Unwin Ltd, 1917, p.9
[3] Description of Sheffield in the 1870s, Hobsbawm, Eric, *The Age Of Capital 1848-1875,* Weidenfeld & Nicolson, 1995, p.210
[4] Hey, David, *A History of Sheffield,* Carnegie Publishing, 1998, p.60
[5] Baines, Edward, *History, Directory & Gazetteer of the County of York,* published by Edward Baines at the Leeds Mercury Office, 1822, p.296
[6] Vickers, J Edward, *A Popular History of Sheffield*, Applebaum, 1987, p.39

Sheffield c1760

Streets in Sheffield in 1700

Balmgreen	Irish cross
Broad lane	Mill sands
Bull stake	Newhall Street
Campo lane	Pinfold Lane
Castlefold	Ratten row
Castlegreen	Red croft
Castlegreen head	Scrag hill croft
Castle hill	Snig hill
Church lane	The Isle
Fargate	The Underwater
Fig tree lane	Townhead street
Hartshead	Waingate
High street	West bar
Hollin lane or Blind lane	West bar green

Many of these thoroughfares had open sewers running down their middle, which also served as household refuse dumps. These were infrequently washed clear, about four times a year, and flushed into the River Dun (Don) using water from Barker's Pool at Balm Green, a reservoir fed by natural springs dating back to 1434.

During the 17th century, it was used on occasions for the ducking of turbulent women on the *cuck stoole*.[7] By the late 18th century, Barker's Pool was a walled water enclosure built by Robert Rollinson measuring 36 yards by 20 yards, although it was not a true right-angled quadrilateral as the eastern end was slightly wider than the other (see map below).[8]

Towards the end of the century, it became unfit to drink and was used purely to flush the gutters and put out fires. James Wills (1774-1827), a Sheffield tailor and poet, described it in a verse in its final days:

> *'The Barker's Pool, noted for nuisance indeed,*
> *Green over with venom, where insects did breed,*
> *And forming a square, with large gates to the wall,*
> *Where the Rev. Charles Wesley to sinners did call.'[9]*

It was removed in February 1793 and houses were built on the site, the first by Mrs Hannah Potter, which was a public house called *Well Run Dimple*, alluding to a horse that had distinguished itself at the Crookes Moor races and may have landed Hannah Potter a decent winning bet.[10]

Samuel Roberts (1763-1848)[11] gives us a contemporary account of the cleansing of the gutters:

> *"All the channels were then in the middle of the streets, which were generally in a very disorderly state, manure heaps often lying in them for a week together. About once every quarter the water was let out of Barker Pool, to run into all those streets into which it could be turned, for the purpose of cleansing them. The bellman gave notice of the exact time, and the favoured streets were all bustle, with a row of men, women,*

---

[7] Leader, Robert Eadon, *Sheffield in the Eighteenth Century*, The Sheffield Independent Press, 1901, p.156

[8] Ibid, p.154

[9] Ibid, p.156

[10] *The Local Register and Chronological Account of Occurrences and Facts Connected with the Town and Neighbourhood of Sheffield,* Robert Leader at the Office of the Sheffield Independent, 1830 (Continued to 1857), hereafter referenced as *Sheffield Local Register,* pp.71-72, also Leader, Robert Eadon (Ed), *Reminiscences of Old Sheffield, its Streets and its People*, Leader and Sons Independent Office, 1876, p.262

[11] Samuel Roberts followed in his father's (also Samuel) footsteps making his wealth from the silver trade, also becoming a Town Trustee, magistrate and alderman for the Brightside ward.

and children on each side of the channel, anxiously and joyfully awaiting, with mops, brooms, and pails, the arrival of the cleansing flood, whose first appearance was announced by a long, continuous shout. All below was anxious expectation; all above, a most amusing scene of bustling animation. Some people were throwing the water up against their houses and windows; some raking the garbage into the kennel; some washing their pigs; some sweeping the pavement; youngsters throwing water on their companions, or pushing them into the wide-spread torrent. Meanwhile a constant, Babel-like uproar, mixed with the barking of dogs and the grunting of pigs, was heard both above and below, till the waters, after about half an hour, had become exhausted."[12]

Flushing the streets with water from Barker's Pool.[13]

Early governance of Sheffield was undertaken by the Court of the Lords of the Manor. In 1297, the people of the town were given some control of affairs by a charter granted by Thomas Lord Furnival and the town Burgesses came into existence. By a charter of Queen Mary in 1554, The Twelve Capital Burgesses

[12] Op Cit Leader, Robert Eadon, pp.156-157
[13] Sheffield Local Studies Library: Picture Sheffield s13279

and Commonality, also known as the Church Burgesses, became a Corporation with a Common Seal.[14]

During the 17th century, the twelve Burgesses became thirteen and formed into a body of Trustees, later becoming the Town Trustees.[15] Whilst purporting to be a representative body of the people of Sheffield the Town Trustees were in essence a board of select and wealthy elite, predominantly land-owners, aristocrats and country gentlemen, driven by self-interest and who were not elected by the people but appointed from amongst their own social circle, and they often generated discontent.

Little changed into the 19th century, as in 1825, an anonymous pamphlet was published and sold in all of the town's book shops for 6d. The author of this pamphlet, calling himself 'A Commissioner', with the subtitle *Secresy* [sic] *in Public Trusts is always either the Parent or Offspring of Mismanagement, if not Peculation,* attacked the methods of the proceedings of local government:

> *The government of this town appears to me to be in the hands of some six to eight respectable families, united by marriages, inter-marriages, and intimate connections, into what may be called a Family Compact, or, perhaps, a Holy Alliance, always able, by their united efforts, to overturn or overbear all measures or individuals opposed to the interests of any member of this self-incorporated body. They are likewise able to carry any measure which they are determined to promote. The ramifications of their influence penetrates every avenue of the town, and can secure the co-operation, when required, of all whom they employ, from the opulent banker, to the most despised and oppressed of the human race, the wretched substitute for a sweeping-machine.[16]*

That the price of this leaflet being 6d suggests that it wasn't primarily aimed at the working class but to bring, what the author thought, were corrupt practices, including the alleged embezzlement of the Trust's money, to the notice of the middle and upper classes, from which the Trustees were drawn, including, by now, the industrial capitalists whose new-found wealth gained them acceptance

---

[14] Hall, T Walter, *A Catalogue of the Ancient Charters,* J W Northend, 1913, p.106
[15] Op Cit Vickers, p.93
[16] Stokes, John, *The History of the Cholera Epidemic of 1832 in Sheffield,* J W Northend Ltd, 1921, p.207

into the realms of government. Throughout the ages, power, corruption and greed have been ready companions.

In 1843, Sheffield was incorporated as a municipal borough with nine wards and governed by a Town Council consisting of a Mayor (the first Mayor of Sheffield was William Jeffcock), 14 aldermen and 42 councillors.[17]

At the beginning of the 18th century, the Town Trustees found it necessary to employ someone, known as a *Scavenger*, to sweep Lady's Bridge, Truelove's Gutter (now Castle Street) and the pavements at the Church gates.[18] The annual salary was 13s-4d but there were other expenses for buying a *muck drag* and *cow-rake* and for *leading away* the rubbish.

In 1769, some colliers were employed to clean Truelove's Gutter and were paid £1-11s-6d.[19] In 1775, James Turton was paid £2-10s to clean the streets of the town but the service was probably limited to the busiest thoroughfares. In April 1795, the Trustees agreed a contract with Robert Taylor to keep the streets of Sheffield clean for one year for which they paid him £80; he was also allowed to keep the manure, which would be plentiful at this time and was a saleable commodity.[20]

By this time, more thought had been given to the job and in 1801, John Hall was paid 8s for devising a cask for the scavengers to water the streets.[21] By 1805, Robert Taylor was also employed to sweep the market on Sunday mornings for 19s-4d.[22] In 1810, Taylor was still cleaning the Sheffield streets but he was now being paid £105. The contract stipulated that he must find his own horse and cart and all necessary tools and implements, but he could still keep the manure.[23]

[17] Drewry, Mick, *Intimidation—The History, The Times And The People Of The Sheffield Outrages,* Austin Macauley Publishers, 2017, p.19

[18] Op Cit Leader, Robert Eadon p.159

[19] Ibid

[20] Leader, John Daniel, *Records of the Burgery of Sheffield*, Sheffield Independent Press Limited, 1897, p.406

[21] Op Cit Leader, Robert Eadon, p.159

[22] Op Cit Leader John Daniel, p.403

[23] Ibid, p.422

Samuel Roberts[24]

There was no street lighting until 1734, when a process of gradually providing oil lamps in appropriate places was introduced. But these were initially few and far between and only lit in the winter months. The Town Trustees paid a Mr Parkin £3-15s-11d for their lighting.[25] In 1747, a job was created to light, clean and take care of the lights at a salary of £4 per year.

By 1778, the annual cost of upkeep for the street lights was £72-5s. In 1809, there were 599 street lights in the town being looked after by Thomas Milner at 11s-4d per lamp, which included the cost for any repairs or replacements.[26]

---

[24] Bradbury, Frederick, *A History of Old Sheffield Plate,* Macmillan and Co Limited, 1912, p.39
[25] Op Cit *Sheffield Local Register,* p.38
[26] Op Cit Leader, Robert Eadon, p.160

Samuel Roberts described the street lighting as *few dirty, dull, oil lamps, far apart, and just within sight of one another, often not lighted or blown out, and supplemented at times by a farthing candle stuck in a shop window, served to make darkness more dark.*[27]

The oil lamps were phased out and replaced by gas lights from 1818 when the Sheffield Gas Company was formed. Gas lighting was introduced in 1798 and first used to light Manchester cotton mills.[28] Electric street lights first appeared in Sheffield in 1882.[29]

Water for domestic use was sourced from wells and natural springs. The first mention of supplying piped water to the town can be traced to 1697 when Peter Whalley, a Nottingham engineer, obtained a lease for a rood[30] of land near Lady's Bridge on the banks of the River Dun between Lady's Bridge and Cawton's weir and a piece of waste land near Barker's Pool for this very purpose.[31]

Peter Whalley died in 1707 and the leases transferred to Messrs. Chapel, Lee, Drake, Terrie and Waterhouse.[32] An engine-house was built to pump water from the River Dun to a reservoir near Barker's Pool but nothing further is known of this scheme other than it was abandoned not long after Whalley's death although another engine or pump was constructed on the Don to feed water to the town by the Derbyshire engineer George Sorocold (1666-1738) in 1727.[33]

The first reservoir for piping water into the town wasn't built until 1712, when work started on a dam near White House at Upperthorpe, financed by John Goodwin, a Bawtry wharfinger, and Robert Littlewood, a Thrybergh millwright.[34]

The White House dam was followed by an intricate system of five dams at Crookes Moor in 1737, then a larger dam completed in February 1785. From this reservoir, water was run through 4½ inch pipes to what was known as a working-

---

[27] Ibid, p.150

[28] Hobsbawm, Eric, *The Age Of Revolution 1789-1848,* Weidenfeld & Nicolson, 1995, p.298

[29] Gretton, R.H., *A Modern History of the English People 1880-1898,* Grant Richards Ltd., 1913, p.95

[30] Rood: measure of land equal to a quarter of an acre

[31] Op Cit *Sheffield Local Register,* p.29

[32] Ibid, p.32

[33] Baines, Thomas, *Yorkshire Past and Present, Vol. 1, Part 2,* William Mackenzie, 1870, p.604. George Sorocold was considered the first 'civil' engineer.

[34] Walton, Mary, *Sheffield—Its Story and its Achievements*, The Sheffield Telegraph & Star Limited, 1948, p.99

dam in Portobello, then to a stone cistern in Division Street, from where it was distributed around the town via more pipes.[35]

The Crookes Moor dams were superseded by the Redmires dams between 1836 and 1854 built by the Sheffield Waterworks Company, which was established in 1830. Between 1830 and 1860, the Sheffield Waterworks Company increased the number of Sheffield houses supplied with water from 12,000 to 36,000.

In 1853, the company successfully obtained an Act of Parliament to allow it to build three further reservoirs to the north of Sheffield at the source of the River Loxley at Bradfield: the Agden, Dale Dyke and Strines reservoirs. The embankment of the Dale Dyke reservoir collapsed on its completion resulting in the Great Sheffield Flood of 1864.[36]

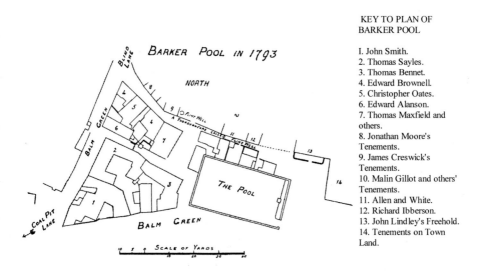

KEY TO PLAN OF
BARKER POOL

1. John Smith.
2. Thomas Sayles.
3. Thomas Bennet.
4. Edward Brownell.
5. Christopher Oates.
6. Edward Alanson.
7. Thomas Maxfield and others.
8. Jonathan Moore's Tenements.
9. James Creswick's Tenements.
10. Malin Gillot and others' Tenements.
11. Allen and White.
12. Richard Ibberson.
13. John Lindley's Freehold.
14. Tenements on Town Land.

From Leader, Robert Eadon, *Sheffield in the Eighteenth Century*, The Sheffield Independent Press, 1901, p.153

The 18th century was the key period for the development of water-powered industry on Sheffield's five rivers and by 1794 all available riparian sites had

---

[35] Hunter, Joseph, *Hallamshire—The History and topography of the Parish of Sheffield,* Lackington, Hughes, Harding, Mavor and Jones, 1819, p.126
[36] For the full story of the Great Sheffield Flood see Drewry, Mick, *Inundation—The History, the Times and the People of the Great Sheffield Flood of 1864,* Youbooks.co.uk, 2014

been developed, on some, particularly on the River Dun, multiple mills had been built.[37]

In 1758 there were a number of carpet manufacturers, more than one hundred looms weaving hair seating and a lead works got underway on the River Porter.[38] Initially, Sheffield's water-powered mills were of diverse use and included corn mills, snuff mills, paper mills, cotton mills, and silk mills.

However, the increase in industrial development through the 18th century brought an overabundance of cutlery grinding wheels, forges, steel-making and rolling mills. As early as the mid-18th century, the town had become known as *Old Smoky Sheffield* with its buildings tainted by the volume of industrial smoke.

Technological advances in steam-power and machinery, later in the century, further expanded the metal trades. David Hey tells us that Bailey, Proctor & Turner, who manufactured optical lenses at the foot of Park Hill, were probably the first Sheffield manufacturers to install a steam engine in 1786 on the River Sheaf.[39] By 1794, over 300 steam-driven grinding troughs were operating in the town.[40]

With the expansion of industry came an increase in the population of Sheffield. In 1700, there were about 6,000 people living in Sheffield, 5,000 in the township and a further 1,000 or so living in the extended parish.[41] By 1801, the population of Sheffield had multiplied seven and a half-fold to 46,336.[42] Stark as this was, the growth in the population of Sheffield in the 18th century was to be dwarfed by that to take place in the 19th century.

By 1851, the population of Sheffield had increased to 135,000 and by 1871 to 240,000; a staggering forty-fold increase on the population of 1700.[43] This compares with a four-fold increase in the population of Great Britain over the same period, 6.5 million in 1700, rising to over 26 million in 1871.[44]

There was a huge increase in trade towards the end of the 18th century and into the 19th century with many new trades being introduced to the town to

[37] Crossley, David (Ed) with Cass, Jean; Flavell, Neville; and Turner, Colin, *Water Power on the Sheffield Rivers,* Sheffield Trades Historical Society and University of Sheffield, Division of Continuing Education joint publication, 1989, p.viii
[38] Op Cit Baines, p.287
[39] Op Cit Hey, p.115
[40] Ibid
[41] Op Cit Walton, p.95
[42] Op Cit Drewry, *Intimidation*, p19
[43] Ibid, p.21
[44] Hill, C P, *British Economic and Social History 1700-1975,* Edward Arnold, 1981, p.2

compliment the traditional cutlery trades, yet surprisingly, some remained static, such as anvil making (4 traders in 1779 and still only 4 in 1828) and bellow making (2 traders in 1779 and 2 in 1828).[45]

In 1750, the first direct trade from Sheffield with continental Europe was claimed by the Quaker merchant and later banker, Joseph Broadbent, and Benjamin Roebuck, also a merchant who turned to banking and who opened the first bank in the town in 1770.[46] In the following year, the River Don was made navigable from Sheffield to Tinsley which opened up other markets and facilitated an increase in the exporting of goods through the port of Hull.

Roads in and out of Sheffield were poor before the first Turnpike roads were built in the 1750s. Ten major Turnpike roads were built between 1759 and 1821.[47] In 1751, Joshua Wright of Mansfield started the first stagecoach out of Sheffield and in 1760 Samuel Glenville[48] at the Angel Inn began the first Sheffield to London stagecoach.[49] The journey from Sheffield to London took three days.

The next big leap in transport technology would be the coming of the railway in 1838, when the Sheffield to Rotherham line opened on 31 October.[50] The Sheffield to Manchester railway opened in December 1845 with the completion of the first Woodhead Tunnel that had taken six years to build at a cost of £200,000[51] and the lives of 32 navvies[52] opening up more markets and a much faster link to Manchester and the port of Liverpool.

---

[45] Op Cit *Sheffield Local Register,* see table, p.xxvi
[46] Op Cit Leader, Robert Eadon, p.89. The bank failed in 1780. Mary Walton dates this event to 1747 and suggests that the Kenyon family also established agencies abroad. Op Cit Walton, p.125
[47] Op Cit Walton, p.129
[48] Samuel Glenville was born in Exeter in 1720 and came to Sheffield as a soldier in a recruiting party in 1741. He met and married a local girl before taking over the Angel Inn. Op Cit Walton, p.130
[49] Op Cit Baines, p.287
[50] Op Cit *Sheffield Local Register,* p.315
[51] Ibid, p.415. A second tunnel was completed in 1852 running parallel with the first. A third, larger bore running on a slightly different course, was completed in 1954. The line was closed in 1981 and the tunnels are now owned by the National Grid, the later tunnel being used as a conduit for power cables.
[52] Coleman, Terry, *The Railway Navvies,* Penguin Books, 1976, p.124. In a later article in a *Railway World Special* magazine on the Woodhead line in 1986, Josephine Rhodes reports that a further death occurred at the tunnel before its completion, subsequent to this official figure, making the total loss of life 33. She also tells us that just one of these deaths was from natural causes. Twenty-nine people died during the construction of the second tunnel, built between 1847 and 1852, including two nurses, as cholera swept

There were three inventions of note by Sheffield men during the 18th century: the art of silver-plating devised by Thomas Boulsover in 1743; the making of cast-steel by the former Doncaster clock-maker Benjamin Huntsman in 1751; and Britannia Metal, composed of tin, antimony and lead, invented by James Vickers around 1769; all three helped to bring more trade to the town.

The introduction of silver-plating helped to increase the manufacture of silver and plated goods and following an Act of Parliament, on 20 September 1773, the Sheffield Assay Office was opened. Thus, rendering it unnecessary for each item to be sent to London to be assay marked.

Thomas Boulsover[53]

through the navvies' camps. Six died during the construction of the third tunnel between 1949 and 1953.
[53] Op Cit Bradbury, p.24

Understandably, such an increase in population along with the technological advances made during this period, engendered many changes to the way people lived but what changed very little were the living standards of the lower classes whose incomes were kept at subsistence levels to allow greater profits for the rich.

The gulf between the poor and the wealthy, which was less marked at the beginning of the century, widened as the new industrial capitalists, with the exception of a small number of philanthropists, took advantage of the new technologies in the latter decades to increase their wealth and with it, their power.

Robert Leader informs us that, *no instances can be found, until after 1750, of large individual prosperity derived from the town of Sheffield by those engaged in the staple trades of the place* and *in the middle of the eighteenth century £100 a year was considered a handsome income, qualifying its possessor for the first rank among his fellows; and £500 was a fortune that justified retiring from business.*[54]

Such dizzy heights of wealth at this time were only achieved by the owners of large-scale forges and foundries that grew towards the end of the century and into the 19th century; and of course, the landowners whose income predominantly and traditionally came from rents. It was noted of Sheffield in *The New Yorkshire Gazetteer* of 1828 that there were, *few of the manufacturers possessing those great accumulations which would now be thought to constitute a large fortune.*[55]

Nationally, the extremes of poverty and wealth in the 19th century can be discerned from contemporary novels such as *Sybil* by the future prime minister, Benjamin Disraeli, in 1845 in which the Chartist delegate character Stephen Morley described Britain as being two nations:

between whom there is no intercourse and no sympathy; who are as ignorant of each other's habits, thoughts, and feelings, as if they were dwellers of different zones, or inhabitants of different planets; who are formed by different breeding, are fed by a different food, are ordered by different manners, and are not governed by the same laws.[56]

He was describing the rich and the poor, which, from a working-class perspective, engendered the *Them* and *Us* scenario that continues to this day.

---

[54] Op Cit Leader, Robert Eadon, p.6
[55] Clarke, Stephen Reynolds, *The New Yorkshire Gazetteer or Topographical Dictionary,* Henry Teesdale & Co, 1828, p.227
[56] Disraeli, Benjamin, *Sybil, or The Two Nations,* Wordsworth Editions Limited, 1995, p.58

Elizabeth Gaskell's *Mary Barton* (1848) also gives a compelling interpretation of the social inequalities of early Victorian Britain. Much can be learnt about prevailing social standards from contemporary literature and from contemporary art.

Sheffield from Crookes Moor by William Ibbitt

Early photograph of the Crookes Moor Dams

There is little doubt that there was much poverty in 18th century Sheffield, as there had been in the 17th century. A survey undertaken on 2 January 1615, found that out of a population of 2,207, 725 were not able to live without the charity of others—the begging poor—and 160 householders were not in a position to relieve others and were close to begging themselves.[57] Poverty grew with the increasing population throughout the 18th century.

The levels of dire poverty and destitution can be measured to some extent by the number of people who found themselves in the workhouse, which was opened in 1733 under the governorship of William Lotas,[58] and the burden upon the ratepayers in providing for their relief under the Poor Relief Act of 1601.[59]

In 1721, 1,320 ratepayers paid £70-9s-1d in poor rates; a little over 1s per head. By the end of the century, the workhouse expenditure was £10,000, which was supplemented by voluntary contributions through organised subscriptions (see chapter on Food Riots). Throughout the 18th century, the number of people registered at the Sheffield workhouse ranged from 24 in 1736 up to 169 in 1788 (see table below).

The fluctuations in the annual figures reflect the state of the local economy at the time and we also have to take into account the growing population as the century progressed. Throughout the 18th century, trade fluctuated for many reasons, not least the Anglo-French wars (1740-8, 1756-63 and 1776-83) that brought embargoes and other forms of commercial warfare, and also in the latter years, the American War of Independence (1775-83).

And from 1793 and into the 19th century, further wars with France greatly impacted on food prices and levels of employment and taxation.[60] Wheat and other agricultural imports from Poland and East Prussia were brought to a halt due to war with France.[61] In 1800, after the loss of successive European markets, Sheffield found itself with no foreign trade at all.[62]

The years 1793 to 1802 were designated *The Years of Endurance* by historian Arthur Bryant. Continued conflict with France in the Napoleonic Wars, which

---

[57] Smith, William (Ed), *Old Yorkshire—Vol. 5*, Longmans, Green & Co, 1884, p.28

[58] Op Cit *Sheffield Local Register*, p.37 On a 1780 map the workhouse is indicated at where West Bar joins West Bar Green. In 1829 an old cotton mill on Kelham Street was bought and adapted to replace the West Bar workhouse. For the story of the Sheffield workhouse see Drinkall, Margaret, *Sheffield Workhouse*, The History Press, 2011

[59] Under the 1601 Act each parish was made responsible for its own poor and paid for by a parish tax. The Act was reformed by a Royal Commission in 1834 and a new Poor Law was introduced which abolished relief for able-bodied paupers, known as 'outdoor' relief, which was replaced by workhouses run by unions of parishes.

[60] Redford, Arthur, *The Economic History of England 1760-1860*, Longmans, 1960, pp.88-105

[61] Court, W.H.B., *A Concise Economic History of Britain—From 1750 To Recent Times*, Cambridge At The University Press, 1958, p.21

[62] Op Cit Walton, p.148

ended at Waterloo in June 1815, further extended Britain's economic problems and the years of endurance were in effect decades of endurance.

On 21 November 1806, for example, Napoleon Bonaparte issued a decree that commerce and correspondence with England, whether carried by French or neutral ships, was forbidden under pain of death in all lands controlled by France. Further, that all English ships and those of her colonies, and their cargoes, would be forfeited.[63] Within two years, English exports to Northern Europe fell in value from £10m to £2m.[64]

Tory Prime Minister, William Pitt, introduced a direct tax on people's income on 3 December 1798: Income Tax was paid on all annual earnings of £60 or more with a top rate of 2s in the pound (10%) on annual earnings of more than £200.[65] Income Tax was introduced not so much to fund Britain's war with France and save the country but as to free Europe from the tyranny of Revolutionary France.[66]

Resorting to the workhouse was the worst possible fate of the Sheffield poor as it was deliberately run in a manner to deter all but the utterly desperate and invariably those close to starvation; life in the workhouse was horrendous. All who entered the workhouse, excepting those who were too ill, had to work, women and children mainly sewing, men stone-breaking or oakum-picking.[67]

Life was regulated, discipline was strict and punishment was savagely cruel. On 12 January 1746, two overseers, John Abbey and John Spooner, were informed that two women had been found to have stolen material to sell to a local pub landlady. Anne Pitt and Hannah Clayton had taken a sheet of linen and three pieces of blue Linsey-woolsey[68] to Mary Woodhouse at the White Horse in Gregory Row.

For this misdemeanour, they were put in the *black hole*, obviously some dark and wretched cell for the confinement of those who transgressed the regulations. The workhouse accounts show that on the following week, 19 January, Anne Pitt and Hannah Clayton were whipped for their crime.

---

[63] Bryant, Arthur, *Years of Victory 1802-1812,* The Reprint Society, 1945, p.231
[64] Ibid, p.245
[65] Bryant, Arthur, *The Years of Endurance 1793-1802,* The Reprint Society, 1944, p.292
[66] Ibid, p.297
[67] Oakum: loose fibre obtained by untwisting old rope, used especially for the caulking of wooden ships
[68] Linsey-woolsey: a strong, course fabric with a linen or cotton warp and a woollen weft

Available Figures for the Number of People Registered at the Sheffield Workhouse 1736-1799

Year	No.	Year	No.	Year	No.	Year	No.
1736	24	1746	108	1785	134	1794	129
1737	34	1750	65	1786	156	1795	144
1738	35	1752	73	1787	164	1796	143
1739	33	1755	74	1788	169	1797	129
1741	78	1761	111	1789	164	1798	147
1742	72	1781	156	1790	173	1799	114
1743	70	1782	146	1791	134		
						Figures from *Sheffield Local Register*	
1744	60	1783	163	1792	121		
1745	94	1784	145	1793	126		

Despite the technological advances of the late 18th century, the nature of Sheffield's staple industries, although expanding, generally retained their small-scale *modus operandi*. The cutlery and edge tool trades, in particular, consisted of a multitude of small workshops run by individuals; small-scale artisans who became known as the *little mesters*, who would employ either a small number of journeymen and/or apprentices.

Very often, a little mester would work alone from his rented workshop, frequently, no better than a shed and described by Leader as *deplorable hovels*[69], buying his own materials, forging, grinding and polishing knife blades, forks, etc, for other manufacturers or, when work was scarce, speculatively making his own pieces on the chance of finding his own customers.

This changed as the century progressed as many masters became more specialised in one of the processes of production with the adoption of a division of labour, becoming a blade maker, blade grinder or handle maker, but still working from his small workshop. For example, a penknife would pass through the hands of sixteen workers with 144 separate stages in the production of a single penknife.[70]

This change in the production of cutlery is further illustrated by employment in the manufacture of scissors. In 1797, there were 56 scissor makers recorded in Sheffield who would undertake all of the work involved in their manufacture. In 1830, there were 887 workers employed in the production of scissors made up

---

[69] Op Cit Leader, Robert Eadon, p.3
[70] *Robson's Birmingham and Sheffield Directory,* 1839

of 158 scissor forgers; 205 scissor filers; 132 scissor dressers; 252 scissor grinders; and 140 scissor finishers.[71]

These changes in Sheffield contrasted with the industrial development of the nearby West Yorkshire woollen industry and the Lancashire cotton industry where capital and commerce-controlled production and ultimately, methods of production, which increased in scale, resulting in huge mills being built, employing more women and children than they did men, thus ending the traditional cottage industries.

In 1741, Britain exported £20,000 worth of cotton goods. By 1790, the value of cotton exports had grown to £1,662,369.[72] The last handloom workers disappeared in the 1850s.[73] The Sheffield artisan was spared the demoralising misery and wage-slavery of the huge mills and factories of West Yorkshire and Lancashire.

The division of labour in production of cutlery also impacted upon the health of many a master and worker, in particular, for those who specialised in grinding. In the early 18th century, grinding was one job in a series of processes that produced a finished item. The table knife maker, for example, would first of all source and purchase his materials, then forge the blanks that formed the blades.

He would then grind them, glaze and polish them, then make and fit the handles, giving them a final inspection to ensure the finished quality that was expected. Once the order was complete he would wrap them and take them to his customer and complete the sale. Consequently, the table knife maker spent only a small portion of his working time undertaking the grinding process.

When a man took up a trade solely in grinding, especially dry-grinding, he was exposed to the dust and, bent over his wheel, he was at risk to serious injury or death should a wheel break, for all of his long working day. Over time, as we especially find in the 19th century, if he survives the dangers of potential accidents at the wheel, the grinder becomes disfigured by his working posture and succumbs to what became known as *grinders' asthma* and meets an early grave.[74]

The prevalence of this disease accelerated with the introduction of steam power and by 1842, 50% of all Sheffield razor grinders in their thirties, 79 % in

---

[71] Op Cit *Sheffield Local Register,* p.xxxix
[72] Op Cit Bryant, *Years of Endurance,* p.22
[73] Op Cit Hobsbawm, *The Age Of Capital,* p.209
[74] Op Cit Drewry, *Intimidation,* pp.36-7

their forties and all razor grinders over the age of 50 were suffering from this condition.[75] Accidents at work were also commonplace in the factories where workers, especially children, were exposed to unguarded machinery.

In 1854, Henry Morley, a London journalist who contributed to Charles Dickens's *Household Words,* reported that nearly twelve thousand accidents had occurred in British factories over the previous three years, many resulting in horrific injuries. This included more than one hundred deaths and his article, entitled *Ground in the Mill,* contained a number of graphic details where limbs were torn from the bodies of children caught by the revolving shafts and gearings of the mills at which they worked.

The gruesome catalogue of deaths and injuries over the three years illustrate the hazards of early mechanised industry: 106 deaths; 142 lost hands or arms; 1,287 fingers; 1,340 broken bones; 549 damaged heads; 8,282 miscellaneous injuries.[76] Many of these accidents occurred late in the long working day when workers were tired and prone to be careless, especially the children. It is worth noting that these statistics were for a period that followed the introduction of a number of Factory Acts.

The lack of concern for health and safety at work extended into the social and domestic domains as the prevailing sanitary conditions and living standards were harbingers for poor health and disease. Neither the Town Trustees of the 18th century, nor the later Town Council in the 19th century, made any serious effort of improving the town's sanitary conditions.

In 1860, the Town Council resolved that *it is not expedient at the present time to consider the most efficient means of improving the sanitary conditions of the Borough.* It was not until 1884 that a comprehensive sewage system was considered by the Council to be an obligation.[77] Health care was almost exclusively the preserve of the wealthy and whenever there was an outbreak of disease it was the lower classes that bore the burden, but not always.

The Cholera epidemic of 1832 affected the whole social spectrum, claiming the lives of 402 Sheffield people of all classes, including John Blake, the Master Cutler. Such conditions were a factor in the short life expectancy for Sheffield

---

[75] Op Cit Hobsbawm, *The Age Of Revolution,* p.206
[76] Harvie, Christopher, Martin, Graham and Scharf, Aaron (Eds), *Industrialisation & Culture 1830-1914,* The Open University Press, 1970, pp.52-5
[77] Briggs, Asa, *Victorian Cities,* Penguin Books, 1975, p.237

people with the average age at death of just 24 years in 1843; another huge factor in this figure was the high level of infant mortality rates.[78]

During the 18th century the national life expectancy rates were pretty equal across the spectrum of social class but by the 1850s the 'folks on the hill' could expect to live 15 years longer than the townsfolk living in the slums and squalor of the courtyards in the industrial suburbs.[79]

Despite this poor life expectancy, the Sheffield area recorded five centenarians during the 18th century and seven more in the early 19th century:[80]

Sheffield Centenarians between 1708 and 1843

1708	William Hunt	102
1739	Mary Bradberry[81]	105
1751	Willam Congreve	111
1770	Ann Hatfield (Tinsley)	105
1795	Aaron Rodgers	101
1809	Mrs Humphries (Elmsall)	103
1817	Ann Carnall	100
1818	Ann Andrews	100
1819	Phoebe Watkinson	107
1821	George Wainwright	107
1830	Thomas Clitheroe	101
1843	Mrs Gray	109

We have no indication of the social status of these people but we may assume that few, if any, were from the necessitous poor or the lower working classes.

Whether a master or a worker, life in 18th century Sheffield was bleak, but the worst existence experienced by those in work was that suffered by the poor young apprentices. Until 1791, apprentices were indentured to their masters and would live with them as one of the family.

---

[78] Op Cit Drewry, *Intimidation*, pp.26-7

[79] Hunt, Tristram, *Building Jerusalem—The Rise and Fall of the Victorian City*, Phoenix, 2005, p.287

[80] Grainge, William, *Yorkshire Longevity*, Thomas Thorpe, 1864. See also White, William, *History, Gazetteer and Directory of the West-Riding of Yorkshire Vol. I*, Robert Leader, Independent Office, Sheffield, 1837, p.8

[81] Recorded as Mary Bradley in *Sheffield Local Register*, p.41

The first step of arranging an apprenticeship was for the lad and his proposed master to get together for a *liking* and if they got on satisfactorily the lad was taken to the Cutlers' Hall where a fee of 2s-6d was paid to the Company of Cutlers in Hallamshire,[82] either by the master or the lad's father, family or friends, and he was then bound to serve his apprenticeship until attaining the age of 21 years.

The master would use his apprentice to do the less-desirable work, sometimes in the place of journeymen so as to cut his costs, and to undertake the most tedious tasks while the master did the skilled work. Up until 1748, when the minimum age was raised to 12 years, boys of 10 or even younger found themselves apprenticed. Relationships could be fraught and disputes between master and apprentice appear to have taken up a fair share of the local magistrates' time.

---

[82] The Company of Cutlers in Hallamshire was formed in 1624 by Act of Incorporation for *'the government of the makers of knives, sickles, shears, scissors and other cutlery wares'*. It consisted of a ruling group of one Master Cutler, two Wardens, six Searchers and twenty-four Assistants. The rest of the company was made up of its members; Sheffield cutlers. The Master Cutler and his cohorts had the lawful right to make laws governing trade and to levy reasonable penalties on those who failed to observe them. The first Cutlers' Hall was built in 1638. It was demolished in 1725 and a new Hall was built on the same site. The second Hall was demolished in 1832 and the present Cutlers' Hall was then built; it was enlarged in 1867.

Old Cutlers' Hall

How much an apprentice was exploited depended upon the nature of his master but a typical 12-14 hour working day for an apprentice was then extended with further chores in the household, like fetching water from the well, especially on a Sunday night as Monday was washing day. Other tasks included tending the chickens or feeding the pigs; fetching coal in for the fire and cleaning out the ashes; and running errands for the *Dame*, the woman of the house who was either the master's wife or his housekeeper, who ruled the household and was the lad's boss at home.

Generally, the master's role at home was simply to administer discipline, which was often brutal.[83] In return, the apprentice was fed and clothed and again, how well was determined by the nature of the master but most were treated appallingly. Typically, he would get a quarter of an oatcake and porridge for breakfast, more often made with water than with milk.

For dinner, there was broth made with fat mutton or beef trimmings. At around four o'clock was what was known as *drinking*[84], for which he had a quarter of an oatcake, which was often stale. Sometimes, the oatcake was mixed with dripping and hot water, and seasoned with salt and pepper. This was known as *brewis* and was a rare treat.[85]

There was more porridge and oatcake for supper. If their food was poor their clothing was worse. Typically, apprentices would be seen in doe-leather or fustian[86] breeches that they continued to wear as they grew older, getting shorter in the leg, tighter round the waist and shinier in appearance from constant wear.

His shirt sleeves would be rolled up often revealing the legs from old stockings on the lower arms. He may wear a flannel waistcoat but stockings on his feet were a luxury and he would wear a pair of old shoes, often passed down from the master, other family member, or even the Dame; his own, best shoes were reserved for Sundays.

He would wear an old hat crown or a cap made of brown paper on his head and a leather apron completed the picture of a cutler's or a smith's apprentice.[87] On Sundays, he looked a little different as James Wills described in verse:

'The church-going clothes of our Hallamshire lads,
Coats twenty years old, and their hair put in pads,
With strong buckskin breeches, and waistcoats of shag—
No wonder they put so much money i' th' bag.
Striped pudding-poke nightcaps, worn all the week long,
With broad buckles at shoes, both easy and strong. [88]

---

[83] Op Cit Leader, Robert Eadon, p.25
[84] Drinking: an old Yorkshire word for an afternoon meal
[85] Op Cit Leader, Robert Eadon, p.20 Described in Addy, Sidney Oldall, *A Glossary of Words used in the Neighbourhood of Sheffield,* Trubner & Co, 1888, p.28: Browis or Brewis—a dish made of scalded oatcake and broth with pepper, salt and butter
[86] Fustian: course cotton or cotton and linen cloth
[87] Op Cit Leader, Robert Eadon, p.22
[88] From a poem by James Wills describing the Sunday best clothes of an 18th century Sheffield apprentice. Wills was a tailor by trade. See Kay, Steven, and Windle, Jack,

With life as such for the apprentice, and with up to nine years to endure, it is not surprising that a good number of them absconded at times, so much so that there was a masters' society set up for the recovery of runaways.[89] The prevalence of runaway apprentices also inspired a local song entitled, *The Sheffield 'Prentice*[90], which told the story of one such unfortunate lad:

I was brought up in Sheffield, but not of an high degree,
My parents doated on me, they had no child but me;
I rolled in such pleasures, just where my fancy led,
Then I was bound apprentice, and all my joys were fled.

I did not like my master, he did not use me well,
I made a resolution not long with him to dwell,
Unknown to my parents from him I ran away,
And steer'd my course to London on an unhappy day.

A wealthy rich young lady from Holland met me there,
And offered me great wages to serve her for a year,
At last, with great persuasion with her I did agree,
To go and live in Holland which proved my destiny.

I had not been in Holland passing half a year,
Before my young mistress grew very fond of me,
"My gold and silver, my houses and my land,
If you'll consent to wed with me shall be at your command."

I said "Dear honoured lady, I cannot wed you now,
For I have lately promised and made a solemn vow
To wed none but Polly, your pretty chambermaid,
Excuse me my dear mistress, she has my heart betray'd."

Seditious Things—The Songs of Joseph Mather—Sheffield's Georgian Punk Poet, 1889books, 2017, p.96
[89] Op Cit Leader, Robert Eadon, p.17
[90] Davison Ingledew, C.J., *The Ballads and Songs of Yorkshire,* Bell and Daldy, 1860, pp.220-1

Then in an angry humour she went from me away,
Resolved within herself to make me dearly pay,
She was so much perplexed she could not be my wife,
She soon contrived a tragedy to take away my life.

One day we were talking in the garden, fine and gay,
A viewing of the flowers that grew so fine and gay,
The gold ring on her finger, as I was passing by,
She slipped into my pocket and for it I must die.

My mistress swore I'd robbed her and quickly I was brought
Before a grave old justice to answer for my fault,
Long time I pleaded innocent but that was all in vain,
She swore point blank against me and I was sent to jail.

Then our royal assizes were drawing on apace,
Presently on me the judge a sentence past,
To the place of execution they brought me to a tree,
And may God forgive my mistress for she has wronged me.

All you who come to see me now, hear before I die,
Don't laugh at my downfall nor smile at my disgrace,
Believe me I'm quite innocent, I bid this world adieu,
Farewell my dearest Polly, I die thro' loving you.

Leader argued, that the apprentice system was *the best ally of the recruiting sergeant* as a good many of the runaway lads took the King's shilling to avoid going back.[91] He goes on to suggest that many a Sheffield lad contributed to the famous naval victories and the battles of the Peninsula Wars after absconding from their master. It is debatable as to which was the worst option.

That Sheffield was a favoured recruiting town, is revealed by a report stating that there were 30 recruiting parties in the town during February 1793.[92] In August that year, war was declared with France.

---

[91] Op Cit Leader, Robert Eadon, p.17
[92] Op Cit *Sheffield Local Register,* p.72

For the ordinary working man and his family, excepting the better-paid, highly-skilled artisans, life wasn't much better than that of the apprentice and much of what little disposable income that they had, and the limited leisure time at their disposal, was predominantly spent in the beer-house.

They were certainly absent from Sheffield's *society* which consisted of the professional class: lawyers, surgeons, apothecaries, clergymen and the gentry (men of independent means) who would come together at assemblies held in rooms at the Boy's Charity School;[93] a clear division of class and culture.

This is not surprising given most of the working class could not read or write (even by the 1840s only between 40% and 50% of the British population were literate[94]). There are a number of references to assemblies and balls in the Burgery accounts but undoubtedly, the working classes were excluded from these.

For those in well-paid regular employment, tradition required their employers to accept that Mondays were likely to be a less productive, often non-productive, day of the six-day working week as those men who had money left over from the weekend would simply take the day off and make up for the shortfall in wages by putting in more work during the rest of the week.

This tradition, known as *Saint Monday*, was prevalent throughout the 18th century and largely practiced in towns like Sheffield and Birmingham, where most work took place in small workshops, often by journeymen, and where it continued into the 1850s.[95]

As inconvenient that this was for the employers, they simply accepted this custom and practice, but the tradition eventually disappeared with the mechanisation of industry, the discipline of the factory system and working to the clock.

Whilst literacy amongst the lower classes of Sheffield's townsfolk of the 18th century was such that only a minority could read or write, oral communication with people from outside the town and its environs was often just as difficult as the written due to the local dialect.

---

[93] The Boy's Charity School was situated at the north-east corner of the Parish Churchyard, founded in 1706 by the vicar, Rev. Drake and instituted in 1710. It was built by subscription and supported by voluntary contributions. Up to 90 boys were clothed, maintained and educated. The school was rebuilt in 1826. A Girl's Charity School was erected on the opposite side of the churchyard in 1786

[94] Op Cit Hobsbawm, *The Age Of Revolution,* p.136

[95] Thompson, F.M.L., *The Rise of Respectable Society—A Social History of Victorian Britain, 1830-1900,* Fontana Press, 1988, p.273

The local gentry, upper- and middle-classes of the town would have been familiar with the broad Sheffield dialect but anyone from wider afield would have had difficulty conversing with the locals. Indeed, people of modern Sheffield, excepting perhaps the local elderly who have lived all their lives in the city, some (like me) who still use some of the old words and terminology, would also have difficulty understanding the vernacular of the 18th and 19th centuries.

It is from this dialect that people of neighbouring townships, such as Barnsley or Rotherham, refer to Sheffielders as *Dee-dahs,* although the term ought to be *Thee-thahs.* Sidney Addy tells of a young lad who moved to Crookes from a village in Mid-Derbyshire and who for months couldn't converse with people due to the stark difference in the dialect from his own.[96]

The following 1870s dialogue is a conversation between two old Sheffield cutlers, entitled *The Apprentice,* comparing the life of an apprentice of the day with their experiences of being apprentices in earlier times:

> **Oud Samma Squarejoint:** O say, Jerra, heah's different toimes for prentis lads nah, thrubbe wot they wor when thee an me wor prentis, isn't ther, oud lad?
>
> **Jerra Flatback:** Hah, they'n better toimes on't nah, booath e heitin and clooas; we'n had menni a mess a nettle porridge an brawis on a Sunda mo'nin, for us brekfast; an it wor nobbut a sup a hot watter tem uppa sum wotcake, we a bit a fat in, at made hear a star, an thear a star: an as for clooas, us coit cloth wor awlis as cooarse as if it had been wovven throo a noin barr'd gate; an us britches made a lether, butten'd rahnd us hips, and raich'd dahn tot cap on us knees: an for all meit wor so cheap, we verra seldom tasted off a Sundiz—yo mut a bowt it at tuppence-hopena a pahnd, an if yo'd twenta pahnd at wonce, they'd a geen ya a sheep heead in. Samma, dusta remember hah menni names we had for a sahwer wotcake?
>
> **Oud Samma Squarejoint:** O kno'nt lad; bur o think we'd foive or six. Let's see: Slammak wer won, and Flat-dick wer anuther; an't tuther wor—a dear, mo memra fails ma—Flannel an Jonta: an-an-an-an—bless me, wot a thing it is tubbe oud, mo memra gers war for ware, bur o kno heah's anuther; o'st think on enah. O, it were Tooa Clate. A, Jerra, heah's menni a thahsand dogs nah days, at's better dun too nor we wor then; an

[96] Op Cit Addy, Sidney, p.xviii

them were t'golden days a Hallamshoir, they sen. An they happen wor, for't mesters. Hofe at prentis lads e them days wor lether'd whoile ther skin wor skoi blue, a clam'd whoile ther booans were bare, a work'd whoile they wor as knock-kneed as oud Nobbletistocks. Thah nivver sees nooa knock-kneed cutlers nah; nou, not sooa; they'n better mesters nah, as they'n better sooat o wark anole. They dooant mezher em we a stick, as oud Natta Hall did. But for all that, we'd none a yer whirligig polishin; nor Tom Dockin scales, with bousters cumin off; nor yer sham stag, nor sham revvits, a sich loik. T'noives wor better made then, Jerra.
Jerra Flatback: Hah, they wor better made; they made t'noives for yuse then, but they mayn en to sell nah.[97]

Whilst we can decipher that there had been some improvements in the life of the Sheffield apprentice during the time since the two old cutlers were apprentices—better fed, better clothed, less beaten and abused, not worked so hard and less deformed by their work.

It is also interesting to note the final comments of Oud Samma Squarejoint and Jerra Flatback concerning the change in quality of the Sheffield knives being made over the same period—inferior polishing (*whirligig polishin*), inferior materials (*Tom Dockin scales, sham stag and sham revvits*), poor finishing (*wit bousters cumin off*) and that they were now being made to sell, not to use: sacrificing quality so as to make more profit; a symptom of an evolving capitalism.

Education of the poor was discouraged in the 18th century so as to maintain their subservience and their low status in the social order, thus keeping them in their place. Attitudes towards the education of the working class changed during the 19th century with the growing number of voluntary schools but with an emphasis on religious instruction, which ironically, were considered a means to engender the preservation of social order by conditioning children to become good law-abiding adults and who would be less inclined to riot.

The first secretary of the committee of Council on Education, James Phillips Kay-Shuttleworth (1804-77), maintained that education was the answer to the threat to social order posed by the protesting mobs, the trades unions and the

---

[97] Ibid, pp.xv-xvi, originally published in Bywater, Abel, *Sheffield Dialect,* 1877. Whilst the characters in this scene are fictitious the piece was written to illustrate reality.

chartists, in that workers would learn to understand the real causes of the conditions they endured.[98]

All of this, of course, only applied to the well-paid workers and was irrelevant to the labourers, other unskilled workers and the poor who didn't attend church, let alone send their children to school for religious instruction. The voluntary schools were more dependent on the working-class parents providing pupils so as to get their government grants rather than parents' dependence on the schools.[99]

Theatre in the early years of the 18th century was provided in the streets by strolling players. The Town Hall was rented out on occasions for public entertainment as in 1724 when a company of comedians paid the Town Trustees a 30s fee for its use.[100] The earliest mention of an enclosed theatre is in 1761 from a handbill advertising a concert on Whit, Monday, 11 May, at *the Theatre in the Angel Yard.*

The concert was for the benefit of Mr Hartley of Old Church Yard. There was a ball following the concert for which admission was 2s in the pit and 1s in the gallery. Songs and instrumental music were to be heard and a violinist, a Mr Shaw, was specially brought in from York.[101]

The first purpose-built theatre in Sheffield was built in 1763, back-to-back with the Assembly Rooms on Norfolk Street, with its frontage on Tudor Place. It had a capacity of 800 spectators and described as being *large and commodious* but it was taken down and rebuilt on a larger scale in 1773 and named the *Theatre Royal.*[102]

Admission prices were 3s for the boxes, 2s for the pit and 1s in the gallery. It was from the gallery that the likes of file-cutter Joseph Mather (1737-1804) and tailor John Blackwell interrupted the performances with barbed compositions of their own, much to the chagrin of the Establishment. John Blackwell, alias *Jacky Blacker*, became known as the *King of the Gallery* (see chapter on Food Riots).

Joseph Mather, who worked for file maker Nicholas Jackson of Shemeld Croft, regularly performed in the public houses, at fairs, at the races and in the

---

[98] Op Cit Thompson, F.M.L., pp.144-145
[99] Ibid, p.148
[100] Op Cit *Sheffield Local Register,* p.36
[101] Op Cit Leader, Robert Eadon, p.134
[102] Ibid, p.135

streets riding a donkey or a bull backwards, facing the tail of the beast as he sang his satirical lyrics and sold his song sheets to the crowds.

This self-imposed humiliation not only emphasised the satire but helped to engrain his message on the conscience of the local community. Mary Walton tells us that Mather's influence on the Sheffield 'commonalty' was immense. His funeral in June 1804 was followed by a huge crowd.[103]

Caricature of Joseph Mather by Sarah Jane Palmer

The public houses also facilitated the games that many of the working men played, such as providing a skittle alley and space to play knur and spell, quoits and cricket. The earliest cricket match of note to take place in Yorkshire was in Sheffield in 1771 when a Sheffield eleven played a Nottingham side.[104] One of the apprentices' pastimes was to kick about an inflated pig's bladder and by the mid-19th century Sheffield became the home of football with the establishment of the world's first football club, Sheffield FC, in 1857.

---

[103] Op Cit Walton, pp.139-140
[104] Op Cit Fletcher, p.29

One or two taverns had a bowling green but, whatever the sport, the working men preferred it was undertaken whilst drinking and gambling. The consequence of this was a high level of drunkenness in the town, not just from the amount people drunk but also from the strength of some of the brews available.

Ale and beer were consumed in high proportions as it was safer to drink than the water. A gallon of beer per day was not considered an excessive consumption for a working man.[105] Interestingly, Dr Arnold Knight observed in 1834 that amongst the Sheffield grinders, those who spent more time getting drunk lived longer than those who didn't, simply because they spent less time at their grinding wheels.[106] The first public Brewery in Sheffield was built by the side of a well at the junction of Campo Lane and Townhead Street by John Taylor in 1756.[107]

The cutler and the blacksmith would have a tankard of beer at hand as he worked so as to clear the *smitha-slek*[108] from his throat. Even the town's dignitaries conducted much of their business in pubs or had drinks brought into their official meetings as any bit of business had to be *wetted*.

The reputation of Yorkshire Ale reached far and wide and was epitomised by Joseph Mather in his song *Shout 'em Down's Barm*, explaining the reason for its potency in the chorus:

> *'The brewer excuses,*
> *For all the abuses.*
> *That range thro' the country exciting alarm;*
> *'Tis not her resentment,*
> *Witchcraft, nor enchantment,*
> *But working her liquor with Shout-'em-down's barm.*[109]

Other amusements for the working men involved animals and were of a cruel nature: bull-baiting, bear-baiting, cock-fighting, rat-worrying and dog-fighting were common spectator sports, not to mention a large element of gambling on

---

[105] Op Cit Bryant, *Years of Endurance,* p.10

[106] Engels, Friedrich, *The Condition Of The Working Class In England,* Penguin Books, 1987, p.215

[107] Op Cit *Sheffield Local Register,* p.47. Also: Bean, J.P., *The Sheffield Chronicles,* D&D Publications, 2008, p.75

[108] Smitha-sleck or Smithy-sleck: a kind of blister which flies off hot steel or iron when the smith hammers it. Op Cit Addy, Sidney, p.223

[109] Op Cit Kay and Windle, pp.100-3

their outcome. For the well-to-do, there was the hunt where the fox was the unfortunate quarry.

Other pastimes of the day were not only cruel but utterly abhorrent to modern sensitivities. It was common to see cockerels tied to a post and used for target practice simply for amusement purposes.[110] In 1757, the Town Trustees paid 14s-6d to support a cricket match on Shrove Tuesday, *to entertain the populace, and prevent the infamous practice of throwing at cocks.*[111]

Dogs were also treated with much cruelty, especially on Statute or *Stattis* day[112] when it was customary to take to the streets with whips, chasing any unfortunate stray mongrel through the streets and alleys thrashing them for pure amusement, sometimes to death. *Dog-whipping day* is said to have originated in York after a dog swallowed a sacred wafer in the Minster;[113] a practice that continued into the 19th century in Sheffield, long after the demise of the Statute day.

Such cruel pursuits were not exclusive to Sheffield and were practiced throughout the country. Horses, overwhelmingly, the means of personal transport and used for hauling the numerous varieties of cabs, coaches, carts and wagons in the 18th and early 19th Centuries, were mistreated and cruelly abused in the towns, as they often were in rural areas where bull-baiting and bull-running were also popular pastimes and regular features of annual celebrations and traditions.

It was not until 1822 that the first legislation forbidding cruelty to animals was successfully proposed by the Irish MP Richard Martin (1754-1834),[114] preventing the ill-treatment of horses and cattle, against much opposition and personal ridicule in the House of Commons. *Humanity Martin,* as he became known, was a founder of the Royal Society for the Prevention of Cruelty to Animals (RSPCA), which was formed in 1824. Bull-baiting and other similar practices were eventually outlawed in 1835.[115]

---

[110] Op Cit Leader, Robert Eadon, p.45
[111] Op Cit *Sheffield Local Register,* p.47
[112] Statute day: held on the Feast of St. Simon and St. Jude, 18 October, when young country lads and lasses were looked over by farmers at the hiring fair. Statute was pronounced 'stattis'
[113] Op Cit Addy, Sidney, p.63
[114] *The Concise Dictionary of National Biography, Vol. II G-M,* Oxford University Press, pp.1964-5
[115] Woodward, Sir Llewellyn, *The Oxford History of England——The Age of Reform 1815-70,* Oxford University Press, 1962, n. p.470

One other spectator sport enjoyed by the working classes in Sheffield, for much of the 18th century, was horse racing. Although participation and administration was, naturally, the preserve of the wealthy, particularly the landed-gentry, whose subscriptions paid for a grandstand. The course, a rough track one and a third mile long and wide enough to accommodate five horses abreast, was at Crookes Moor and horse racing was first recorded there in 1711.

The last racing took place in 1781 and the grandstand was dismantled in 1790 with the proceeds from the sale of the salvaged material being distributed amongst the original subscribers.[116] A house was built on the site that was given the name *Stand House,* which in 1829 was occupied by merchant William Middleton, who had his office in George Street,[117] and later by Sir Arthur John Hall, the eminent surgeon and consultant.

This too was later demolished and the Hallam Towers Hotel was built on the site in the 1960s. The Hallam Towers Hotel was demolished in 2017 to make way for housing development. The course was eventually lost to the Sheffield Enclosure Act and let for building plots.[118]

From the songs of Joseph Mather we discern the Sheffield races as being a festival enjoyed by all social classes that lasted for three days culminating in the prestigious winning of the 'Plate' on Friday.[119] There is also mention of winning the 'Cup' on Thursday, another celebrated trophy for a winning owner.

Church bells announced the first day's racing and the crowds would make their way to Crookes Moor where they would enjoy the assembled fair, with much drinking, music and revelry, often to excesses that invariably ended in fighting and rioting. Mather's songs on Sheffield Races conjure up a picture of 18th century Sheffield partying at its best:

> *Come ye lads and lasses gay,*
> *Lay aside your toil and labour,*
> *Joy and mirth begin to-day,*
> *Call upon each friend and neighbour;*
> *All as one united be*

---

[116] Op Cit Leader, Robert Eadon, p.45
[117] In 1845, Mrs Sarah Middleton is registered at Stand House, probably Williams' widow, or perhaps daughter. In 1871, Stand House was occupied by Alfred Rowbotham, Gentleman.
[118] Addy, John, *The Agrarian Revolution,* Longmans, 1967, p.62
[119] Op Cit Kay and Windle, pp.49-51

To partake of things diverting,
At the races you will see
Man and horse their powers exerting.[120]

A Lift of the H O R S E S, &c.

Entered to RUN on *CROOKS* MOOR, near *SHEFFIELD*,

On *Wednefday, Thurfday, & Friday the* 28th, 29th, & 30th *of May*, 1777.

Program for the Sheffield Races in 1777.

[120] Ibid, pp.50-1

A List of the HORSES, &c.

Entered to RUN on *CROOKS MOOR*, near *SHEFFIELD*,

On Wednefday, Thurfday & Friday the 28th, 29th & 30th of May, 1777
Wednefday, Fifty Pounds, by Four Year Olds; Colts carrying 8ft 3lb, Fillies 8ft, the beft of three Two mile Heats. Winners of one 50l Plate in the prefent Year to carry 4lb each more.

MARQUIS of Rockingham's Bay Colt, Brufh
Mr Swinfen's Brown Colt, Royal
Mr Vernon's Chefnut Colt, Varano (1 Plate)
Mr Pearfe's Bay Colt, Cacambo
Mr Sidebotham's Chefnut Filly, Mermaid
Mr Steer's Bay Filly, Flycatcher

Thurfday, a Silver Cup, value 70l by any Horfe, Mare or Gelding, that never won 50l at any one Time, Matches excepted. Four Years Old to carry 7ft. Five Years Old 8ft Six Years Old 8ft 10lb, and Aged 9ft 2lb. The beft of three Four Mile Heats.

MARQUIS of Rockingham's Bay Mare, 5 Years old
Howell Lloyd, Efqr's Bay Mare, Coufin Beffy, 5 Years old
Mr Hudfon's Bay Mare, Florella, Aged
Mr Vernon's Bay Colt, Bellimore, 4 Years old
Mr Swinfton's Brown Horfe, Volvus, Aged
Mr Garforth's Bay Mare, Squirrella, 4 Years old
Mr Smith's Chefnut Horfe, Why Not?, 5 Years old

Friday, Fifty Pounds, by Five years Old, Six Years Old, and Aged Horfes, &c. Five-years Old to carry 8ft 5lb, Six-years Old, 9ft and Aged, 9ft 6lb, the beft of three Four Mile Heats. Winners of one 50l Plate in the Prefent Year, to carry 4lb each more.

LORD Thomas Clinton's Horfe, Coronet, 6 Years old
Marquis of Rockingham's Bay Horfe, 5 Years old
Mr Singleton's Roan'd Horfe, Soothfayer, 6 Years old
Mr Robinfon's Bay Mare, Caffandra

To Start precifely at Four o'Clock

The STEWARDS have ordered, that proper Perfons (with Staffs) be appointed
to keep the Courfe clear.

N.B. All Perfons are defired to keep their DOGS at Home; and if any be found upon the Race Ground
it is hoped the Populace will deftroy them.

List of horses for the three main races, including the Silver Cup.
Note the message to dog owners at the bottom (Courtesy Chris Hobbs).

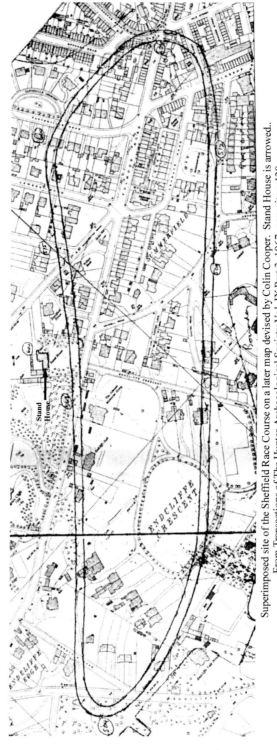

Superimposed site of the Sheffield Race Course on a later map devised by Colin Cooper. Stand House is arrowed.
From Transactions of The Hunter Archaeological Society Vol. IX Part 3, 1967, opposite p.128

Despite the raucous behaviour of Sheffield's workers, there was relatively little serious crime in the town. As Mary Walton relates *Drunkenness was rife; bad manners, disorderly conduct and bullying were common; but real crime was comparatively rare.*[121]

But with high levels of poverty and frequent shortages of provisions, for diverse reasons at various times during the century, high levels of drunkenness and a growing resentment of the injustices of the times, both perceived and real, petty crime and the propensity for protest and to riot is understandable.

Notwithstanding, there were just 13 Sheffield men found guilty of a capital felony during the whole of the 18th century out of a total of 223 people executed at York Castle.[122] Of these, just two were hanged for murder (see table below). This was the age of the *bloody code* when over 200 criminal offences were punishable by death and property was deemed to be more important than people in the eyes of the law.

On 30 March 1775, John Vickers was hanged for assaulting and robbing John Murfin on the night of Saturday 11 February near the Blue Ball public house at Attercliffe, and for assaulting and robbing John Staniforth, to whom he had been apprenticed, on the same night near the Glass House at Attercliffe.

Vickers stole a breast of mutton, ½lb of butter wrapped in a handkerchief, a *bad shilling* and 3½d from John Murfin; and 3s-6d, a sack of horns for knife scales, a leg of mutton, 6lb of sugar and some flax from John Staniforth. John Booth, an alleged accomplice and one of a gang that Vickers associated with, was also tried for the crimes but was acquitted.[123]

The bodies of two of the Sheffield men hanged at York Castle were gibbeted: Bradfield file-smith and murderer Francis Fearn's body was gibbeted on Loxley Common in 1782;[124] Spence Broughton, hanged for robbing a mail-boy between Sheffield and Rotherham, was gibbeted on Attercliffe Common in 1791.[125]

---

[121] Op Cit Walton, p.136

[122] Op Cit Leader, Robert Eadon, p.52 In the 17th century just 2 out of 185 people executed at York Castle were from Sheffield

[123] Knipe, William, *Criminal Chronology of York Castle,* C.L. Burdekin, 1867, pp.88-9 See also Bentley, David, *The Sheffield Hanged 1750-1864,* ALD Design & Print, 2002, pp.44-5

[124] The hanging of Francis Fearn prompted Joseph Mather to write a ballad titled *Frank Fearn* and a further song related to the murder called *Loxley Edge.* He also wrote a ballad on John Stevens and Thomas Lastley: *Stevens and Lastley's Executions.* Op Cit Kay and Windle, pp. 59-60 and pp.62-3

[125] Ibid, pp.111-128, also Bentley, pp.63-72

Date	Name	Crime committed
6 March 1766	Isaac Turner	Burglary
30 March 1775	John Vickers	Assault and Robbery
23 July 1782	Francis Fearn	Murder of watchmaker Nathan Andrews
19 August 1786	William Bamford	Robbery
19 August 1786	William Sharp	Robbery
3 August 1789	John Barker	Burglary
17 April 1790	John Stevens	Highway Robbery
17 April 1790	Thomas Lastley	Highway Robbery
17 April 1790	George Moore	Burglary of a shop in York
6 September 1791	John Bennett	Riot and Arson[126]
12 April 1792	Spence Broughton	Robbing the Mail
9 August 1793	John Hoyland	Bestiality
18 July 1796	James Beaumont	Murder of Sarah Turton

Not all 18th century murderers were simply hanged; there was a particular death awaiting any woman convicted of murdering her husband. In the legal terminology of the day, mariticide was classed as *petty-treason* and the penalty was death by strangulation and burning. There was no such case recorded in Sheffield but the last case in England was at Bury St Edmunds on 15 June 1788.[127]

No Sheffield women were hanged in the 18th century and only one, Mary Thorpe, was hanged in the 19th century, which was for a crime committed in the 18th century. Mary Thorpe was hanged on 17 March 1800 for the murder of her one-week-old illegitimate baby son in November 1799.[128]

There was no police as such in Sheffield during the 18th century. Under the Statute of Winchester of 1285, the whole township was collectively responsible for enforcing the King's peace and for apprehending and punishing any offenders. One or more men would be appointed, in Sheffield's case by the

---

[126] See chapter on Enclosure Riots
[127] Op Cit Smith, pp.98-99
[128] Op Cit Bentley, pp.73-75

Burgers, to be responsible for this collective task and to raise the *hue and cry* in which everyone had to join.

These men gained the title of *constables* and it was they who would bring the offender before the courts. The term *constable* originates from the medieval times and was the title given to the governors of Royal castles. There are many references in the Burgery accounts through the 16th and 17th centuries for payments to the constables for various things and they were clearly responsible for maintaining public order.

They were also responsible for the collection of the Hearth Tax. References to the constables in the accounts disappear in the early 18th century when their responsibility for maintaining public order fell upon the *waits*: the town minstrels and official musicians who, sometime during the 17th century, also adopted the role of town night-watchmen.

Throughout the 18th century, the home-based army, supplemented by the local militia and the yeomanry, was increasingly used to contend with the *riotous mob*. It was not until 1818 that Sheffield was provided with a regular police force by Act of Parliament, which consisted of a police surveyor (later Chief Constable), a deputy, 5 sergeants, 16 day-policemen and 56 night-watchmen.[129]

The first police surveyor was Colonel Francis Fenton. The judicial and administrative authority rested with the magistrates, also known as Justices of the Peace (JPs), whose original functions were formalised by the Justices of the Peace Act of 1361. Prior to 1361, and from the reign of Richard I, these powers were vested in certain knights, who were appointed to keep the King's peace and they became known as Keepers of the Peace.

Like their predecessors the JPs, who were exclusively from the gentry and were unpaid, were appointed by the Crown.[130] By 1822, there were eight Sheffield magistrates but none of them actually lived in the town.[131]

There are numerous references to riots throughout the 18th century recorded in the Burgery accounts. Below are some examples:

---

[129] Op Cit Vickers, p.179
[130] Bunyan, Tony, *The Political Police in Britain,* Julian Friedmann Publishers, 1976, p.59
[131] Op Cit Baines, p.360

1 January 1755—Paid 10 men watching 2 nights on disturbances committed in the town: 1s each and for drink 4s-6d. Paid Simpson, Brownell and Saunders same.

21 August 1755—Paid for horse hire to Justice Wrightsons concerning riot: 7s-6d.

13 June 1757—Paid Mr Battie and James Witham the expenses of obtaining the discharge of the rioters committed to York Castle: £43-14s-6d.

19 May 1758—Paid Joseph Hancock's bill on account of the riot: £1-12s-6d.

28 June 1758—Paid Benjamin Broadbent, the constable, for horse hire and attendance at York Assizes on account of rioters: 11s-6d.

29 June 1758—Paid R Dent his disbursements on account of riot: 9s-6d.

3 May 1799—To Samuel Rabey for loss in potatoes occasioned by riot on Tuesday last: £11-7s-7d (several other payments for same cause and for butter).

7 June 1799—To Thomas Taylor for posting and distributing handbills on account of the riot and an address to His Majesty: 15s-8d

Such references are to be found in the Burgery accounts well into the 19th century, thus indicating that there were frequent occurrences of riot throughout the period. Many were small scale, inconsequential events but they nevertheless, indicate a predisposition for the townsfolk to take to the streets to protest about, and to seek redress of their grievances, and there were many of them.

A number of these mid-18th century riots were against the Methodists and David Price tells us that up until around 1760, when this form of religious expression eventually gained acceptance, a number of Methodists' meeting houses were destroyed by angry mobs[132] (see chapter on anti-Methodist riots below).

As for the general propensity for Sheffield's townsfolk to riot, Ebenezer Elliott, the *Corn Law Rhymer*, put his particular observations of the Sheffield grinder, perhaps, typical of the Sheffield artisan, into verse:

---

[132] Price, David, *Sheffield Troublemakers—Rebels and Radicals in Sheffield History*, Phillimore & Co, 2012, p.6

There draws the grinder his laborious breath;
There, coughing, at his deadly trade he bends.
Born to die young, he fears nor man nor death;
Scorning the future, what he earns he spends;
Debauch and riot are his bosom friends.

The propensity to protest and to riot in Sheffield, and the early establishment of workers' organisations in the town which were perceived a threat to law and order, led to the government and the King to consider Sheffield a hotbed of Radicalism. The first recorded combination of workers or trade union in Sheffield was the Tailors' Society in 1720 followed by numerous others in subsequent years.

The Sheffield Society for Constitutional Reform was founded in December 1791 and one of the first British workmen's clubs was established in Sheffield in 1792. Later, in 1848, between 10,000 and 12,000 Sheffield people took to the streets to celebrate the Paris revolution.[133]

Later still, in 1883, a proposed exhibition on explosives in Sheffield was barred in the public's interest due to the prevailing Anglo-Irish troubles, probably as there was a large Irish community in the town; there had been a number of 'dynamite' incidents in London following convictions for the brutal murder of two members of the cabinet, Thomas Burke and Lord Frederick Cavendish, in Phoenix Park, Dublin.[134]

King George III was heard to call Sheffield *a damned bad place.*[135] Even so, and despite the display of support for the Paris revolution, Sheffield didn't really pose the threat that the monarch and the government had imagined.[136] The eminent Victorian historian, Asa Briggs, tells us that although Radicalism was strong in Sheffield it had little impact on life in the town and that the influence of the working class in local politics was actually slow to establish itself.[137]

---

[133] Op Cit Hobsbawm, *The Age Of Revolution*, p.212
[134] Op Cit Gretton, p.106
[135] Op Cit Price, p.xi
[136] Op Cit Bryant, *Years of Endurance,* p.61
[137] Op Cit Briggs, pp.36-37

Engraving showing the first brick houses built in Sheffield in Pepper Alley c1696.

Coal Riots

Black I am, and much admired,
Men do seek me till they're tired;
When they find me, break my head,
And take me from my resting bed.[138]

1728 and 1774

There was nothing more likely to incite a riot in Sheffield during the 18th century than a perceived unfair increase in the price of provisions. As we shall see later, the price of foodstuffs was the biggest cause of social disturbance but the price of coal, another one of life's essentials for cooking and keeping warm in the winter months, and for firing the smithies from which most people earned a living, was another sensitive issue that could ignite disorder in the town.

Thomas Howard, 8th Duke of Norfolk in his ceremonial robes

At the beginning of the 18th century, most of Britain's coal was obtained through surface mining but there were some shafts driven underground, some over 200 feet deep.[139] The amount of coal hewn from British collieries rose from around 2,500,000 tons in 1700 to 10,000,000 tons in 1800.[140]

By 1850, output had increased to an estimated 56,000,000 tons.[141] Coal was an

---

[138] A Sheffield riddle for coal: Op Cit Addy, Sidney, p. xxvii
[139] Op Cit Hill, p.26
[140] Ibid, pp.25-26
[141] Op Cit Court, p.49

important commodity to trade at home and for export and would become even more important as the fuel that essentially sparked, then drove the huge transformation of Britain via what we now know as the Industrial Revolution; without coal it simply would not have happened, it was the most important source of industrial energy.

Coal, also needed and attracted high levels of capital investment that in turn engendered increasingly high profit as demand and capacity of supply was driven up by the expansion of industry in the late 18th century. Across Britain, the capital invested in coal, and iron, established some of the most important men of their day.[142] As the 18th century progressed into the 19th century, so did the power of industrial capitalists in Parliament.

The collieries were predominantly outside of the towns and cities on sites owned by the wealthy landowners. There is a reference to *coalepyttes* in the Burgery Accounts for 1587, when 2s 7d was paid to the constable, William Shemelde, to bury a man who died there.[143]

Chief amongst the pit owners in and around early 18th century Sheffield, principally, because he was the biggest landowner in the town, was the Duke of Norfolk, whose colliery was at Sheffield Park, for which we find an early reference in 1636.[144]

In 1728, the 8th Duke of Norfolk, Thomas Howard, incited the wrath of the populace by increasing the price of a pack-horse load of coal by a halfpenny to pay for work to improve the road from the colliery to the coal depot in the town. He argued that such an improvement would be beneficial to the people and well worth the increase in the price of coal, despite the Duke monopolising the road by stopping other coal-owners at Handsworth and Gleadless from using it, causing them to take a longer and more costly route.[145]

Similar circumstances prevailed in 1762, when the 9th Duke of Norfolk, Edward Howard, who succeeded Thomas Howard on his death in 1732, prevented the Spencers from transporting coal from their colliery at Attercliffe,

---

[142] Ibid, p.57

[143] Op Cit Leader, John Daniel, p.54

[144] Op Cit Leader, Robert Eadon, p.83 Most aristocratic landowners with coal reserves leased their land for a fixed rent plus a percentage of the profits: see Hammond, J.L. and Hammond, Barbara, *The Town Labourer 1760-1832——The New Civilisation,* Alan Sutton Publishing Limited, 1995, p.9

[145] Op Cit Leader, Robert Eadon, p.84

across his land at Attercliffe Common, again forcing his competitors to take a longer, more costly route to Sheffield.

It would appear that the Duke of Norfolk used his privileged status of Lord of the Manor to disadvantage the competition by bringing a case of trespass against the Spencer's colliery tenants. His counsel declared that:

> *'Spencer's tenants of the said colliery sell a deal of coal into the town of Sheffield, in prejudice of the Duke's colliery in Sheffield Park, and they carry the coals upon horseback, also in wagons and carts over that part of the Common belonging to the Duke, because it is a great deal nearer Sheffield than the common high road is.'*[146]

The cost of transporting coal from the local collieries stymied the development of the Sheffield coal industry in the 18th century, making some pits, such as one at Handsworth, unprofitable.[147] However, those that were profitable had a monopoly in Sheffield up until 1819 when the canal was brought into the town from Tinsley. This reduced the cost of transporting coal from across the wider south Yorkshire coalfield, which developed at a great pace from this time. The Earl Fitzwilliam was quick to take advantage of the new canal and opened up a colliery at Tinsley.[148]

By 1774, Edward Howard had turned his attention to other means of gaining an advantage over the competition presented by the Spencers and the other coal-owners, some of whom were his own tenants. Instead of incommoding the movement of their coal, with the help of his superintendent of works, J B Furness, he commissioned the building of a wooden railway to convey coal on wooden wagons from his colliery to the coal depot in town; a system extensively used at the time in the Newcastle area that can be traced back to the 16th century.

The wooden track, built by Townsend & Furness, was about two miles in length, terminating at the coal depot at the bottom of Park Hill near to where Duke Street and South Street join Broad Street. The use of such a system negated the employment of the carters who had traditionally conveyed the corves[149] of coal using horse-drawn carts and pack-horses.

---

[146] Ibid
[147] Op Cit Walton, p.113
[148] Ibid, p.152
[149] Corves or corbs: baskets used for carrying minerals in mines.

Not surprisingly, this new-fangled railway was met with derision and hostility, particularly when it was rumoured that the price of coal would be increased to pay for it, not to mention the impact it had on the physical environment; an issue that is omitted from contemporaneous accounts. One contemporary letter proclaimed that the coal-owners were 'merciless wretches' seeking to almost double the price of coal and that they would refuse to sell it in quantities less than a horse-load.[150]

Peter Machan conjures up the thought that this letter was pinned to the Town Hall door to deliberately incite public unrest and that it was probably written by the popular satirical rhymester, Joseph Mather.[151] As is customary with technological advances on this scale, the developer, in this case the Duke of Norfolk, would promote the benefits of the scheme, omitting that it would increase his profits but by emphasising that such a grand scheme would benefit everyone in the town, far outweighing its impact on a few carters, and it would reduce the price of coal, not increase it. But the sceptical Sheffield folk were having none of that.

The cost of the new railway would have to be met from somewhere and the only plausible inevitability that the people foresaw, was that it would come from them, the customer. As the work on the wooden railway was nearing completion, the simmering cauldron of contempt, stirred up no doubt by the carters whose livelihood it threatened, boiled over and a mob attacked the object of their resentment.

---

[150] Op Cit Leader, Robert Eadon, p.85
[151] Machan, Peter, *Sheffield's Time Trail: True Tales From The Norfolk Heritage Trail*, Green Estate Ltd., 2004, pp.52-53

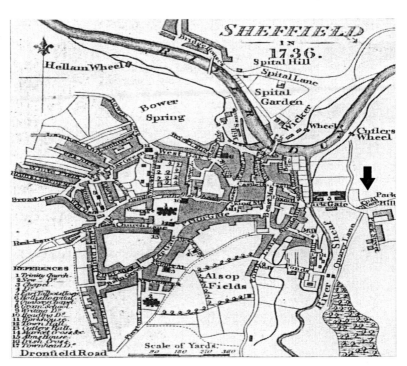

Sheffield in 1736 showing the Duke of Norfolk's coal yard at the bottom of Park Hill arrowed.

A gathering of malcontents advanced upon the Duke's coal depot to protest and destruction ensued in no time at all. The wooden wagons with low wheels designed to run on the wooden rails were the first target of the mob. Several of them were turned over and destroyed and the new loading stage was broken up and set on fire. A watch-box and counting-house within the yard were demolished and a good portion of the wooden rails were broken up and set alight.

One of the trucks was dragged through the streets of the town as a trophy before being torched and then shoved down the embankment into the river. In Norfolk Row, the mob attacked the Lord's House, the home of Henry Howard, the Duke's cousin and the agent for his Sheffield estate. A pitched battle ensued with the police and watchmen and at one point the law-enforcers had to barricade themselves in the Parish Church until help arrived. One man called Shaw later died of his injuries after being struck by a policeman.[152]

On reaching Fargate, the rioters dispersed after being confronted by soldiers who fired musket shot over their heads.

---

[152] Op Cit *Sheffield Local Register,* p.53

The Lord's House, home of Henry Howard   Arms of the Duke of Norfolk

In response to the rioting, Henry Howard quickly put together a handbill for distribution amongst the townsfolk stating that it was never intended to raise the price of coal and explaining that the new transport facility actually allowed him to keep prices low.

At a public meeting, the duke's agent was backed up by assurances from Joseph Roberts, the Town Collector, Joseph Kenyon, the Master Cutler, and other town dignitaries. However, the people were not appeased by these representations and more trouble erupted in the months that followed causing such alarm that an association for the protection of property and person was set up to deal with the situation.

Meanwhile, a new engineer called John Curr, whose innovations and inventions would later contribute significantly to the expansion of Britain's coal mining industry, was brought in and work began on restoring the railway.[153] Being mindful of the ease by which the mob had destroyed the wooded facilities, John Curr replaced the wooden rails with cast-iron plates, first of his own design, which proved inadequate, then with plates designed by James Outram of Ripley. These plates had a flange to keep the wheels of the trucks on the track and were called *edge-rails*.[154]

---

[153] For a detailed account of John Curr's life see Medlicott, Ian R., *John Curr, 1756-1823, Mining Engineer and Viewer,* in Jones, Melvyn (Ed.), *Aspect of Sheffield 2,* Wharncliffe Publishing Limited, 1999, pp.63-78

[154] It is from these plates that the term 'plate-layer' is derived: a worker on the railways whose job it is to fix the rails to the sleeper and to maintain and repair the line.

The rails were laid on wooden sleepers and this track system became known as an *Outram-way*, which soon, and henceforth, became known simply as a *tramway*.[155] Whilst the new tramway worked satisfactorily, the wooden sleepers were still vulnerable to attack and having been torn up by objectors, they were replaced first with cast-iron box sections, which suffered the same fate, and then by solid stone blocks.

Discontent amongst the townsfolk continued but evidently, receded as there are no further reports of violent attacks upon the tramway. Whilst these attacks upon this technological advancement in the transportation of coal in Sheffield, at this time, predated the Luddite Rebellion of the early 19th century, which incidentally, did not affect the Sheffield area, they were perhaps, the nearest that Sheffield came to adopting Luddism.

Example of an early tramway on the Derby Canal using James Outram's flanged plates or edge-rails.

We have no way of knowing how or even if the 1774 coal riot affected production at the Park colliery. The work of the miners may not have been affected at all if the coal was simply stock-piled at the pit; there was probably plenty of room for it as the colliery site was in an open rural area. Or perhaps

---

[155] Op Cit Leader, Robert Eadon, p.341

transporting the coal reverted to the employment of local carters whilst the tramway was being rebuilt.

As for maintaining the supply of coal to Sheffield, any shortfall in supply from the Park colliery would undoubtedly have been made good by other local coal-owners taking advantage of the situation. However, the trouble seems to have had an effect upon the Duke of Norfolk's interest in the Park colliery as in the following year he let the site to Townsend & Furness. He took back control of the pit in 1781, working it up until 1801, when he then let it to a company that became the Sheffield Coal Company.[156]

Whilst these were the major incidents of riot connected to the coal mining industry in Sheffield, nationally, the industry was often subject to disturbances due to conflict between colliers, who were regarded as being uncivilised and primitive, even by the standards of the day, and the colliery owners. Sheffield had its fair share of these disputes, particularly in the 19th century. Most of these were due to prices and the level of wages.

Also, as with all industry during our period, safety at work was a major issue but in the coal-fields the risks were far greater than most industries due to the nature of the work and death and severe injuries were accepted as a way of life by both mine workers (including women and children as young as seven years) and employers alike: the ability to earn a living by the former and to make a profit by the latter were more important than the risk to life and limb.

Coal mines were susceptible to fire and explosions, flooding and tunnel-collapse, any of which could cause a major disaster and loss of life. Statistically, there were more deaths and serious injuries amongst miners than amongst the men who took the king's shilling and joined the army; the history of coal mining is littered with disasters, some claiming hundreds of lives.

Between 1856 and 1886, the number of miners killed in accidents in British pits was around 1,000 per year.[157] No major disaster is recorded in Sheffield in our period but one incident was recorded in 1841 when, on 8 March, there was an explosion at the Soap House Pit, owned by the Sheffield Coal Company, where four men and three boys were severely burnt.

---

[156] Op Cit Walton, p.114
[157] Hobsbawm, E.J., *Industry and Empire,* Penguin Books, 1975, p.116

Samuel White was so badly burnt that he died later that day.[158] Another accident is recorded on 17 July 1855 when two young men were killed at the same pit after being thrown from a corve as it ascended the shaft.[159]

In March 1844, there were strikes at collieries around the country and Sheffield miners were preparing to join in the dispute so as to reduce coal stocks. This resulted in a disturbance at the Tinsley Park colliery on 21 March.[160] Later, on 11 May, over 600 men of the Sheffield Coal Company went on strike over pay. They were joined by men from other Sheffield collieries including Soap House, Intake and Tinsley Park.

At some of these pits, strike-breakers were brought in from other areas. However, at some pits the employers gave in to the men's demands. A mass meeting of the striking miners was held in Paradise Square on 13 May to demonstrate their resolve. On 22 May, a letter from Alderman Thomas Dunn[161] of the Sheffield Coal Company was published outlining the wages that the men were earning and that they had demanded increases of 50-60%.

Dunn also made a point that the company employed union men only. Four days later the striking miners responded by stating they sought only a 20% rise.[162] On 4 July, a number of men brought in to work the Soap House pit were attacked and seriously injured by a mob in buildings at the pit where they had been lodged. On this occasion, the military were called out and three men, William Mason, George Taylor and Richard Winker, identified as ringleaders, were committed to York Assizes on charges of riot and assault. They were hastily tried and convicted on 19 July and sentenced the next day to be transported for 15 years.[163]

By the end of July, the Soap House pit was back in production and entirely worked by new, non-union men. At Birley pit, 12 striking miners had returned to work on the pre-strike terms and prices. The Handsworth colliery did not re-open as it was abandoned due to a fault found in the strata.[164] Thomas Dunn

[158] Op Cit *Sheffield Local Register,* p.531
[159] Ibid, p.539
[160] Ibid, p.396
[161] Alderman Thomas Dunn was the son of Thomas Dunn senior who was Master Cutler in 1832 and the returning officer in the 1832 election (see chapter on Election Riots below). Thomas Dunn junior became Mayor of Sheffield in 1844. Both were coal owners
[162] Op Cit *Sheffield Local Register*, p.398
[163] Ibid, p. 399
[164] Ibid

suffered a severe injury to an ankle at one of the riots at his pit from which he suffered for many years.[165]

On 25 August 1844, the boiler of No. 2 engine at Deep Pit, at the Manor, was blown up with gunpowder.[166] William Bolton was arrested nearby soon after and Thomas Crichlow, who had been seriously injured in the explosion, was also arrested at his brother John's house in the Park. Thomas died of his injuries at the Infirmary on 11 September, whilst still in police custody.

On 17 September, John Crichlow was apprehended in Manchester and charged with the explosion and sent to York. On 3 October, Thomas North Stocks was also arrested and committed to York charged with being an accessory after the fact at the Deep Pit explosion in assisting John Crichlow.

On 6 December, William Bolton was convicted of blowing up the Deep Pit boiler and sentenced to 18 months imprisonment; John Crichlow was acquitted and no evidence was offered against Thomas North Stocks. Although Thomas Crichlow died as a result of the explosion, there is no mention of manslaughter or any other charges in relation to his death. Coroner's verdict was most probably, a misadventure.

Another notable disturbance in the Sheffield coal-field occurred on 10 July 1869, at the Manor Castle colliery owned by the Tinsley Coal Company. Trade union miners were locked-out during a dispute and once more non-union men were brought in to work the pit. These men, some armed for their own protection against the union men, were given a police escort to the pit.

However, the police officer escorting the men had to return to Sheffield after arresting a man for stealing a fawn along the way leaving them to continue the last quarter of a mile to the pit without a police presence. The resulting inevitable clash between the non-union men and the locked-out union men led to two people being shot and wounded, one, a woman named Sykes, came near to death but she eventually recovered.[167]

By the mid-19th century, the demand for coal had increased with the growing use of steam-power to drive industrial machinery and the locomotives of the expanding railway network, itself a bi-product of the coal mining industry; the first steam locomotive to run on rails was built by mining engineer Richard

[165] Op Cit Leader, Robert Eadon, p.334
[166] Op Cit *Sheffield Local Register*, pp.400-404
[167] Op Cit Drewry, *Intimidation,* p.334

Trevithick (1771-1833) in 1804 and experimented with in the South Wales and Tyne coalfields.[168]

In 1814, George Stephenson, who also devised a miner's safety lamp, built the first steam locomotive railway to carry coal from the Killingworth colliery near Newcastle to the River Tyne.[169] By 1855, there were nearly 8,000 miles of railway across Britain.[170] The gauge of the railway lines (the distance between the rails: 4ft 8½in) used by Stephenson, became and remains the standard of British railways today.[171]

Richard Trevithick's steam locomotive.

The ever-increasing demand for coal, both at home, where two-thirds of it was being burnt in domestic fireplaces,[172] and for export often led to shortages, which in turn led to increases in the price. Such was the case in Sheffield in 1853 and 1854. This led to the owners of local steam-power increasing rents, which in turn impacted upon trade.

---

[168] Op Cit Court, p.47
[169] Op Cit Hill, p.76
[170] Ibid, p.78
[171] Op Cit Court, p.47. The only exception was the Great Western Railway built by Isambard Kingdom Brunel in 1841 which had a gauge of 7ft. The British railways were standardised on the narrow gauge in 1846
[172] Op Cit Hobsbawm, E.J., p.69

On 17 January 1854, a Coal Consumers Company was established and on 27 January, a meeting of steam-power owners raised rents by 10%.[173]

By 1868, there were 35 collieries in the Sheffield coalfield producing 1,075,500 tons of coal, most of it used locally. The total output of coal in the UK in 1868 was 103,141,157 tons, of which 9,740,510 tons was produced in Yorkshire.[174]

Industrial conflict would haunt the British coal-fields well into the 20th century and take on a more political dimension, circumstances that brought about the General Strike of 1926; the toppling of the Tory government in 1974; and a year-long miners' strike in 1984-5, after which the government embarked on a programme of pit closures, eventually leading to the demise of the British coal industry in the 21st century. The last deep coal mine, Kellingley in North Yorkshire, closed in 2016.

---

[173] Op Cit *Sheffield local Register, Continuation,* p.1
[174] Baines, Thomas, *Yorkshire Past and Present Vol.1, Part 1,* William Mackenzie, 1870, pp.38-9

Anti-Methodist Riots

By rule they eat. By rule they drink,
By rule do all things but think
Accuse the priests of loose behaviour,
To get more in the layman's favour,
Method alone must guide 'em all
When themselves Methodists they call.[175]

'As there is no King in Israel—I mean no magistrate in Sheffield—every man doth as seemeth good in his own eyes.'[176]

1743-6

The theologian and hymn writer Charles Wesley (1707-88) was a student at Christ Church, Oxford in 1726 where he was joined by some fellow-students, including his brother John, in a strict method of religious observance and study calling themselves *The Holy Club* but acquiring the derisory nickname of *Methodists,* a term originating in the 17th century for those leaning towards an extremely structured devotional existence, amongst the other undergraduates who considered them to be quite mad; one of the group, William Morgan, literally, did go insane and died in 1732.[177]

This perceived madness of the Methodist preachers extended to their congregations at their open-air meetings. Their enthusiastic preaching provoked much frenzy and shouting-out from the most fanatical amongst their congregation.

As the group spread their message amongst the wider public, gaining support amongst the working classes who refrained from going to church, the notion of Methodism being associated with madness also gained ground, so much so that

---

[175] Rhyme of Oxford undergraduates on the Wesley brothers. Landsdown, Richard, *Method in the Madness* in *History Today, Vol.68, Issue 9*, September 2018, p.58
[176] Charles Wesley on the destruction of the third Methodist chapel in Sheffield. Op Cit Leader, Robert Eadon, p.330
[177] Op Cit Landsdown, p.58

Methodism was officially registered as a cause of insanity. Between 1772 and 1787, ninety deaths (accounting for 10% of the total) caused by insanity recorded at the London Bethlem Hospital (Bedlam) were attributed to *Religion and Methodism.*[178]

In 1738, one of the Oxford Methodists, Rev. Benjamin Ingham, was living in Sheffield at Fulwood with a Mr Wardlow when he met and converted David Taylor, a Sheffield minister, to Wesley's Evangelical preaching. David Taylor began to preach Wesley's gospel in and around Heeley and James Vickers, the inventor of Britannia metal, was one of his early converts.[179]

In 1742, Charles's brother, John Wesley (1703-1791), made his first visit to Sheffield and spent a week helping Taylor to organise his small but growing congregation of converts and to establish the Sheffield Methodist Society.[180] One of Taylor's converts was a Sheffield cutler called James Bennet[181], who organised subscriptions for the building of a little preaching-house next door to his house in Cheney Square, the first Methodist chapel in the town.

John Wesley visited Sheffield three times in 1743 and in the spring of that year Charles Wesley also paid a visit to the town. All of these visits were met with opposition from the local clergy who preached a series of sermons in the Parish Church against this *new schism and heresy.*[182]

As had been the case in other parts of the country, the Sheffield Methodists were subjected to violent opposition and persecution; even the local magistrates connived in this harrying, seeing them as a threat to the established order. During his visit to Sheffield on 5 May, Charles Wesley joined David Taylor in conducting a service at the Cheney Square preaching-house where the converts were joined by what Wesley termed *fellows of the baser sort.*

This growing mob, egged on by an army captain, who on any other day and with other underlying objectives, would be suppressing the insurgents, began brawling with the converts and a full-scale riot ensued. Wesley *sang on* until stones were hurled, striking his desk and the people standing nearest to him. As things escalated Wesley moved from his desk and retreated outside only to be followed by some of the rioters and the army captain, who prodded him with his

---

[178] Ibid, p.54
[179] Op Cit Leader, Robert Eadon, p.82
[180] Seed, Rev. T Alexander, *Norfolk Street Wesleyan Chapel, Sheffield,* Jarrold & Sons, 1907, p.15
[181] Recorded in *Sheffield Local Register* as Edward Bennett, p.41
[182] Op Cit Seed, p.16

sword as the frenzied mob seized him and pelted him with brickbats and filth from the gutter.

Despite the recital of the Riot Act the mob continued to threaten him as he further retreated into James Bennet's house next door. Here, Wesley held a prayer meeting with the converts who had been able to escape the mob and join him. As the Methodists joined in prayer in Bennet's house, the mob turned its attention back on the little chapel. The foundations were undermined and ropes and poles were used to pull the building down, demolishing it completely.

When Wesley returned to the chapel the following day, he found that *not one stone remained upon another.*[183] Charles Wesley had experienced violent opposition before on many occasions but what he had witnessed in Sheffield was beyond anything he had previously endured:

Hell from beneath was moved to oppose us. Those at Moorfields, Cardiff and Walsall were lambs to these.[184]

Charles and John Wesley

In 1744 a second Methodist chapel was built at the end of Pinstone Lane, near Burgess Street. This too was paid for by private subscriptions and was also attacked and damaged by the mob. Although it was not utterly destroyed as was the first chapel, the Methodists moved out and a third preaching-house was built further along Pinstone Lane in 1745. This chapel was associated with the

---

[183] Ibid, p.17
[184] Op Cit Leader, Robert Eadon, p.330

Sheffield optician, John Wilson, a descendent of the Wilsons of Sharrow, and like its predecessors, had a short and turbulent history.[185]

On 9 February 1746, a crowd of 400-500 people gathered near St. Paul's churchyard then proceeded to attack the new Methodist chapel. The scene repeated itself the following night despite the presence of two constables and the Riot Act being read out to the hollering mob; no magistrates were available to undertake the proclamation.

John Wilson appealed to two local magistrates to issue warrants against the rioters but was ignored and no action was taken to stop the destruction; it seems that opposition against the Methodists also ran deep amongst the local gentry. As Robert Leader commented, *All was complacent lethargy when a Methodist Chapel, and not the Lord's mill, was attacked.*[186]

The attack upon the third chapel persisted each night until, by the end of the week, it too was completely destroyed. Weeks later, John Wesley arrived in Sheffield and remonstrated with the local Justices of the Peace only to be rebuffed. Gaining no redress from the Sheffield magistrates, John Wesley took his case to York Castle where he was received more sympathetically. The York judges handed out heavy fines to the ringleaders of the mob and ordered that the Sheffield magistrates rebuild the chapel.

---

[185] Op Cit Seed, p.18
[186] Op Cit Leader, Robert Eadon, p.330

The second Sheffield Methodist preaching house, Pinstone Lane.[187]

It is at this point that the history of Sheffield Methodism becomes a little obscure. Following the York judgement, the violent attacks by the mob appear to have ceased but it isn't clear whether the sentences handed out at York were actually implemented. There is no record of the chapel being rebuilt and it is not until 1757 that we find reference of a new Methodist chapel on Mulberry Street, which was a converted factors' warehouse.[188]

Before moving to Mulberry Street, the Methodists worshipped for a time in a chapel in West Street that belonged to the Calvinists.[189] The threat of further violence may have sent the remaining converts underground as little is known of where and how often they met in the town. However, there is evidence to suggest that meetings took place in villages surrounding Sheffield in 1748. In Ecclesfield, described at the time as, *a rough and brutal village, a very Sodom.* There are records of Methodist preaching that year.[190]

Following this period of the persecution in Sheffield, the fortunes of the Wesleyan Methodists changed dramatically for the better as the new religion

[187] Op Cit Seed, p.17
[188] Ibid, p.332
[189] Taylor, John (Ed), *The Illustrated Guide to Sheffield*, Pawson and Brailsford, Sheffield, 1879, p.89
[190] Op Cit Seed, p.19

gradually became accepted and the number of converts overtook all other Nonconformist sects, trumping the Independents, the Presbyterians and the Quakers.[191]

The Mulberry Street chapel was enlarged in 1763 and again in 1765 to accommodate the growing congregation: *The house is twice as large and so is the congregation.*[192] By 1779, we find John Wesley, who visited Sheffield thirty-five times,[193] preaching to the largest congregation that he ever saw on a week-day in Paradise Square.[194]

By 1796, the recorded Methodist membership in Sheffield was over 3,000.[195] This figure included the break-away Methodist Connexion which, in the following year, saw a further secession with the Methodist New Connexion being created by Alexander Kilham.[196] The Norfolk Street Chapel was built in 1780 and in 1804, a further Methodist Chapel was built in Carver Street.

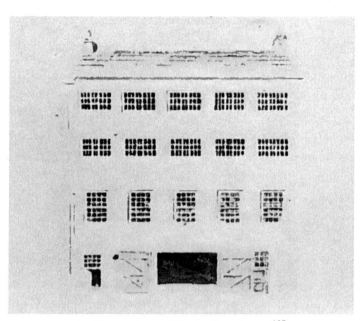

Mulberry Street Methodist Chapel[197]

---

[191] Mercer, Malcolm, *Rev. James Wilkinson and the Church in Sheffield, 1754-1805* in Jones, Melvyn (Ed.), *Aspects of Sheffield 2,* Wharncliffe Publishing Limited, 1999, p.40
[192] Op Cit Leader, Robert Eadon, p.332
[193] Op Cit Taylor, p.90
[194] Op Cit Leader, Robert Eadon, p.332
[195] Op Cit Mercer, p.42
[196] Ibid.
[197] Op Cit Seed, p.17

Norfolk Street Methodist Chapel[198]

There certainly was a revival in Wesleyan Methodism in Sheffield between the years 1795-1797 when the Rev Seed informs us that there were some 1,800 people now converted to the sect: *One of the largest and most fruitful revivals, probably, ever known in the history of Yorkshire Methodism.*[199] Across Britain, just 59,000 Methodists were recorded in 1790 and the Sheffield revival claimed by Seed appears to have been replicated nationally, as between 1800 and 1830, the number of Methodists in Britain rose by more than 200%.[200]

By 1850, there were well over half a million Wesleyan converts.[201] The Methodists seem to have bucked the trend in religious activity in industrial towns and cities during this period. In 1843, records show that less than 5% of Sheffield families of the skilled artisans attended church or chapel.[202]

The religious census of 1851, the earliest reliable statistical evidence, showed that church attendance in Sheffield was well below the national average of 54%, with just 29,000 Sheffield people out of a population of 135,310 attending church, chapel or Sunday schools. That nearly half of the population

---

[198] Op Cit Seed, frontispiece
[199] Ibid, p.151
[200] Op Cit Hunt, p.85
[201] Op Cit Hobsbawm, *The Age Of Revolution*, p.225
[202] Op Cit Drewry, *Intimidation*, p.23

of Britain failed to attend church at all, raised great concern within the Establishment. However, the same census indicated that there were only church places for 34% of the total population of Sheffield.[203]

Historians have long-argued over the influence of Methodism on social discipline within the working classes, a debate that has produced differing opinions over the years. E P Thompson, for example, argued that Methodist societies in industrial areas played a counter-revolutionary role and was a major factor in there being no British Revolution equivalent to that of the French.

Even after the death of John Wesley, Methodist Conferences continued to reaffirm their, *unfeigned loyalty to the King and sincere attachment to the Constitution.*[204] On the other hand, the 19th century philosopher, Friedrich Engels (1820-95), argued that Methodism or indeed any other church had only a minor influence on averting revolutionary inclinations amongst the industrial workers and that it was the employers' role that disciplined the urban masses via both sanction (the threat of the sack, the blacklisting of difficult men, fines for minor misdemeanours such as being late for work, etc.) and incentive (especially increases in wages and bonus payments): the carrot and the stick.

As John Kent points out, these pressures affected every worker whereas Methodism, or any other religion, influenced but a small minority.[205] From the religious census of 1851, we find that less than one in ten Sheffield folk attended church on census day and that most of them were from the middle and upper classes.[206]

Contemporary Methodists would have supported E P Thompson's view as we find in a letter from one George Heap to the Mayor of Leeds, requesting a ticket for the opening of the new Town Hall by Queen Victoria and Prince Albert in 1858, in which he outlines why he was deserving of the honour to attend and that he had been a good Methodist for a number of years and that he *fully believed*

---

[203] Op Cit Hobsbawm, *The Age Of Revolution*, p.221

[204] Thompson, E.P., *The Making of the English Working Class*, Pelican Books, 1968, p.45

[205] Kent, John, *Feelings and Festivals* in Dyos, H. J., and Wolff, Michael (Eds), *The Victorian City-Images and Realities Volume 2*, Routledge & Kegan Paul, 1973, p.856

[206] Ibid, p.857 The 1851 Religious Census did not distinguish those who attended once from those who attended twice or three times which means the actual number of individuals attending church may well be even lower; one estimate by as much as one third. Ibid, Note 5, p.868.

there would have been a revolution in this country but for the Sabbath School and the benefits both Children and Parents have from them.[207]

In addition to the notion that the Methodists in their early period were tinged with insanity, there was also a hint of Jacobinism amongst them that the Establishment was concerned about, although the official line of the Methodist leaders was one of loyalty to King and country. Charles Wesley was brought before Yorkshire magistrates for praying for *the Lord's absent ones,* what some alleged referred to the Stuarts.

However, John Wesley distanced himself from such leanings and went out of his way to assure his allegiance to the reigning House of Hanover and to the Church of England.[208] The Methodists' split from the Church of England came four years after his death in 1795. What we can say with confidence is that the introduction of Methodism in Sheffield, despite its popularity amongst the working classes (62% of male members in the 1790s were artisans),[209] was met with more violent opposition than it was anywhere else in Britain.

However, by 1850 the riots had ceased and the only disturbances that occurred in the Sheffield Methodist chapels were now those of religious frenzy engendered by the newly converted. By this time, Yorkshire had the strongest following of Methodism. A table published in 1824 indicated that 1 in 23 Yorkshire persons were Methodists, compared, for example, with Surrey, where there was 1 in 249.[210]

Whilst researching the Sheffield Methodists, I came across a couple of interesting anecdotes. The first was about Mr Henry Longden, one of their original members:

A person came to Mr Longden, of Sheffield, one day and said, "I have something against you, and I am come to tell you of it." "Do walk in, sir." he replied; "You are my best friend. If I could engage my friends to be faithful with me, I should be sure to prosper. But, if you please, we will both pray in the first place, and ask the blessing of God upon our interview." After they rose from their knees, and had been much blessed together, he said,

---

[207] Op Cit Briggs, pp.172-173
[208] Op Cit Lansdown, p.60
[209] Ibid
[210] Op Cit Hammond and Hammond, p.268

"Now, I will thank you, my brother, to tell me what it is that you have against me."

"Oh," said the man,

"I really now don't know what it is; it is all gone, and I believe I was in the wrong."[211]

This story quite obviously infers the Lord's intervention in quelling any animosity towards Methodism aroused in this potential adversary that was Mr Longden. In another anecdote I came across, this divine intervention in the promotion of Methodism is taken to Biblical proportions of divine retribution:

At Sheffield the captain of a gang who had long troubled the field-preachers, was bathing with his companions. 'Another dip' he said 'and then for a bit of sport with the Methodists'. He dived, struck his head against a stone, and appeared no more.'[212]

This story was one of a number of similar anecdotes from around the country circulating at the time, which emphasised God's support of Methodism and to instil the fear of God in its opponents and adversaries.

Contemporary sketch of Anti-Methodist Riot 1750.

---

[211] Taylor, Rev. R.V., *Yorkshire Anecdotes,* Whittaker & Co, 1883, p.238
[212] Lecky, William Edward Hartpole, *England in the Eighteenth Century, Vol III,* Longmans Green and Co, 1892, p.93.

Enclosure Riots

Our fenceless fields and village greens
The sons of wealth divided,
And e'en the blue-belled 'by-paths'
Were denied us.[213]

1791

One of the most notable riots to have taken place in Sheffield was that which occurred following the 1791 Sheffield Enclosure Act, although the unpopularity of the Act, particularly at the loss of Crooks Moor, where up until 1781 horse racing had taken place, was not the only grievance to incite the wrath of those who participated in the rioting at this time.

There had been a growing resentment at how justice was being administered by local magistrates and the harsh nature of punishments being metered out, particularly on the lower classes, not least of which was the dubious conviction and execution of button makers Thomas Lastley and John Stevens in 1790 for robbery, which, in the eyes of most people, was not criminal intent but merely a foolish prank.[214]

At that same time, many people were still most aggrieved at the removal of some graves from the Parish Church yard during work to widen Church Street in May 1785: interference with the dead was a highly sensitive issue for the people of Sheffield and this sacrilege was still fresh in their minds. They were reminded

---

[213] Paulus, Carolus, from an account on the Enclosure Acts that covered Sheffield and district in *Some Forgotten Facts in the History of Sheffield and District*, Sheffield Independent Press, 1907, p.12

[214] Op Cit Bentley, pp.48-52. The execution of Lastley and Stevens sparked disturbances in the town and attacks on the house of John Wharton, the man that they allegedly robbed due to suspicions that Wharton gave false evidence against them for a statutory reward of £40 which he allegedly shared with the arresting officer, Constable Eyre. Wharton escaped the mob disguised in women's clothes. Joseph Mather wrote a song about the unfortunate pair entitled *Stevens & Lastley's Execution*. See Op Cit Kay and Windle, pp.62-63

by Joseph Mather with his song *The Black Resurrection,*[215] which some argued actually incited the riot.

The anger and resentment bubbling under the surface, burst through to shatter the peace of Sheffield streets following the legalised robbery of 6,000 acres of common land by the town's already land-rich, wealthy elite, particularly, the Duke of Norfolk, who was not surprisingly a keen promoter of enclosure, and the Vicar of Sheffield, Rev James Wilkinson, who had also gained land out of previous enclosure legislation. The resentment against James Wilkinson was compounded by him also being an unpopular magistrate, and that he had permitted the removal of the graves to facilitate the widening of Church Street.

The enclosure of common land across Britain had been practiced since the 14th century as a means of generally improving farming and protecting, and increasing, landowners' income from rents at the expense of the rural population. Many small farmers and farm labourers and their families were dispossessed of their homes and lost their means of making a living as the practice increased throughout the 15th and 16th centuries, resulting in revolts in 1536, 1569 and 1607.

The first enclosure by Act of Parliament enclosed land at Radipole in Dorset in 1604.[216] Into the 18th century, further improvements in farming were made by notable inventions such as Jethro Tull's (1674-1741) seed drill and horse-hoe, and Viscount Charles 'Turnip' Townshend's (1674-1738) development of root crops that enabled four-year crop rotation instead of three, which in turn provided animal food for the winter.[217]

Incentivised by these improvements and increased profits, the wealthier landowners made calls for further enclosures and throughout the 18th century and well into the 19th century, Parliament—a Parliament stacked with wealthy, land-rich gentry and the aristocracy that still formed the absolute majority as late as 1885[218]—enacted no less, that 4,000 Enclosure Bills covering approximately 10 million acres of common land.[219]

In total, between 1604 and 1914 there were over 5,200 enclosure bills passed enclosing 6.8 million acres of land, which amounts to a fifth of the total area of

---

[215] Op Cit Kay and Windle, pp.90-93
[216] www.parliament.uk/livingheritage
[217] Op Cit Addy, John, *Agrarian,* pp.21-23
[218] Op Cit Hobsbawm, E.J., p.196
[219] Op Cit Paulus, p.14

England.[220] Of these, over 63,000 acres of common land within a radius of around 12 miles of Sheffield were enclosed by 35 different Enclosure Acts between 1767 and 1839:

Year of Act	District to which Enclosure Act refers	Number of acres enclosed
1767	Anston (North)	1100
1769	Laughton-en-le-Morthen	1160
1774	Rawmarsh	1250
1777	Killamarsh	410
1778	Bolsterstone	3000
1779	Ecclesall	1000
1779	Anston (South)	1685
1781	Stoney Middleton	500
1784	Ecclesfield and Southey	600
1784	Loxley Chase and Wadsley	2600
1788	Brightside	150
1791	**Sheffield**	**6000**
1795	Eckington	1070
1795	Barlborough	900
1796	Beighton	600
1797	Dalton	450
1798	Ulley	220
1802	Handsworth	470
1803	Eyam	3000
1806	Bakewell	2800
1809	Dronfield and Dore	5000
1810	Attercliffe	285
1811	Langsett	4000
1812	Bradfield	14000
1812	Brinsworth	245
1813	Thurgoland	400
1813	Whitwell	940
1814	Wentworth	260
1814	Wickersley	540
1815	Wisewood	90
1816	Whiston	230
1816	Holmesfield	3000
1821	Whittington	284
1823	Baslow and Froggatt	3900
1839	Totley	1200
	Total	63339

---

[220] www.parliament.uk/livingheritage

The greatest beneficiary of this land-grab in Sheffield was the Duke of Norfolk, who was allotted more than 1300 acres of waste and common land. Next was the Vicar of Sheffield, Rev James Wilkinson, who was also a magistrate and one of the three Sheffield enclosure commissioners working with the Government's Commissioner, Arthur Elliot, who oversaw the process,[221] a conflict of interest not lost on the dispossessed and displaced people, thus making him all the more resented by them.

Wilkinson added another 80 or so acres of land to his estate in 1791[222], having previously gained 200 acres from the 1779 Ecclesall Enclosure Act.[223] Should anyone wish to object to enclosure, they would have to travel to London and employ a skilled lawyer to make their representations to Parliament; a process well beyond the means of the casualties of the Enclosure Acts.

James Wilkinson had become Vicar of Sheffield in 1754, preaching his first sermon on 3 November and he remained in the post until his death on 18 January 1805, aged 75.[224] As a magistrate, appointed in 1763, he held court in the ground floor rooms of the Cutlers' Hall, known as *Low Street* or, as portrayed by Joseph Mather, *Bang Beggers Hall*.[225]

Wilkinson was nicknamed *Old Niddlety Nod* due to an affliction of involuntary nodding, probably palsy, or perhaps a consequence of his early days as an amateur boxer. Mather dubbed him *the Old Serpent* and referred to him as *that black diabolical fiend* in *The Black Resurrection*,[226] reminding the people of his approval for the removal of graves to widen Church Street in 1785.

---

[221] The other two commissioners were Vincent Eyre, the Duke of Norfolk's agent, and Joseph Ward, the former master cutler (1790) and father of Thomas Aisline Ward (see chapter on Election Riots)
[222] Op Cit Paulus, p.78
[223] Op Cit Vickers, p.94. Also Derry, John, *The Story of Sheffield*, S. R. Publishers Ltd., London, 1981, p.236
[224] For a detailed account of James Wilkinson's life see Op Cit Mercer
[225] Op Cit Vickers, p.186
[226] Op Cit Leader, Robert Eadon, p.60 For the lyrics to *The Black Resurrection* and a summary of the episode see Op Cit Kay and Windle, pp.90-93

Reverend James Wilkinson

Notice of the intention to enclose Commons and waste grounds of Upper Hallam, Nether Hallam and Stannington was given in the *Sheffield Local Register* on 6 September 1787 and trouble was predicted.[227] The Sheffield Enclosure Act was passed on 24 June 1791 and it was reported in the *Sheffield Local Register* that the enclosure of waste and common land at Upper and Nether Hallam, principally Crooks Moor, *'caused some commotions but they soon subsided.'*

Nevertheless over the following weeks, as the consequences of the Act were gradually realised and discontent spread, the magistrates must have been concerned that things might come to a head and they sought urgent assistance from the Home Office on 23 July. A detachment of Light Horse Dragoons commanded by Captain Polhill was sent to Sheffield from Nottingham. On

---

[227] Op Cit Addy, John, *Agrarian,* p.58

Monday, 27 July, a crowd had gathered outside the Tontine Inn[228] when the Dragoons appeared in the town, the glint of their swords indicating that they meant business.

Trouble erupted when the bailiff at the debtors' gaol, Joseph Schofield, unwisely attempted to arrest a man in the crowd.[229] The man ran off in the confusion with the bailiff in pursuit. Schofield caught up with the fugitive near to the gaol house in Pudding Lane (now King Street) and tried once more to apprehend the man.

Fully aware of what was happening, the crowd once more intervened and the man made his escape again. This time Schofield dodged into the gaol as the crowd began throwing some stones that were at hand, which were meant for use on nearby road works. The Dragoons followed the protesters but this only added to the frenzy and the mob attacked the outer gate of the gaol and the house of the gaoler, Godfrey Fox, smashing the windows and doors.

Before the Dragoons could disperse the crowd, the keys to the two rooms that held the prisoners had been taken from the house and used to release the 19 or 20 prisoners.[230] In a press report of 1 August, it was stated that some of the rioters were known to have come from Birmingham. It is not known whether they came on a mission or simply joined in the disorder for the fun of it.

---

[228] The Tontine Inn, No. 14 Haymarket, was built on the site of the Castle Barns (between Exchange Street and Dixon Lane) in 1785 and was Sheffield's largest coaching house. In 1838, thirteen coaches per day left the Tontine for various destinations: York, Derby, London, Manchester, Birmingham, Leeds, Doncaster and Retford & Worksop. The opening of the railway that year engendered the decline and eventual demise of coaching and the Tontine Inn was bought by the Duke of Norfolk in 1850 to be demolished to make way for a new market. Op Cit Vickers pp.49-50

[229] Op Cit Bentley, p.53. The philanthropist John Howard (1726-1790) undertook a tour of the country's prisons, 1775-1776, and calculated that of the 4,084 prisoners, 2,437 were debtors: *State of the Prisons,* 1777, see Moore, J.M., *Behind Victorian Bars* in *History Today, Vol.69, Issue 1,* January 2019, p.62.

[230] The debtor's gaol, where men and women were locked up together, was demolished in 1818 and a converted warehouse in Scotland Street was used for the gaol. The site at Pudding Lane was used to sell fruit and fish and became known as 'The Green Market'. In September 1837, the *Sheffield Local Register* reported *Prisoners in Sheffield and Ecclesall gaols for debt: without a child 32; with 1 child 12; with 2 children 12; with 3 children 13; with 4 children 3; with 5 children 1.* The report does not specify whether the children were in gaol with them. The Scotland Street gaol also closed later in the 19th century and the building was taken over by the Sheffield Socialist Society in 1887. The ground floor was opened as a café called the Commonwealth Café on 21 February and the rooms upstairs used for meetings: see Lee, Andrew, *The Red Flag of Anarchy—A History of Socialism & Anarchism in Sheffield 1874-1900,* Pirate Press Sheffield, 2017, p.54

The Dragoons' horses cleaved through the crowd sending people in all directions. However, the determination of the ring-leaders was not stalled for long and soon the dispersed crowd re-formed and a cry went up, *'All in a mind, for Broom Hall!'* the house of the Rev James Wilkinson. The stream of shouting people made its way towards Broom Hall from where, having been forewarned of the trouble, Wilkinson had already fled leaving his servant, John Gregory, to face the mob.[231]

Despite Gregory closing up the shutters, windows were smashed and the house was broken into. Furniture was damaged and the library was set on fire destroying a number of books. In the grounds at the rear of the house, Wilkinson's eight haystacks were set alight and four of them totally ruined.

It wasn't long before the Dragoons caught up with the action and once more the crowd was dispersed with the people generally making their way back to the town. On their way, some attacked the home of Vincent Eyre, the agent of the Duke of Norfolk, and also an enclosure commissioner in Fargate, where it was reported that every window of the house was broken before the Dragoons intervened again. Windows were also broken at the nearby Roman Catholic Chapel.

There were shouts of *'Liberty or Death'* and shots were fired but there were no casualties. No further disruption occurred that night but on the following day, the town's magistrates arranged for the swearing-in of hundreds of special constables, and two troops of Heavy Dragoons were drafted in from York.[232] Business in the town was at a standstill and clearly the town's leaders feared further trouble.[233]

Overnight thirteen men had been arrested in connection with the riot. All appeared before Major R A Athorpe JP at the Tontine Inn and five of them were committed to trial at York Assizes. The other eight were questioned but released due to lack of evidence against them. John Bennett, an 18-year-old apprentice of limited intellect, who lived in Waingate, had been apprehended on his return from Broom Hall and on being questioned, he implicated another man named William Ellis.

Benjamin Johnson had been accosted in the church yard in the early hours of the morning, having not gone home in fear of being dragged from his bed to

[231] Op Cit Bentley, p.58
[232] Ibid, p.59
[233] Press cutting provided by Chris Hobbs

answer for his part in the riot. Thomas Furniss had been seen at the gaol and arrested on suspicion of riot. The fifth man committed to York was Ellis Froggatt. All were young men of no more than 19 years of age.

At York, after being interviewed, Froggatt was discharged. William Ellis, no doubt in retaliation for his being implicated by Bennett, turned King's evidence against him. Bennett had seemingly been cajoled into participating in the firing of the library and was described by Robert Leader as *'a half-witted fellow who had been employed by the mob as the monkey used the cat to take the chestnuts from the fire'*.[234]

Nonetheless, Bennett was found guilty of riot and arson and sentenced to hang. Johnson and Furniss were acquitted. The young simpleton John Bennett was hanged on Saturday, 6 September 1791 alongside John Minitor, a Rotherham flax-dresser, hanged for arson, and Abraham Robertshaw, a Bradford butcher, hanged for forgery.[235]

Broom Hall

That there was civil unrest following the Enclosure Acts is not surprising as, in the words of one writer, they brought *'harsh, bleak and grinding poverty and*

[234] Op Cit Leader, Robert Eadon, p.61
[235] *Criminal Chronology of York Castle,* published by C. L. Burdekin, 1867, pp.109-10

injustice'.[236] The common people not only lost their right to roam and to use common land, many of the rural population lost their living as they had to give up the rights of pasture for their animals.

They also lost their access to wild herbs and fruits, and the practice known as 'gleaning'—the gathering of left-over grain after harvest that kept many poor families in grain for anything up to a year[237]—came to an end. Farm labourers in enclosed villages saw their income drop dramatically, as did their access to cheap butter, eggs, milk and poultry.[238]

The enclosures also engendered an increase in the poor rates. Many poor farmers, farm labourers and their families also lost their homes and were forced to move to the towns to find work. Many more found themselves driven into poverty and destitution, becoming dependent on the Poor Law or the workhouse, a situation exacerbated by the increase in population and, into the 19th century, by economic depression following the Napoleonic Wars.

In some areas, enclosure added to the troubles of those who earned their living from the declining cottage industries as they were replaced by the factory system.[239] Adding salt to the wounds, the Duke of Norfolk and his ilk increased their income from ground rents generated by the acres of land added to their estates. I wonder how many Sheffield people today continue to pay ground rent to the Duke of Norfolk estate for that very same land.

Some historians have argued that the benefits of enclosure outweighed the suffering and that farm labourers who lived in enclosed villages actually saw improvements to their standard of living with more employment, higher wages and better food.

However, the Sheffield Enclosure wasn't undertaken with the intention to improve local farming but to provide land for more factories and to build houses for the workers. Brightside (1778) and Attercliffe (1810) to the east of the town are prime examples of enclosed land being used for industry. The debate for and against enclosure continues to this day.

---

[236] Bryant, Arthur, *Years of Endurance*, p.7
[237] Evans, Eric J, *The Forging of the Modern State—Early Industrial Britain 1783-1870*, Longman, 1996, p.152
[238] Op Cit Bryant, *Years of Endurance*, p.8
[239] Op Cit Court, p.22

Gleaners by Frederick Morgan (1856-1927)

The Sheffield Enclosure riot of 1791 had a profound effect on the town's instruments for law-enforcement and civic authority. Mindful of the revolution in France, the government was growing concerned about the restlessness of

Sheffield's working class and sent Colonel Oliver de Lancey[240] of the 17th Dragoons to assess the situation. He reported that *'there were few persons with sufficient influence to resist them* [townsfolk] *in case of riot.'*[241]

The latest uprising persuaded the magistrates that when the use of the military was required to keep the peace; it was not close enough to hand. They needed to be better prepared for any future unrest and it was decided that Sheffield would have its own garrison.

On 27 July 1792, work began on building Sheffield's first military barracks at Philadelphia. Up until this time, it was the custom to billet soldiers in alehouses. The new barracks, capable of housing and stabling two troops of cavalry, opened in 1794 at a cost of more than £2,000. This was not the sole financial cost attributed to the 1791 riot. We find in the *Accounts and Minutes of the Burgery of Sheffield* (commonly known as the Town Trust), that a payment of £542-10s-1½d was made in respect of *'expenses incurred by the magistrates, constables, &c, during the Riots of 1791'.*[242] Compensation was also paid out to those whose property was damaged in the riot as we find in a report of 19 March 1792 in the *Sheffield Local Register*:

> *'Paid by the county, to defray the loss occasioned by the riot in Sheffield, (July 29, 1791); to the Duke of Norfolk, £54. 5s. 8d.; to Mr Wheat £185. 14s. 5d.; to the Rev. Mr Wilkinson,* (exclusive of a claim for £409. 10s. for hay destroyed) *£190. 5s.1d.'*

The Mr Wheat referred to in the above report was the lawyer and Town Trustee, James Wheat, who had his office in Paradise Square, although I can find no mention of him or his property being involved in any of the reports of the riot. However, Wheat did receive £876-9s in legal fees for the implementation of the Sheffield enclosure.

It is also possible that he represented the Duke of Norfolk's interests and those of Vincent Eyre, whose property was damaged but is not one of those

---

[240] Later Major-General de Lancey, 1794; MP for Maidstone, 1796-1802. In 1804, he was removed for *carelessness in the keeping of his accounts as barrack-master.* See *The Concise Dictionary of National Biography—Vol. I A-F,* Oxford University Press, 1994, p.769

[241] Addy, John, *A Coal and Iron Community in the Industrial Revolution,* Longman, 1969, p.79

[242] Op Cit Leader, John Daniel, p.397

recompensed by the Trust. It is also interesting to note that Wheat, Eyre and the Duke of Norfolk were themselves Town Trustees and what Mary Walton terms *'Sheffield rulers'.*[243] James Wheat was elected Clerk to the Trustees on 14 February 1805.[244]

The Rev James Wilkinson's award did not cover the cost of the lost hay burnt during the riot but he must have been reimbursed from the public purse as J Edward Vickers informs us that Wilkinson was compensated with nearly £600.[245] There is little doubt that Wilkinson was shaken by the riot and Colonel de Lancey, in his report to the government, on the efficacy of Sheffield's magistrates, stated that *'since the mob burned part of his property,* [Wilkinson] *comes very seldom to Sheffield.'*[246]

Whatever the general population of Sheffield felt about Wilkinson, the town's dignitaries continued to honour the Reverend as we find in the *Sheffield Register* that 130 of them attended a public dinner at the Tontine Inn to celebrate his 70th birthday on 5 August 1800. This was the first of six annual celebratory dinners that were organised in his honour, the last taking place on 6 August 1805, the year of his death.[247]

Hailed as *'Father of the town of Sheffield',* a portrait and a bust of Wilkinson, both by Sir Francis Leggatt Chantrey,[248] were commissioned; the portrait by the Company of Cutlers and the bust at public expense for a memorial in the Parish Church. Medals were also struck in commemoration on his death. I can't imagine many of the working class making a contribution.

---

[243] Op Cit Walton, p.134

[244] Op Cit Leader, John Daniel, p.411

[245] Op Cit Vickers, p.180

[246] Op Cit Addy, John, *Coal,* p.79

[247] Op Cit *Sheffield Local Register,* p.108

[248] Sir Francis Leggatt Chantrey (1781-1841); born at Norton, son of a Sheffield carpenter; started work as a grocer's boy; apprentice to a Sheffield wood-carver, 1797-1802; learned drawing, stone-carving and painting in oil; portrait painter in Sheffield, 1802; lived in London from 1802 but made visits to Sheffield till 1808; exhibited pictures at the Royal Academy, 1804-07; worked mainly at carving statues from 1804; paid 300 guineas by King George IV for his bust, 1822; knighted, 1835. See *The Concise Dictionary of National Biography—Vol. I A-F,* Oxford University Press, 1994, p.522

Commemorative medal on the death of Rev James Wilkinson.

The financial costs of the riot were added to the cost of professional fees and expenses for the implementation of the Sheffield Enclosure Act:

	£	s	d
Legal fees for James Wheat	876	9	0
Parliamentary expenses	219	11	8
Commissioner's fees	1,284	9	4
Commissioner's expenses	251	7	10
Surveyors' fees	934	18	0
Roads, causeways and paths	1,030	11	4
Stakes and fences	184	1	1
Miscellaneous	916	2	3
Total	**5,694**	**10**	**6**

The miscellaneous items included £141-10s for stamping the award, £295 for repaying a loan from the Rotherham Bank, and a payment of £166 to James Watson, the landlord of the Tontine Inn.[249] The latter was probably to settle the account of Arthur Elliot, the Government's Commissioner, who resided at the Tontine for the duration.

---

[249] Op Cit Addy, John, *Agrarian,* p.62

A final anecdote on the 1791 Sheffield Enclosure riot, which epitomises the nature of the gentry and Sheffield's ruling class at the time and exemplified by the Rev James Wilkinson, is told by William Swift, alias *'Twiss'*:

> *'A little girl in the street was incited by some mischievous fellow to go up to a gentleman as he walked along and to say:*
>
> > *"They burnt his books*
> > *And scared his rooks*
> > *And set his stacks on fire"*
>
> *—the well-known doggerel relating to the rioters' attack on Broom Hall. The child innocently went in front of the gentleman, and, bobbing a curtsey, lisped out the lines.*
> *"What, my dear?" asked the Vicar, for it was none other. The child repeated it.*
> *"Yes, my dear," said he, "come along with me!" and, leading her by the hand, he took her to the Church Gates and had her put into the stocks, to her great distress.'*[250]

[250] Op Cit Leader, Robert Eadon (Ed), *Reminiscences*, pp.64-65

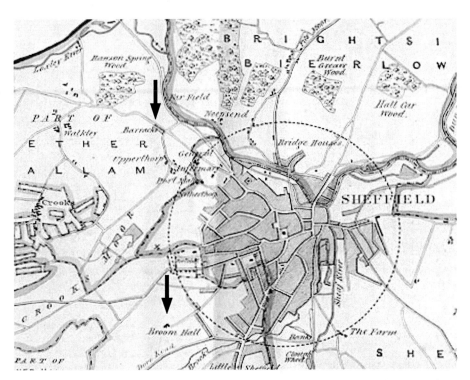

1832 map of Sheffield with the first Barracks and Broom Hall arrowed.

The Norfolk Street Riot

Corruption tells me homicide
Is wilful murder justified,
A striking precedent was tried
In August, 'ninety-five.
When armed assassins dressed in blue
Most wantonly their townsmen slew,
And magistrates and juries too
At murder did connive.[251]

1795

Nationally, 1795 was a year of much agitation by political reformers and the number of incidents of riot increased with the bad harvest of that year due to the hard winter that lasted into March and wheat crops were damaged by late frosts. In March, there were food riots in the Midlands, Cornwall and Sussex. Between April and July wheat more than doubled in price.

In some parts, in particular Portsmouth, Plymouth and Chichester, the military, instead of suppressing them, joined the rioters and even led them.[252] So alarmed was the government, that two new Acts were introduced in response. The Seditious Meetings Act prohibited meetings of more than fifty persons except by licence and under control of magistrates.

Lectures outside of universities were also banned except by similar licence and magisterial control. The Treasonable Practices Act extended the scope of treasonable activities to include those who plotted to help invaders, those who sought to coerce parliament and those who *'devised evil'* against the king.[253]

---

[251] From Joseph Mather's song, *The Norfolk Street Riots* in Op Cit Hey, p.138 See Appendix for the full song
[252] Op Cit Gilmour, p.409
[253] Watson, J. Steven, *The Reign of George III 1760-1815,* Oxford at the Clarendon Press, 1992, p.360

Most riots were generally put down by the military but on Tuesday, 4 August 1795, a disturbance on Norfolk Street in Sheffield began with a dispute amongst the military. A new regiment of 600 men, commanded by Colonel Duncan Cameron, based at the recently built Sheffield Barracks, had been parading in the town that evening.

At the end of the parade, at half past six, the Colonel ordered his recent recruits to dismiss and return to their quarters but instead an argument ensued between the privates and the colonel over non-payment of wages, a common state of affairs in the British army of the 18th century. About 300 local people, who had been watching the parade, gathered around to view the spectacle and it wasn't long before some became agitated and got involved in the squabble.

There was a general anathema towards the military amongst the people, it being seen as an agency of oppression. This seemingly innocuous altercation lit the fuse of a powder-keg, an explosion of anger at the prevailing injustices amongst the people that had been simmering for some time.

It wasn't long before the crowd had grown into several thousands and stones were being thrown and what started as a minor dispute turned into a full-scale riot. The Sheffield Independent Volunteers were called out and their commanding officer, lieutenant-colonel Robert Athorpe (that was his full name and not a repetition error), was sent for.

Col R A Athorpe was also a Sheffield magistrate, the very same who committed the five Broom Hall rioters to trial four years previously and a very unpopular gentleman. Col Athorpe was apparently enjoying dinner with the Earl Fitzwilliam at Wentworth Woodhouse when he got the despatch requesting his attendance at Sheffield.[254]

There were reports that he had had his fair share of wine and brandy, and that his actions that night were stimulated by drink. He rode to Sheffield with a furious haste, not sparing his horse, which apparently died the following day. On his arrival, according to *The Sheffield Iris,* edited by James Montgomery, the local poet and hymn writer, he *'plunged with his horse among the unarmed, defenceless people, and wounded with his sword, men, women and children promiscuously'.*[255]

---

[254] Op Cit Hey, p.137
[255] Op Cit Walton, p.140

Conversely, the Tory paper *The Courant,* reported that he merely rode about asking people to disperse.[256] A witness by the name of James Hinchcliffe, a drummer with the Volunteers, better known to his contemporaries as 'Jemmy Queer', confirmed that stones were thrown at the Volunteers and in particular he recalled the crushing of Major Greaves cocked-hat by a particularly large stone.[257]

Hinchcliffe was well-known in the town, as was his father, John Hinchcliffe, a police constable and landlord at the Greyhound in Gibraltar where James was born. James Hinchcliffe was of the ilk of Joseph Mather and John Blackwell and acquired his Jemmy Queer moniker from his talents as a mimic, poet, singer, comic and teller of many 'queer' stories.[258]

One thing that was agreed upon by all the reports, is that Athorpe read the Riot Act and the Volunteers discharged their muskets killing two, Benjamin Bradshaw and a man named Sorsby, and wounding several others, on his orders. In the confusion, Colonel Cameron's horse was shot from under him.

Most recorded accounts of the Norfolk Street riot that I have come across, have ignored the connection with the discontent amongst the local people due to inflated prices of wheat and other provisions, that there was also much agitation for political reform at the time, and that the outcome of the enclosure riots just four years previous was fresh in their minds.

Few writers have made a direct causal link between these prevailing social factors and the Norfolk Street riot. However, it was not lost on some commentators at the time and one such person wrote to the *Morning Post* expressing that there had been what they called a *'preconcerted plan'* to incite the riot.

On the morning of the riot, a pamphlet had been distributed amongst the townsfolk designed to incite anger amongst the discontent, and there were many:

---

[256] Ibid

[257] Kay, Steven, and Windle, Jack, *Seditious Things—The Songs of Joseph Mather-Sheffield's Georgian Punk Poet,* 1889 books, 2017, pp.84-5

[258] See Chris Hobb's website, Sheffield 3, No.9. There are a couple of Jemmy Queer's songs in Op Cit Kay & Windle: *Rotherham Fair,* pp.154-5, and *Dr. Shinar's The Lad For The Ladies,* PP.176-7

Treafon! Treafon! Treafon!
Againft the People.

The people are humbug'd! A plot difcovered! Pitt and the Committee for bread are combined together to ftarve the poor into the Army, and Navy! and to Starve your Widows and Orphans!

God help you! Labourers of the Nation! you are held on requifition to fight in a bad Cause! a Cause that is blafted by Heaven and damned by all Good Men! ! !

Every man to his Tent O Ifreal! fharpen your weapons and fpare not! for all the Scrats in the Nation are united againft your blood, your Wives and your little ones! ! !

Behold good Bread at fix fhillings per ftone and may every wearer of a bayonet be ftruck with Heaven's loudeft Thunder that refufes to help you—Fear not your lives—Ariftocrats are Scoundrels, Cowards; Curfed be the framers and promoters of the Corn Bill and let all the People fay Amen.

The author of this pamphlet certainly had incitement in mind and the military was certainly the target they had in mind, but were they aware of the potential dispute amongst the military that would play out that very day? One might think this is very unlikely and that the riot was indeed spontaneous. But was it?

A report in the *Reading Mercury* infers that not only was the riot planned, but that some of Cameron's troops were complicit with it and that the altercation with the Colonel had been contrived to ignite the riot and that they were party to it, some having replaced the wooden dummy flint of their muskets with real ones to use them against the Volunteers,[259] others coming on parade armed with stones in their pockets.

The same article relates that the Adjutant of the Volunteers had been forewarned of the plot and after consulting fellow officers, armed and readied the Volunteers in anticipation. The *Morning Post* correspondent, who says they witnessed the events as they unfolded, went on to say that they heard denunciations of the *'Scrats'* and a shout of *'Aye, damn then! bluff as they look, wee'l* [sic] *do them before twelve to night however.'*

---

[259] *Reading Mercury,* 17 August 1795, Vol. XXXIV, issue 1752, p.4, (courtesy Chris Hobbs)

They go on to defend the Volunteers, who had assembled in the street some three-quarters of an hour before the Riot Act was read, and Athorpe and Major Greave, who warned the mob of the fatal consequences should they remain another hour.

As for Athorpe's conduct, he describes that after he had *'prayed them to disperse'*, he *'brandished his sword and rode backwards and forwards amongst them without any military assistance',* refuting Montgomery's version of events published in the *Sheffield Iris.* Colonel Athorpe was acquitted of any wrong-doing at the ensuing Coroner's inquiry.

Colonel Robert Athorpe.

Robert A Athorpe Esq of Dinnington Hall, took command of the Regiment of Loyal Independent Sheffield Volunteers on 19 June 1794 with the rank of major, then being promoted to lieutenant-colonel on 15 December 1794 and also taking command of the West Riding Yeomanry Cavalry on 4 June 1795.

Instituted in April 1794, the Volunteers were known as *'The Blues'* from the colour of their uniform: blue coats with red facing worn over white waistcoats and black leggings.[260] Joseph Mather satirised them as *Ruddle-neck'd tups* and Col Athorpe as *Beef-headed Bob*.[261]

Mather's satire was popular with the people as it exposed corruption and the abuses of authority that they were powerless to challenge. Joseph Mather was a thorn in the side of the Establishment and was fortunate not to find himself arrested under the prevailing circumstances. It is reported that Mather was present and witnessed the whole affair; there is no doubting how he viewed the event.

For some time afterwards, he entertained drinkers in the local pubs with his ballad, *The Norfolk Street Riots*, claiming, *arm'd assassins, dressed in blue, who wantonly their townsmen slew, and magistrates and juries too, murder did connive* and on Athorpe, *What the bloody tyrant meant, was murder without precedent*.[262]

James Montgomery was not so fortunate. His published account of the Norfolk Street riot in *The Sheffield Iris* led to a £30 fine and six months in York Castle gaol for libel against Col Athorpe, his second conviction in twelve months. Previously, on 22 January 1795, he had been convicted for the printing of a ballad on the fall of the Bastille in the French Revolution, containing a libel *'of and concerning the war, and his Majesty's conduct therein,'* for which he was fined £20 and gaoled for three months.

Montgomery was tried once more at the West Riding Quarter Sessions on 21 January 1796 and was convicted of the criminal libel of Col R A Athorpe, whose fellow Sheffield magistrate, Rev James Wilkinson, sat on the bench that heard the case. The full article that condemned Montgomery described the events of the night:

> '*On Tuesday evening, a disturbance, trifling indeed in its commencement, but dreadful in its progress, and fatal in its consequences, happened in this town. The privates of Colonel Cameron's newly raised regiment refused to disperse after the evening exercise. The colonel remonstrated with them upon the impropriety of their conduct, but the men in return complained that part of their bounty*

---

[260] Op Cit Leader, Robert Eadon (Ed), *Reminiscences*, p.280
[261] Ibid, pp.279-280 For lyrics to *Raddle-Neck'd Tups* see Op Cit Kay and Windle, pp.93-96
[262] See Appendix 1

money had been hitherto withheld, and arrears of their pay were due. Of the justice of this complaint we cannot pretend to speak; but in consequence of the circumstances, a number of people assembled in Norfolk Street and upon the parade, R A Athorpe esq, Colonel of the volunteers, who had previously been ordered to hold themselves in readiness, now appeared at their head, and, in a peremptory tone, commanded the people instantly to disperse, which not being immediately complied with, a person, who shall be nameless, plunged with his horse amongst the unarmed, defenceless people, and wounded with his sword men, women and children promiscuously. The people murmured and fell back in confusion. The Riot Act was read. The people ran to and fro, scarcely one in a hundred knowing what was meant by these dreadful measures; when, an hour being expired, the volunteers fired upon their townsmen with bullets, and killed two persons upon the spot; several others were wounded, and the rest fled on every side in consternation. The whole town was alarmed, and continued in a state of agitation all night long. It is our duty to say, that, during the whole of this bloody business, no violence was committed upon any man's person or property by the people, no symptoms of a riotous disposition were manifested, except by one enraged individual, who threw a few stones, by which several of the volunteers were bruised.' [263]

In 1839, it came to light that Montgomery was the victim of persecution by the State. A book-seller named John Innocent unearthed some legal papers in a shop that he had bought at 22 Paradise Square which had previously been a lawyer's office, that of a Mr Charles Brookfield of Brookfield & Gould.

Within these documents it was stated that, *'briefs were to be given to counsel with the Attorney General's compliments'* and *'that this prosecution is carried on chiefly with a view to put a stop to the associated clubs in Sheffield; and it is to be hoped, if we are fortunate enough to succeed in convicting the prisoner, it will go a great way towards curbing the insolence they have uniformly manifested.'[264]*

---

[263] Op Cit Bentley, p.182. Bentley includes a potted biography of James Montgomery, including some of his hymns, as an appendix.
[264] Op Cit Leader, Robert Eadon (Ed), *Reminiscences*, p.7

His predecessor at the *Iris*, then called the *Sheffield Register*, Joseph Gales, had to flee the country in 1794 to avoid arrest for writing a letter to the London Corresponding Society critical of the government, a letter he denied writing but his political views were well known.

He fled to Germany and from there to America, where he started a printing business in Philadelphia and in 1797 bought the local newspaper, the *Independent Gazetteer*.[265] Montgomery had been Gales' clerk and he took over the newspaper following Gales' flight and renamed it *The Sheffield Iris*.

Montgomery's fortunes improved after his release from gaol as *The Sheffield Iris* improved its circulation and his poems and hymns gained in popularity. His standing steadily grew over the subsequent years and he was recommended a government pension of £150 per annum[266] by the Prime Minister, Sir Robert Peel, on 10 April 1835.[267]

Was this for his literary achievements or as recompense for his undeserved persecution? A statue of James Montgomery was erected over his grave in the General Cemetery following his death on 30 April 1854, aged 82, at a cost of £3,500.[268] His remains and the statue were later removed to the Cathedral churchyard.

Colonel Robert Athorpe resigned his commission on 31 October 1799 and died on 23 February 1806.

---

[265] Ibid, p.13
[266] Other accounts state that Montgomery received a pension of £200, Op Cit Taylor, pp.193-194
[267] Op Cit *Sheffield Local Register*, p.275.
[268] Ibid, p.530

James Montgomery and the Montgomery Monument

Food Riots

'The economic problems of men begin in the scarcities and inequalities of nature, although they may be sharpened beyond measure by the unwisdom and injustice of human arrangements.'[269]

'Bread or Blood'[270]

1756—1816

Shortages of food or unaffordable high prices caused more riots than any other public grievance during the 18th and early 19th centuries, accounting for well over half the public disturbances that occurred in Britain.[271] In his maiden speech in the House of Lords in 1812, Lord Byron commented on the riot of Nottinghamshire weavers that *'nothing but absolute want'* could have driven them to such excesses.[272]

There were widespread food riots at times when the harvests failed, such as in August 1756, when there were four days of rioting in Sheffield that required *'stout men, all armed with bludgeons'* to put down.[273] A mob attacked the Pond Corn Mill pulling slates off one side of the roof and taking away two loads of corn.

The Marquis of Rockingham and Mr William Battie JP came to the town and swore in ten new constables. From a contemporary letter dated 28 August 1756, we find that *'A very good scheme was formed by raising a company of stout, able men, who assembled last night well-armed with bludgeons, guns, and bayonets, knocked down all before them they knew to be of the gang of the mob, patrolled the town round and seized all the ringleaders, some in bed, some in the streets,*

---

[269] Op Cit Court, opening line of Chapter 1, p.3
[270] Slogan on a placard carried by Sheffield tailor John Blackwell, 3 December 1816
[271] Gilmour, Ian, *Riot, Risings and Revolution——Governance and Violence in Eighteenth Century England,* Pimlico, 1992, p.224
[272] *Hansard,* House of Lords, 27 February 1812, quoted in Fraser, Antonia, *Perilous Question——Reform or Revolution? Britain on the Brink, 1832,* Public Affairs, 2013, p.13
[273] Op Cit Gilmour, p.291

brought them in prisoners to the Town Hall, and this morning has escorted about 30 persons to ye Marquises, where Justice Battie and Sr. Rowland Wyn attends. All the best of the people in town is ready for its defence, and the mob is not able to stand them. All is at present very quiet.[274]

Inflated prices aggravated the food shortages, not least due to the introduction of the Corn Laws to protect the interests of the landowners, the first being introduced in 1791, which kept the price of grain high by restricting imports and exports by way of tariffs.

Further riots due to a poor wheat harvest in 1795, the year of the Norfolk Street riot, were averted by the foresight of some local dignitaries who organised a public meeting on 29 June where a Corn Committee was set up, chaired by Dr John Browne,[275] and a subscription of £8,100 was raised to purchase corn to distribute to the poor at cheaper prices.[276]

Between 4,000 and 5,000 applications for relief were made. Flour was retailing at 4s-11d per stone but the Corn Committee sold it on from the Town Hall at 2s-6d per stone for fine flour and 2s for bread flour.[277] Instead of riots there were public celebrations at the sudden fall in the price of corn and Dr Browne was hailed a hero by the poor but he declined the honour of being carried through the streets of the town *'as it would invert the order of things, and be ungallant.'*[278]

He was later honoured by his peers, in 1810, with the commissioning of a bust by Sir Francis Chantrey that stood in the boardroom at the Infirmary and later in the Cutler's Hall and is now part of the archives collection at the Northern General Hospital.

---

[274] Op. Cit, Leader, Robert Eadon, p.59

[275] Dr John Browne was one of the public benefactors instrumental in building the General Infirmary, the first stone of which was laid on 4 October 1794. He died 10 April 1810 aged 70

[276] Mayhall, John, *The Annals of Yorkshire Vol. 1,* Joseph Johnson, 1865, p.184

[277] Op Cit *Sheffield Local Register,* pp.79-80

[278] *The Courant,* 22 August 1795

Dr John Browne (1740-1810)

The year 1800 was a year of want for Sheffield's *'necessitous poor'* due to the price of provisions exceeding their ability to pay for them, once more due to a bad harvest but also due to a growing inequality between the workers and the landed and commercial classes, largely as a result of the wars with France.[279]

Even though the year saw a record high in the value of wheat imports (wheat imports reached a record value of £2,675,000 in 1800, three times that of pre-war years[280]) and that there had been improvements in farming following the enclosures, there was not enough to feed an ever-increasing population.

It was reported in the House of Commons that one-sixth of the population was living on charity.[281] By October 1800, there were *'bread riots'* up and down the country, aggravated in many instances by the reactions of unsympathetic and

---

[279] Op Cit Redford, p.88
[280] Op Cit Bryant, *Years of Endurance,* p.345
[281] Ibid, p.354

dogmatic magistrates and judges, which so much concerned the government that in November troops were recalled from Portugal to quell the unrest in industrial towns.[282]

This was the age of the *'Dual Revolution'*: the Industrial Revolution in Britain and the political revolution in France which *'left no aspect of human life unchanged'*.[283]

The price of wheat in Sheffield had increased from 17s to 19s-6d a load in 1797, to 38s to 48s in 1800. The price of oats had risen from 17s to 18s a quarter to 45s to 55s in the same period.[284] A soup kitchen had opened at the Cutlers' Hall on 5 December 1799 selling soup at 1½d per quart (2 pints) to alleviate the hardship on the run-up to Christmas.[285]

On 13 February 1800, the Sheffield Independent Volunteers, who had of late presented their recently retired Colonel, R A Athorpe, with *'an elegant gold cup'*, voted £100 towards a subscription for the relief of the necessitous poor and, if necessary, a further £100 for the relief of its own members *'exposed to the pressure of the time'*.[286]

On 1 April, a second subscription of the year was rendered necessary *'by the great scarcity and dearness of all the necessities of life'*.[287] On the following day at a public meeting, the town's millers, bakers, meal and flour sellers resolved *'to use all lawful means in their power to suppress the selling of corn by sample, particularly that sold by petty-fogging corn-jobbers, being convinced that their trade is thereby greatly imposed upon, the public in general injured, and the labouring part of mankind most shamefully oppressed'*.[288]

Whilst the tradesmen professed action by legal means, it wasn't long before the necessitous poor turned to illegal means in response to their situation.

On 22 April 1800, there were disturbances in the town and a riot in Queen's Street. A flour warehouse was attacked and meal shops, butter dealers and potato merchants were raided by the hungry populace. Whatever legal means were attempted by the town's tradesmen and dignitaries, including the prosecution of *'forestallers'* for rigging the market, they clearly failed to curtail the unrest as

---

[282] Ibid, p.344
[283] Op Cit Hobsbawm, *The Age Of Revolution,* p.2 and p.296
[284] Op Cit *Sheffield Local Register*, p.83 and p.91
[285] Ibid, p.90
[286] Ibid, pp.90-91
[287] Ibid, p.91
[288] Ibid Petty-fogging: to practise legal deception or trickery

later in the year, on 2 September, meal and flour sellers' shops were attacked again by mobs in consequence of high prices.[289]

On 23 October, the *Sheffield Register* reported that the Rev James Wilkinson presented fifty guineas to the Infirmary and forty guineas to the boys' and girls' charity schools *'in consideration of the difficulties under which public charities labour, from the extreme dearness of the necessities of life.'*[290]

The same paper reported a meeting of around 2,000 people in a field in the Park area on the night of 1 December *'to consider the distress arising from the high price of provisions.'*[291] On 15 December, a public meeting at the Town Hall raised another subscription of £1,200 for the relief of the poor people *'in great distress'* due to high prices of provisions.

In March 1801, it was reported that upwards of 10,000 people had received benefit from the subscriptions. The population of Sheffield at this time, including the outlying parishes, was 45,755.[292]

Contemporary cartoon depicting the mob dealing with a forestaller.

There appears to have been a lull in the occasions of disturbance and riot in the town over the price of provisions, despite the continuing problem of high

[289] Ibid, p.92 see also Op Cit Leader, Robert Eadon, p.337
[290] Ibid, p.93, a guinea is £1-1s (£1-5p)
[291] Ibid
[292] Parliamentary Census 1801

prices, until January 1809, when it was deemed necessary to raise another subscription for the relief of the poor *'in consequence of the unprecedented stagnation of trade, the very high price of provisions, and the extreme difficulty of collecting the parochial rates'.*[293]

A committee was appointed and on 20 January; it announced the receipt of £1,300, and that 10,000 applications for relief had been made.[294] However, it is not until April 1812 that we find further reports of civil unrest in the town due to the high price of provisions, and the assistance of the militia to keep the peace.

On 14 April 1812, several hundred people congregated and paraded in Market Place protesting at the price of food. The source of the gathering was reported in the *Leeds Mercury* as being a number of unemployed skilled and semi-skilled workers who, being short of regular work in their trades, were being employed to create a new burial ground at St George's church off Broad Lane, to the west of the town.

One report suggests that they numbered around a hundred and were actually inmates of the Sheffield Workhouse.[295] As they approached the Corn Market around mid-day, they were joined by others, mainly women and boys, to protest at the newly-raised price of potatoes.

At the Corn Market, some attacked the potato stores, breaking windows and throwing produce in all directions. Many more joined in the rioting and potatoes were scattered in the street, two or three sacks of corn were split open and their contents strewn about, butter was taken and a barrel of herrings was broken and the fish thrown about.[296]

What wasn't used for missiles was destroyed or taken away. The Riot Act was read by a magistrate, attended by a number of police officers, causing a pause in the disturbance and some to disperse, and then a voice from the crowd called out *'All in a mind for the store-room in the Wicker!'*

At this, they set off to target the Militia Stores at the bottom of Spital Hill. The building was an old warehouse previously occupied by one Jonathan Hobson that had been given over to the Volunteers for the storage of arms and equipment.

Being used for such a purpose one would expect the building to have been relatively secure but on this day it was guarded by just two soldiers, Captain Best

---

[293] Op Cit *Sheffield Local Register,* p.120
[294] Ibid
[295] Priories Historical Society website
[296] *Leeds Mercury,* April 1812. See The Victorian Web and Chris Hobbs' websites.

and Sergeant Thomas Flathes, despite there being more soldiers in the town than was usual due to an ill-advised anticipation of a Luddite rising.[297]

Thomas Flathes lived in a house nearby with his wife and children. The first indication of what was about to unfold was a group of around forty young lads accompanied by five or six men approaching the depot from the direction of the town. They paused in the road about 50 yards away until they were soon joined by four to five thousand others following on from behind.

On the arrival of the mob, all described as being young men, the two soldiers were threatened with their lives. Armed with musket and bayonet, Sgt Flathes did his best to hold them back but he was pelted with stones and it wasn't long before the doors were broken open and the rioters were ransacking the place.

Flathes retreated to his house where he led his wife and children upstairs from where he witnessed the plundering of the stores from his bedroom window. The depot contained 900 stands of arms and the same number of uniforms.

Muskets were removed and smashed on a low wall nearby. Drums, trumpets and uniforms were thrown out of the windows and strewn over the road, being kicked about as the screaming mob went on the rampage. Thirty stands of arms were destroyed.[298] In total, 198 firearms were destroyed and 78 muskets were stolen.[299]

---

[297] Bailey, Brian, *The Luddite Rebellion,* Sutton Publishing, 1998, p.74
[298] Op Cit *Sheffield Local Register*, p.132
[299] Op Cit Bailey, p.38

Market Place

Some of the muskets were shouldered by a small contingent of rioters, mimicking the soldiers, who were considered agents of oppression, as they marched up the Wicker. They were met by a troop of the 15th Light Dragoons from the barracks and they fled in all directions, dropping the muskets as they scurried away.

On their arrival at the stores, it didn't take the Dragoons long to bring the rioters to order. Ten people were apprehended: William Rodgers, aged 16; Mary Gibbons, aged 48; Joseph Wolstenholme, aged 17; John Rowen, aged 15; Thomas Wilson; William Groom; William Shirtcliffe; William Denton; Charles Parker; and William Bowen.[300]

William Rodgers was found with a military sword hidden under his apron and Mary Gibbons was apprehended with a bundle of two pairs of pantaloons and a pair of gaiters. The following day, magistrates ordered a parade of special constables throughout the evening and into the night with orders to apprehend anyone refusing to disperse. All public houses had to close at 10:00 pm prompt.

Things settled down for a few days, but further disturbances were reported in the town on 20 April. Although there was no Luddite rising in Sheffield, this

---

[300] The *Leeds Mercury* reported seven people being arrested but gave no names.

particular riot may have been incited by the deaths of two men, 24-year-old Samuel Hartley and 19-year-old John Booth, following a Luddite attack at Rawfolds Mill at Liversedge, near Dewsbury, on the night of 11/12 April.

News of the nature of their deaths (both were seriously wounded by armed soldiers guarding the mill and died hours later after being interrogated and there were suspicions of them being tortured) and a verdict of *'justifiable homicide'* caused widespread rioting across the north, including at Sheffield.[301]

On 16 May, more special constables were sworn-in at the Town Hall *'for the preservation of the peace'*.[302] The people arrested on 14 April were tried at York Assizes on 1 August. William Rodgers and John Rowan were each sentenced to 6 months for rioting and breaking flintlocks; Mary Gibbons received the same sentence for the same offences but also received a further 6 months for stealing breeches and a pair of gaiters; Joseph Wolstenholme was acquitted.

I have found no records of the sentences handed down to the others but Thomas Wilson was found guilty of assaulting a JP and rioting; William Groom, guilty of stealing potatoes; William Shirtcliffe, guilty of rioting. Curiously, William Denton was found guilty of inciting a mob to attempt the rescue of four prisoners at York, but I have uncovered no details of the event.

Although Charles Parker and William Bowen were sent to York Assizes, I have found no record of their fate. Whilst this event coincided with Luddite riots in nearby Huddersfield and Leeds the government were confident that the Sheffield incident had no association with Luddism.

General Grey, commander of the West Riding, wrote on 18 April that, *'It is evident that this affair was without plan or system, and I should suppose totally unconnected with the proceedings at Leeds, Huddersfield, etc., particularly as everything has since been perfectly quiet at Sheffield.'*[303]

Despite the riots, food prices continued on the increase with the price of fine flour rising above 5s per stone and a public meeting was held on 13 August 1812 where it was decided to raise the weekly allowances of the poor. On 18 August, crowds assembled in the town again and marched on the meal and flour dealers determined to make them reduce their prices.

---

[301] Op Cit Bailey, pp.53-6
[302] Op Cit *Sheffield Local Register*, p.133
[303] Hammond, J.L. and Hammond, Barbara, *The Skilled Labourer 1760-1832,* Alan Sutton Publishing Limited, 1995, p.309

Once more, the Riot Act was read in a number of parts of the town and once more, the military was called out and more arrests were made.[304] A further public meeting on 20 August provided another subscription for the relief of the poor of the town and the parishes not in receipt of relief from the Overseers of the Poor. The amount raised was £1,883-17s. There was no respite in price hikes as on 11 September, flour was reported as being sold at 6s-4d per stone.

Ironically, a fall in prices due to a return of imported wheat as the Napoleonic wars drew to a close caused a severe agricultural depression between 1814 and 1816[305] but prices in the domestic market were kept artificially high by a further Corn Law that restricted imports of wheat, thus increasing the price of bread.

In 1816, there were further riots in the town and a ringleader comes to the fore by way of a colourful character called John Blackwell, a tailor, also known as *'Jacky Blacker'* and *'King of the Gallery'* due to his regular outbursts from the gallery at the Theatre (see Ch1). On Tuesday, 3 December, John Blackwell led a mob along Broad Lane protesting at the price of bread. The price of flour at this time was 7s to 7s-6d per stone.[306]

To make the point, Blackwell carried a drawn sword thrust high in the air and at its point was pierced a penny loaf dripping with blood. In his other hand, he carried a large placard bearing the inscription *'Bread or Blood'*. The spectacle was observed by Mr James Archibald Wortley JP[307] (later to become Lord Wharncliffe) who took it upon himself to apprehend Blackwell, pulling him from the crowd and then dragging him before the magistrates' court, which committed him to York Assizes.

He was tried there on 19 March 1817, found guilty of public order offences and sentenced to two years imprisonment. On his release, it wasn't long before Blackwell found himself once more facing the judges at York, at the Summer Assizes of 1820, for *'behaving in a riotous manner at Sheffield, and encouraging other disorderly persons to riot, and having in his possession a loaded pistol, a pike and other unlawful weapons.'*

---

[304] Ibid, p.134
[305] Op Cit Court, p.161
[306] Op Cit Leader, Robert Eadon (Ed), *Reminiscences,* p.270
[307] James Archibald Stuart-Wortley-Mackenzie (1776-1845), first Baron Wharncliffe, 1826; grandson of John Stuart, third earl of Bute; served in the army, 1790-1801; Tory MP for Bossiney and for Yorkshire; lord privy seal in Peel's ministry, 1834, and president of the council, 1841. See *The Concise Dictionary of National Biography—Vol. III N-Z,* Oxford University Press, 1994, p.2893

This time he was gaoled for two and a half years. John Blackwell died aged 53 on 14 April 1839 in the Sheffield Poorhouse, where he spent the last eight years of his life.[308]

There are a couple of incidental events during the Sheffield food riots that are worth relating that add a bit of levity to the dire situation, although not a laughing matter for the victims concerned. The first concerns Charles Clegg, the Trumpet-Major to the Yeomanry Cavalry and a member of the Theatre Royal orchestra who, on being ordered by the magistrates, sounded *'the call'* for the military to assemble as trouble was brewing in the town.

Mounted on his trusty steed, he first blew his trumpet outside the Tontine Inn, then rode to the vegetable market and repeated the call. It was here that a potato was thrown from the crowd at some force and with faultless aim, right into the mouth of Clegg's trumpet. The force of the missile knocked the trumpet back into Clegg's mouth taking out two of his teeth and rendering him unable to play the trumpet ever again; Trumpet-Major Clegg had blown his last call.[309]

At around the same time of the assault on Charles Clegg, there was another incident involving the use of a potato as a projectile. A crowd of *'roughs'* had gathered outside the Yellow Lion Inn on Haymarket, and a number of police constables attended opposite the Tontine Inn accompanied by Hugh Parker JP[310], one of the less resented Sheffield magistrates.

Through the air from the mob came a large potato destined for the ranks of authority, which hit Justice Parker squarely on his chest, knocking him back a pace. From his reaction, the impact of the potato had obviously caused the magistrate some discomfort and alarm. Then, from the mob stepped forward a burly man wearing a leather apron, signifying that he was either a blacksmith or a forge man, who called out *Mester Parker, I didn't intend that to hit yo; I meant it to hit Tom Smith.*

Thomas Smith[311] was one of the constables standing beside Justice Parker. One can imagine the cheers and laughter from the crowd, which no doubt took

---

[308] Op Cit *Sheffield Local Register,* p.321

[309] Op Cit Leader, Robert Eadon (Ed), *Reminiscences,* p.214. Charles Clegg died on 29 November 1842

[310] Hugh Parker of Woodthorpe, a country gentleman and partner in Parker, Shore & Co Bank; qualified as a magistrate on 2 September 1799; father of John Parker who became one of Sheffield's first members of parliament in 1832 (see Election Riots below)

[311] Thomas Smith was a Sheffield constable for thirty years, eighteen of which he served as Deputy Bailiff of Hallamshire and Bailiff of the Court of Requests. He is also recorded as being keeper of the Debtors' Gaol in 1822. He died on 3 June 1832 aged 64

some of the heat out of the situation; it probably brought a smile to Constable Smith's face too. Hugh Parker survived the potato, but I have not found any information relating to the fate of its thrower.

Of course, food riots were not unique to Sheffield as at times of harvest failure and economic blockade in the first decades of the 19th century (harvests failed in 1800, 1801, 1810, 1812 and 1813, years when wheat prices were described as being little short of famine prices[312]) the impact was felt nationwide and with it the inevitable disturbances arising out of protest.

Neither are the above food riots the only ones to occur in Sheffield but they remain the best documented. I have little doubt that other disturbances would have occurred in the 1840s, a period of the worst harvest failures to affect Great Britain, especially in Ireland where hundreds of thousands suffered starvation and famine-related deaths,[313] and thousands more emigrated to escape what became known as the Great Irish Famine due to the successive failures of the potato harvest.

Between 1846 and 1851, the population of Ireland reduced by 20% and the 1851 census tells us that 25% of the population of Liverpool, the nearest port of call, were born in Ireland.[314] A number of Irish immigrants made their way to Sheffield. The price of wheat at Sheffield Market fluctuated immensely between 1836 and 1857 hitting a peak of £5 7s 5d per quarter (2 stone) on 18 May 1847; the lowest price recorded in these years was £1 19s 9¾d per quarter on 11 March 1851.

The Sheffield townsfolk that took to the streets when food was short or prices were high, did not suffer hunger as the Irish did. Such extremes would have made them physically incapable of the actions that they took. I have found no evidence of anyone in Sheffield actually starving to death but that doesn't mean people didn't die of hunger-related diseases, as undoubtedly some did.

Friedrich Engels tells us that during the first two years of his time living in England (between 1842 and 1845) at least twenty or thirty persons died of starvation *'under the most revolting circumstances.'*[315] He goes on to say that

---

[312] Op Cit Court, p.36

[313] The traditional death-toll of the Great Irish Famine is around 1million. Most of these deaths resulted from hunger-induced dysentery and typhus: O'Grada, Carmac, *Ireland— A New Economic History 1780-1939,* Clarendon Press, 1995, pp.173-209. Similar conditions, although not so dire, prevailed in the Scottish Highlands at this time.

[314] Op Cit Hobsbawm, E J, p.310

[315] Op Cit Engels, p.69

coroners' juries wouldn't declare a verdict of death by starvation, despite overwhelming evidence, for *'The bourgeoisie dare not speak the truth in these cases, for it would speak its own condemnation.'*[316]

Many more people died from illnesses they might otherwise have survived but were exacerbated by malnutrition.

Hugh Parker JP (Courtesy of the Company of Cutlers in Hallamshire) and the arms of the Parker family.

---

[316] Ibid, p.70

Pentrich Rising The Sheffield Connection

Every man his skill must try,
He must turn out and not deny;
No bloody soldier must he dread,
He must turn out and fight for bread.
The time is come you plainly see
The government opposed must be.[317]

1817

Whilst most of the Sheffield food riots were a spontaneous reaction to a sudden increase in prices or an unexpected shortfall of supplies, there were a small number of Sheffield men willing to organise themselves into an army of rebellion with the objective of overthrowing the government to achieve a fairer society.

In January 1817, someone either threw a stone or fired an airgun at the Prince Regent whilst on his way to parliament. In the previous months, a number of large public meetings up and down the country seeking political reform had alarmed the government.

With explicit memories of the 1789 French Revolution and the subsequent abolition of the French monarchy and execution of Louis XVI in 1793, the cabinet called secret committees in both the houses of parliament and presented evidence from their spies of a revolutionary plot to seize the Bank and the Tower.

The government suspended the Habeas Corpus Act[318] and took measures against the holding of seditious meetings. This sparked protests across the country, including a march of petitioners from Manchester to London in March. This became known as the march of the Blanketeers from their carrying of

---

[317] Verse sung by Jeremiah Brandreth on the march from Pentrich to Nottingham: Op Cit Thompson, E.P., p.724
[318] *Habeas Corpus* literally means *you must have the body.* The Habeas Corpus Act is a safeguard against illegal detention.

blankets to sleep in overnight. Their leaders were arrested and the march petered out at Macclesfield.[319]

On 9 June, four hundred stockingers, quarrymen and ironworkers from Pentrich, Ripley and Alfreton in north-east Derbyshire, many armed with pikes, scythes, guns and bludgeons set off to march on Nottingham, with the belief that many more would join them on the road.

Led by 31-year-old framework knitter Jeremiah Brandreth, the men and boys were to join up with hundreds more from the north to take Nottingham as part of a general uprising across South and West Yorkshire, Derbyshire and Nottinghamshire with the ultimate aim of overthrowing the government in London.

The general uprising failed to materialise and within 12 hours of setting off, the Pentrich Uprising, termed *'England's Last Revolution'* by John Stevens,[320] was routed and 80 rebels were in gaol. Brandreth and two of his lieutenants, 52-year-old stone getter, Isaac Ludlam and 46-year-old stonemason, William Turner were hanged for treason on 7 November 1817, their bodies then taken down and beheaded; the quartering was remitted. Fourteen others were transported: eleven for life and three for 14 years.[321]

The government had been kept informed of this seditious plot through the work of their agent *'Oliver the Spy'*, real name W J Richards, who had estimated that 216,000 men could be raised by the rebel leaders in the north and the midlands; 10,000 of them in the Sheffield area.[322]

---

[319] Op Cit, Woodward, pp. 63-64.

[320] Stevens, John, *England's Last Revolution—Pentrich 1817,* Moorland Publishing Company, 1977

[321] Ibid, p.11

[322] Ibid, p.39 The use of undercover agents by agencies of the State has been a regular factor during times of unrest in Britain and almost certainly continues today. During the General Strike of 1926 the Secretary of the Lewisham Unemployed Workers' Movement, a man named Johnson, was an informer in the pay of Scotland Yard. Johnson committed suicide when his pay was stopped. See Attfield, John, and Lee, John in the chapter on Deptford and Lewisham in Skelley, Jeffrey (Ed), *The General Strike, 1926,* Lawrence and Wishart, 1976, p.265

Following a meeting of a rebel group on 5 May at the Joiner's Arms in Wakefield, where one of the leaders, Benjamin Scholes, was the landlord, Oliver sent a list of names of the attending delegates to the Home Secretary, Viscount Sidmouth. Amongst the names was that of William Wolstenholme, a Sheffield joiner who was a relative of the curate at Pentrich, Rev Hugh Wolstenholme, who was a supporter of the reforms sought by the rebels.[323]

Jeremiah Brandreth

Oliver, who was believed by those at the meeting to be directing the regional uprisings on behalf of the London insurrectionists, visited Sheffield on 14 May and met with Wolstenholme at the Blue Bell public house.[324] At this meeting, Oliver advised that the planned uprising, which was originally to take place on 26 May, should be postponed until 9 June as *'the nights would be dark and the whole country would be in a more perfect state for rising.'*[325]

Oliver's regular reports to Sidmouth were relayed to the relevant local magistrates in the towns where the uprising was being planned. Hugh Parker, Sheffield's chief magistrate, who was employing a spy of his own, a silver-plater's assistant called Thomas Bradley, and who had also attended the meeting on 14 May, was informed of Wolstenholme's involvement.

Neither Hugh Parker nor Thomas Bradley was aware that Oliver was Sidmouth's *agent provocateur,* and like the other rebels thought him to be one of their leaders. Oliver returned to Sheffield on 29 May and once more met with Wolstenholme and Bradley at the Blue Bell.

Wolstenholme asked Oliver to stay around for another meeting of the *'Leaders of Ten'* (each delegate was thought to have at least ten further rebels behind him)[326] planned to take place at the Rawson grinding wheel of Mr Chandler just outside of the town but Oliver gave his apologies as he had a seat booked on the Leeds coach.

---

[323] Ibid
[324] The only Blue Bell in directories around this time was at 13 Jehu Lane.
[325] Op Cit Thompson, E.P., p.718
[326] Ibid, p.720

It was fortunate for Oliver that he didn't attend Rawson's wheel as Bradley had already informed Hugh Parker about this meeting and he in turn had planned a raid to capture the insurgents. There were around thirty delegates at the Rawson wheel, but the alarm was raised by lookouts as a troop of dragoons attempted to surround the mill.

Most of the rebels were able to escape into the nearby woods but four, including Wolstenholme, were apprehended. Although they all initially denied seditious activity, one of them, William Bradwell, eventually talked. On Bradwell's information, three other insurgents were later arrested, including William Wolstenholme's two sons, James and Thomas. The other three rebels apprehended were Rowland Hartley, James Rowin and George Robinson. All seven were charged with High Treason and held at the Town Hall.

On 10 June, the day after the Pentrich rebels had been routed on their way to Nottingham, the seven Sheffield men were transferred from the Town Hall to London on the True Briton coach under a substantial escort of dragoons. There, they were 'delivered into the custody of the Constable of the Tower.'[327]

On apprehending the seven rebels, Parker was dismayed in the knowledge that Oliver, who he believed to be the chief plotter, had not been seized and considered sending a constable to Leeds to seek him out but decided instead to write to the mayor with a description of this major player for him to be apprehended by the Leeds police. Parker also wrote to Sidmouth informing him of Oliver's escape and his intentions in pursuing him at Leeds:

> I am furnished with an exact description of this man, and did time admit I would dispatch a Constable to endeavour to take him at Leeds tonight tho' there is not time for this purpose I will write to the mayor by mail.- if not taken at Leeds, I am sure he may be taken when he calls to see Mitchell at Cold Bath Fields prison which he means to do.-Your Lordship shall have a description of O sent. P S Bradley our informer seems to think O will not stay at Leeds longer than he did at Sheffield.[328]

The Home Secretary received Parkers message with some trepidation. To him, it was fortunate that his spy had evaded capture as, if Parker's 'Vigilance,

---

[327] Op Cit Sheffield Local Register, p.150
[328] Op Cit Stevens, p.44 The man Mitchell referred to here was Joseph Mitchell, a constant companion of Oliver before being arrested on 4 May near Huddersfield.

Zeal and Promptitude' engendered Oliver's arrest, his cover would be blown and the government's biggest asset in the field would be lost. Sidmouth quickly wrote back to Parker to inform him of Oliver's true role and that on no account must he be arrested. In fact, he wanted no more arrests until Oliver had reported back to London.[329]

The seven Sheffield men, although initially charged with High Treason, spent months in gaol under the suspension of Habeus Corpus. William Wolstenholme and his sons spent six months in Winchester gaol; they were released in December 1817.

We must assume that the other four insurgents were treated the same. The problem for the authorities was that the only evidence against the seven Sheffield men was the word of Oliver, the spy and the informer Thomas Bradley. Oliver was exposed by the *Leeds Mercury* less than a week after the Pentrich rising and the government, whose reputation now lay in tatters, suffered a number of defeats in the courts when the juries learned of the role of Sidmouth's spy.[330]

The failure of the Pentrich uprising, a good harvest and a revival of trade in 1817 brought an end to the disturbances and the plotting, and an end to the government's consternation for a while. James Wolstenholme would continue his campaigning for political reform and become a prominent figure in the Sheffield Chartist movement (see chapter on the Chartist Uprising).

Oliver, the spy, escaped potential retribution by going to South Africa in 1820 taking a new identity; he became William Oliver Jones and was given employment as Inspector of Government Buildings.[331]

---

[329] Ibid
[330] Op Cit Thompson, E.P., pp.726-7
[331] Op Cit Stevens, p.144

Viscount Sidmouth

Election Riots

No paltry fray, no bloody day,
That crowns with praise the baby great;
The DEED of Brougham, Russell, Grey,
The DEED that's done, we celebrate!
Mind's great charter! Europe saved!
Man, forever unenslaved![332]

1832

The Reform Act of 1832 is regarded by some to be one of the most important pieces of legislation of the pre-Victorian era, arguing that it prevented a revolution on the lines of those encountered by many European states in the 1830s and 1840s. Eric Hobsbawm tells us that, *'The Reform Act of 1832 corresponds to the July revolution of 1830 in France, and had indeed been powerfully stimulated by the news from Paris'.[333]*

There were many incidents of riot up and down the country preceding the Act being passed, the worst being at Bristol on Sunday and Monday, 30 and 31 October 1831, following the House of Lords' rejection of the Bill. Although the official estimate of deaths at Bristol was twelve, around four-hundred people were in fact killed.[334]

Even after the Bill was passed the Duke of Wellington, who had vehemently opposed Reform, was attacked by the mob on 18 June, the anniversary of the Battle of Waterloo.[335] Despite this proclaimed historic significance of the 1832 Act, it engendered little change in how Britain was governed or who it was that governed; although the wealthier middle-class elected at the December election

---

[332] From a hymn by Ebenezer Elliott celebrating the 1832 Reform Act sung during the procession of 18 June; Brougham, Russell and Grey being the leading MPs who brought about Reform
[333] Op Cit Hobsbawm, *The Age Of Revolution,* p.110
[334] Op Cit Fraser, p.169
[335] Ibid, p.265

held the balance of power, parliament was still made up of the wealthy, the nobility and the gentry, and the working classes were still excluded from the franchise.

However, significantly for Sheffield, the Act gave the town the right to elect members of Parliament for the very first time. Like many of the growing industrial towns and cities like Manchester, Birmingham, Bradford, Leeds and the phenomenon that was Glasgow, Sheffield had no Parliamentary representation until the 1832 Reform Act, which was the beginning of a journey towards a genuine democracy; a journey that we are still on.

There were no political parties as we know them today. There were the Tories and the Whigs, names given to the factions that supported or opposed the Hanoverian succession in 1714 but they were not political parties in any formal sense outside of Parliament and inside Parliament, they were best described as *'rolling coalitions of shifting interests.'*[336]

Before the 1832 Reform Act, there was a notable diversity of the franchise in Britain. Qualification for voting varied from borough to borough. These included the 'Rotten' borough or 'Pocket' borough with very few voters, and the right of election was usually restricted to a local patron or 'borough-monger', a wealthy man, usually a landowner, who bought and sold the parliamentary representation of the borough[337] (Old Sarum, described as a lump of stone and a field, had no voters at all yet returned two Members of Parliament[338]).

The 'Potwalloper' franchise was restricted to people occupying dwellings with their own fireplaces and cooking facilities, also described as *'a parliamentary voter who was admitted to vote on proof that he had boiled a pot within the borough bounds during the six months preceding the election';*[339] the 'Scot and lot' franchise restricted voting to occupiers of houses and shops and who were also local rate-payers.

The 'Freeholder' or 'Freeman' franchise, the largest share of the electorate, gave qualification to vote to men owning a freehold property with an annual

---

[336] Chase, Malcolm, *Chartism——A New History,* Manchester University Press, 2007, p.180

[337] The effect of this meant that the 'borough-monger' took his seat in Parliament without an election at all. In the county of Devon for example, there were only two polls between 1690 and 1800. See Loft, Philip, *Power to the People* in *History Today Vol69, Issue 5,* May 2019, p.15.

[338] Op Cit Fraser, p.19

[339] Virtue's English Dictionary, 1952, p.668

rental value or income of forty shillings (£2).[340] All of these voting systems were open to abuse and corruption, particularly the Freeholder franchise where honorary freemen were created for electoral support and indiscriminate bribery was rife.

People who do not exercise their democratic right to vote today should reflect upon how things used to be not so long ago and recognise that universal suffrage was won through struggle and that their apathy is a slight on those who endured that struggle.

The 1832 Act was introduced to eradicate these abuses but it also restricted the franchise to men who had been resident in the borough for six months, be householders of property with an annual rental value of £10 that they must have occupied for at least twelve months, and they must have paid their rates.

Eligible men also had to claim their vote to be placed on the electoral register every year, each time paying a fee of one shilling. The net result of the changes to the franchise within the 1832 Act increased the number of men eligible to vote, increasing the electorate by 63%, but for the first time, it totally disenfranchised women.[341]

However, the new qualifications to vote also drew a defining line between the working class and the middle class and fuelled the rise in Chartism. The UK electorate in 1831 was 497,197; in 1833 it had risen to 811,443.[342] The population of the country was around 22 million.

---

[340] Salmon, Philip and Rix, Kathryn, *Who should have the Vote* in *History Today Vol.68, Issue 8* August 2018, pp.26-30
[341] Ibid, p.31
[342] Ibid, p.33

Medal struck to celebrate the 1832 Reform Act

On 18 June 1832 the Sheffield townsfolk celebrated the passing of the Reform Bill with a procession around the town. Some 30,000 people joined 5,000 members of the Political Union assembled in the Wicker. Accompanied by flags and music the procession crossed Lady's Bridge and took a circuit of the town.

A medal struck for the occasion was distributed to members of the Political Union. In the general election of December 1832, Sheffield elected its very first members of parliament. Whilst initially, this was received as something for the town to celebrate, the poll of 1832 turned out to be anything but a celebration and, ironically, led to rioting that resulted in six Sheffield men and boys losing their lives.

The election for the representation of the Borough of Sheffield was to provide two members of parliament and the process began at temporary hustings erected opposite the New Corn Exchange on Wednesday, 12 December. Proceedings were overseen by the Master Cutler and returning officer, Thomas Dunn, a colliery owner and actuary who lived at 60 Solly Street.[343]

An estimated 30,000 people were in attendance[344], although only 3,504 Sheffield men had the necessary £10 householder qualification that allowed them

---

[343] Thomas Dunn was the first Dissenter admitted to the office of Master Cutler. He was a director of Hounsfield, Wilson & Co, the Sheffield Coal Company when he died on 28 August 1839 at Warwick, aged 65

[344] *Sheffield Local Register*, p.246 *The Poll Book of the Borough of Sheffield, December 13 and 14 1832,* A Whitaker and Co, Iris Office, *Companion section,* 1833, hereafter referenced as *Poll Book, Companion,* states 'above 20,000 persons'

to vote. The male population of Sheffield in 1832 was 43,458; just one in thirteen men had the right to vote. Sheffield was one of many two-member constituencies where each qualifying voter had two votes and the candidates with the highest and second-highest number of votes were elected.

The election was decided by a show of hands at the hustings, where anyone was allowed to attend whether a qualified elector or not. Only if a defeated candidate demanded a poll did one take place. General elections could take a number of weeks and there was nothing to stop candidates standing in more than one constituency.

Early in the morning of the hustings, preparations were made by the followers of all candidates to show their support. Coloured favours of orange, green and pink were worn and displayed in the streets to indicated support for each of the candidates.

Buckingham's supporters displaying their pink ribbons assembled in Paradise Square and at around 8:30am they were joined by the candidate and members of his committee. Led by Buckingham's carriage, which also contained his principal nominators William Vickers and Mr W Ibbotson, the procession commenced and made its way along Bank Street to the bottom of Angel Street where it was joined by a music band of volunteers that took its place behind the two carriages playing as they marched along.

The second carriage contained Mrs Buckingham and several other ladies, probably the wives of the nominators and principal committee members. Behind the band marched Buckingham's committee and supporters. The procession continued along Angel Street to High Street, then along Fargate to Barker's Pool where it turned down Burgess Street, along Union Street, Norfolk Street and Market Street to Haymarket where it was joined by many more of Buckingham's supporters in front of the Corn Exchange.

Two of the other candidates, Thomas Asline Ward and Samuel Bailey with their committees and supporters, were already present at the hustings and John Parker, the other candidate, and his supporters arrived soon after with rather less ceremony. Well over 20,000 people gathered in the area in front of the Corn Exchange to witness the event, which was pure theatre and occasionally pantomime.

At 10:00am Thomas Dunn read the official order that he had published calling for all the interested parties in the election to come together at the day's hustings. This was followed by Mr James Wilson, the Law Clerk to the Cutlers'

Company, reading at length the writ authorising the election. Thomas Dunn then opened the hustings with a speech in which he advised the electors:

> 'If you take care to choose men of sound judgement and independent principles, a removal of many of the evils which now unhappily distress the country—and that it is deeply distressed all must agree—may be reasonably expected. This distress, I believe, is not the consequence of the natural order of things, but the consequence of misgovernment. A reform in the representation of the people, I feel, is the only means of obtaining a removal of grievances; and I am fully satisfied that if men of principle be returned, that the time will speedily arrive when the workmen will have sufficient labour, at good remuneration prices.'[345]

Dunn went on to state that it wasn't just the workers affected by the many evils of society; he also acknowledged that merchants, master manufacturers and farmers had their share of distress. He listed among the *'chief evils that afflict the country commercial monopolies, the Corn Laws* [and] *the deficiencies in the circulating medium'* (the latter I assume was the press). He also made reference to the need for the regulation of infant labour in factories.

He approached his conclusion by outlining the official order of proceedings: each candidate would address the meeting without interruption. Questions to each candidate would only be allowed following the conclusion of his speech. Once questions were exhausted, the next candidate would be called upon to make his speech. No further questions to previous candidates would be permitted.

We learn much about the social conversation and political topics of the time from Dunn's statement and the content of the candidates' hustings speeches, which are recorded *ad verbatim* in the *1832 Poll Book Companion,* from where all the following quotes from the candidates are sourced: from the Corn Lawns to tithes, from slavery to crime and punishment, on taxation and trade, and on the corruption and deficiencies of the political system, both national and local.

Thomas Dunn concluded his opening statement:

> 'I conclude by expressing my confident opinion, that you, the men of Hallamshire, will prove by your conduct during the week, that you are

---

[345] Op Cit *Poll Book Companion*, p.16

worthy of the long-desired and long-withheld privilege you are this day called upon to exercise.[346]

Dunn's statement was followed by loud cheers. He then proceeded to call for the official nominations of the four candidates:

John Parker[347] of Woodthorpe, the son of local magistrate, Hugh Parker, proposed by Dr Arnold Knight,[348] seconded by Mr Joseph Read Esq

Samuel Bailey[349] of Burn Greave, known as a philosopher and litterateur, proposed by Mr Edward Smith, seconded by Mr Fisher

Thomas Asline Ward[350] of Park House, proposed by Mr Ebenezer Elliott,[351] seconded by Mr Edward Bramley, solicitor

James Silk Buckingham[352] of London proposed by Mr William Vickers, seconded by Mr W Ibbotson

---

[346] Ibid

[347] John Parker (1799-1881), barrister, Lincoln's Inn, 1824; Whig MP for Sheffield 1832-52; secretary of the Admiralty, 1841 and 1849-52; privy councillor, 1854. Op Cit *The Concise Dictionary of National Biography—Vol. III,* p.2298

[348] Dr. Arnold Knight oversaw the building of the first Sheffield Medical School on the corner of Surrey Street and Arundel Street, completed on 2 July 1829 (see chapter on Resurrection Riots)

[349] Samuel Bailey was a philosophic writer who Ebenezer Elliott described as 'The Bentham of Hallamshire'. A Town Trustee at the age of 37 and a founder of the Sheffield Banking Company, Bailey made his fortune in manufacture leaving £80,000 to the Town Trustees for public use on his death on 18 January 1870. The Burgery Accounts state the amount was £101,526-10s-1d. See Op Cit Taylor, p.196, Op Cit Derry, pp. 181-2, and Op Cit Leader, John Daniel, p.lxii

[350] Thomas Asline Ward, cutlery merchant, a Liberal and president of the local Political Union.

[351] Ebenezer Elliott (1781-1849), known as the 'Corn Law Rhymer'; born at Masborough, Rotherham, 17 March 1781, one of seven children (3 boys, 4 girls); from 16 years of age until 23 he worked for his father at the New Foundry in Rotherham; started in business in the Rotherham and Sheffield iron trade, at first unsuccessful but started again on £150 borrowed capital operating from 61 Burgess Street in 1821, then 31 Gibraltar Street from 1833; lived at Upperthorpe, 1834-41 then moved to Hargot Hill, Great Houghton, near Barnsley, where he died 1 December 1849 and was buried at Darfield Church; involved in local politics and supporter of the Anti-Corn Law league and the Chartist movement; first came to prominence as a poet in 1831, is best known for his verses on early 19th century Sheffield and surrounding areas. See chapter on Chartist Uprising

[352] James Silk Buckingham (1786-1855), author and traveller; journalist at Calcutta, 1818; expelled from India for attacks on the government, 1823; journalist in London,

Thomas Dunn (Courtesy of the Company of Cutlers in Hallamshire)

The first candidate to come forward to address the crowd was John Parker who was met with hisses and groans from the opposition and cheers from his supporters as he took the oath in respect of his qualification to stand for parliament; contrasting sounds that would continue throughout his excessively drawn-out speech.

He began by emphasising the importance of the day's events reminding his audience of the odious (Borough) system that had been abolished by Reform—*now buried in the "tomb of all the capulets"*—and that it was now their duty to elect the best men for the job of representing Sheffield at the *Legislative Councils of the Nation.*

Having been a supporter of Reform, he would make it his priority to continue to support and maintain it. On parliaments, he professed that the optimum length should be for three years and that elections must be by free ballot. On the laws of the land, on which he assured the crowd, he was well-educated, he advocated amendments to eradicate what he considered the defects in civil, commercial and

---

1824-30; MP for Sheffield, 1832-7; travelled in America, 1837-40; received a pension, 1851. Op Cit *The Concise Dictionary of National Biography—Vol. I,* p.382

ecclesiastic laws and to *'place them in a position of usefulness, economy and perspicuity'.*

Commercial law, he argued, must be simplified to reduce the currently unavoidable expense of recourse to the courts. On the criminal law, he advocated a system of secondary punishments *'whereby society may be protected, by punishments short of death, from evil-doers and the delinquents be visited at a much earlier period, and with an unerring aim than hitherto has been the case with condign punishment'.*

Parker was clearly concerned with the underlying causal factors of crime and criminal tendencies, although he offers no actual policies to deter or distract potential offenders. On the Church, he advocated reform to *'restore it to its primeval purity'.* Parker continued to give a lengthy expression of his reasons for supporting the abolition of slavery, a high-profile topic of the period.

He then turned his attention to finance, commerce and trade declaring himself an enemy of restrictive practices and that, amongst other things, reform of the Corn Laws was required. As for foreign policy, Parker opined that the country must embark on a peaceful future rather than wasting resources and expending the blood of its people in wars in distant lands

> *'Let other nations seek aggrandisement by conquest—let them seek glory, if so they call it: but the sound of war is not musical to me. Let others pursue a warlike course, but let my country decide for peace'.*

He defended his pacifist position by relating the objectives of other nations and how they differ from Britain's. At this, he concluded his speech by thanking everyone for listening and confirming that, if elected, he would pursue the policies that he had outlined.[353]

Thomas Dunn then asked for any questions for John Parker. A question was put regarding tithes and he responded by saying he would support the abolition of them; this brought cheers from the crowd. A second question was about currency,[354] which he considered *'not sufficiently comprehensive for the wants*

---

[353] Full transcripts of all the candidates' hustings speeches are included in the *Poll Book Companion.*

[354] The issue of currency revolved around its stability. At this time there were many small provincial banks that issued their own notes and many of these banks—which increased in number during the wars with France—failed, mainly due to an irresponsible over-issue of notes. See Op Cit Redford, pp.99-103

of the country', and a third on the monopoly of the East India Company to which he replied that he was against all monopolies. Further cheers emanated from the audience.

Thomas Dunn then invited the next candidate to make his address and Samuel Bailey rose and stepped forward to speak amid cheers from the crowd; there is no mention in the Poll Book accounting the hisses and groans that greeted John Parker.

Samuel Bailey (Artuk.org)   John Parker (Picture Sheffield s08454)

Samuel Bailey began by reminding the people that he had given details of his political sentiments on the great questions of general interest to the public at a previous rally in Paradise Square and that now, he would concentrate on other issues that he had not previously given his opinion.

First on his list of issues, was that of assessed taxes, in particular house and windows taxes. The window tax, he opined, should never have been imposed, *'it is a disgrace and injurious and a stain upon our statute book. It has led to the erection of ill-constructed, ill-ventilated and ill-lighted houses.'*

On the house tax, he gave an example of its unequal application by comparing his own house with the stately home of the Marquis of Hertford in Sussex. The Marquis's mansion cost £400,000 and the amount of house tax he paid is £14-3s-4d. Bailey's more modest abode cost less than one-hundredth of that and he paid £7.

This inequality, he said, must be rectified. Of course such taxes had little impact upon most of those present as the poor and the labouring classes were not people of property. Bailey recognising this went on to state that there were other taxes *'that press upon the industry of the country, and retard upon the enlightenment of the people'* that should be repealed first. This brought cheers from his audience.

From the imposition of taxes, Bailey moved on to issues of moral consideration. Like Parker, he supported the abolition of slavery, to which he added, for the very same reason, his support for the abolition of the impressments of seamen—both being a violation of the principles of moral justice:

> *'If it is a violation of the principles of moral justice to seize a Negro, to hurry him across the ocean, and to force him to labour under the fear of the whip, it is a violation of the same principles to take a man, a white man, an Englishman, to force him on board a vessel, and to compel him not only to toil but to expose his life in battle.'*

Once more, the crowd cheered in support despite Sheffield being about as far away from the sea and the threat of the press-gangs as it could possibly get. To support his argument, like Bailey, he cited America for setting a good example, being a country that raises its navy without the use of press-gangs:[355]

> *'Not a seaman treads the deck of an American ship but by his own free will and consent. I would have it so in the British Navy.'*

Bailey went on to raise another issue of moral justice; that of child labour: *'the slavery of children in our cotton and woollen factories'*. Again the crowd cheered in support although it wasn't such a relevant issue for Sheffield, there being no great textile concerns and few large factories.

Child labour was prevalent in the local trades but it was not an issue high on the political agenda as at this time it was a necessity, both for the employer (cheap labour) and the children whose families depended on their earnings. Children were deemed of greater value if they were earning, as demonstrated by the assessments for children's lives lost in the Great Sheffield Flood of 1864.

---

[355] The use of press-gangs to man the British Navy had actually ceased by 1832 but it was not illegal

Next, Bailey turned his attention to capital punishment. Although many of the previous capital felonies of the 'bloody code' had been abolished, forgery remained a capital offence on the statute book. Bailey professed that he would reserve the death penalty solely for crimes against the person and life.

On the international scene, he argued that relations between countries was best confined to the interchange of commodities and knowledge and not unlike John Parker, he detested war and he argued that we shouldn't interfere in distant conflicts, but when a small country is oppressed by a more powerful neighbour, we have a moral duty to protect the weak from the strong.

Here, he was referring to the ongoing dispute between Holland and Belgium that both Britain and France had become embroiled. For the rest of his oration, he spelled out all the reasons for his personal suitability for election to parliament in which he touched upon his attendances at Westminster to listen to the speeches of ministers and other high-profile figures such as David Ricardo.[356]

He concluded his speech *'amid hearty cheers'*. Samuel Bailey was asked two questions from the floor, identical to two answered by John Parker in relation to tithes and Negro slavery. To the former, he said that they should be abolished, and to the latter that he was a decided enemy to slavery. Thomas Dunn asked for any further questions but the only response was *'no, no, we are satisfied'*.

There was another statement of interest for students of political history that was contained in Bailey's speech as he made the point that the successful candidates would need to have the time to actually fulfil their duties in parliament; being a gentleman, he had all the time in the world. Of particular interest are the various figures he quoted in respect of the work of the Houses of Parliament.

During the previous seven years, parliament had passed 2,100 Acts, which averaged 300 Acts per session. During one session in this same period, there were 3,184 petitions heard and debated; petitions being the only opportunity for the common people to raise issues in parliament. In addition to this workload, there were many various committee meetings; as many as 32 different committees meeting in a single day.

Members often found that their committee responsibilities required them to be in a number of meeting rooms at the same time. However, despite this heavy workload, the aristocrats and wealthy land-owners that made up the greater

---

[356] David Ricardo (1772-1823), English economist and wealthy stockbroker, writer of influential economic theory: *Principles of Political Economy and Taxation* (1817)

number of MPs still found plenty of time for the balls, the hunts and the other events on their social circuit.

Next to address the crowd was Thomas Asline Ward who, on taking the oath, informed all that he was in possession of properties in Sheffield and Liverpool, the annual proceeds of which amounted to £300. Ward opened his address by commenting on the people's struggle to achieve Reform, congratulating them on that achievement and that he hoped to see further extension to the franchise so as to give the vote to those men currently excluded by lack of property.

This naturally appealed to the greater part of the crowd and it was met by loud cheering. Indeed, he offered himself as one of them, one of the people, one united with them in feeling and interest; this, he said, was his great advantage. Proclaiming himself a Benthamite,[357] he sought to provide the greatest happiness for the greatest number for the greatest length of time.

Like Bailey, Ward too had already outlined his political thoughts at a previous rally and would not take up time reiterating what was already well-known. He did, however, reconfirm his call for reform of the Church and for the abolition of tithes.

On slavery, he admitted that he once thought that the emancipation of the slaves would be injurious to them, that they might starve without their owners. Now, he was persuaded that slavery should be abolished:

> *'Yes, my friends, disguise it as men may, slavery is a bitter draught that cannot be made palatable, and I am convinced that more misery will be produced—more blood shall be shed by the continuance of slavery, than by its entire and immediate abolition.'*

He next endorsed John Parker's declaration with his own support for the ballot and for triennial parliaments. The ballot, he argued, worked well in France and America and would work as well in Britain. Comparisons with America were used to make their case on a number of issues by the candidates but Ward also emphasised the growing threat that America posed to British overseas trade, in particular, in competition for trade in the East Indies since the East India

---

[357] Jeremy Bentham (1748-1832), the founding father of utilitarianism

Company's monopoly on trade with India was withdrawn in 1813, and in the markets opening up in China.[358]

Nevertheless, Ward nailed his flag to the Free Trade pole and he too sought the abolition of the Corn Laws. Government interference and regulation of trade was simply a means to raise revenue to fight wars or to protect the wealthy land-owners who, of course, made up most of the Government.

Thomas Ward now turned his attention to local issues and to defend his record as a Town Trustee. He refuted what he termed *'anonymous accusations'* that he tried to increase the powers of the Town Trustees or that he tried to suppress the publication of their accounts.

On the contrary, he declared that he always contended for the rights of the electors and that he always advocated publicity of the Trust's accounts, which were customarily only displayed at the Town Hall for freeholders to see. He denied that Sheffield's Trustees were corrupt, yet admitted that other corporations were and criticised the selfish and extravagant abuse of their power.

He went on to pledge that he would propose to the Trustees that their accounts be published for the convenience of everyone. From this, we can discern that there was some distrust of the Town Trustees among the wider town population (see chapter 1) and that Ward felt he needed to defend his own reputation as a Trustee.

Next, he turned his attention to the local judiciary and the inconvenience, and expense, of having to travel to York Court of Assize for criminal cases. If one could not be provided in the town, then at least there should be an Assize Court provided for the West Riding. The Criminal Law, he argued, was also in need of further reform with an emphasis on *'preventing vice and reforming the vicious'*—crime prevention and the rehabilitation of criminals—and that sentences given out were *'too severe for the spirit and feelings of the age.'*

---

[358] The East India Company's monopoly of trade with China ended in 1834 and the company was abolished by The India Act of 1858.

Thomas Asline Ward (Staniforth Family)

Thomas Asline Ward now brought his speech to a conclusion by pledging that, should he be elected, every issue brought to him by his constituents would receive his immediate consideration and that no individual would be disregarded:

> *'However humble and lowly a man may be, he shall not be despised, and however proud and lofty, he shall not command undue influence over my mind. I will endeavour to observe the strictest impartiality between contending interests.'*

It would appear that no-one had a question for Thomas Asline Ward as only *'loud cheers'* is recorded after his speech in the *Poll Book* account before the final candidate, James Silk Buckingham, was asked by Thomas Dunn to come forward to give his address.

On doing so and after greeting his audience to more loud cheers, Buckingham opened up by commenting that he was at a disadvantage by being the last candidate to speak as he would be covering much that had already been said by his opponents. However, what was more important was that they ensure that they chose the most suitable person to represent them, disregarding all other considerations.

He then set about persuading them that, of course, it was he who was the most suitable man for the job and he did so by providing, by far, the more articulate and attention-drawing oration of the proceedings. Whilst expressing the notion that speaking last was a disadvantage, he was actually in a position of better-judging the mood of the crowd and in reality, using it to his advantage.

He saw from the reception of the previous speakers what was popular and what was not. Armed with this knowledge, his speech demonstrated that whilst the other candidates might be sincere and committed to do their best for Sheffield in Parliament, he was the authentic politician; a master of the profession. He began, not by seriously outlining his credentials and his policies but, by bringing some levity to the occasion at the expense of his opponents.

He hadn't heard a word of John Parker's speech due to the *'cordial reception'* he received, alluding to the hissing as well as cheering that drowned out much of what he had to say. Bailey was his next target, mocking his use of Greek mythology and maritime metaphors in his speech to illustrate the desired qualifications for a Member of Parliament, turning them around to ridicule Bailey and to illustrate his own, superior qualifications, which brought more laughter and cheering.

Only Thomas Asline Ward escaped his derision as he was at one with him in being a Benthamite and, as he turned to his political objectives, was singing from the same hymn sheet on a number of issues. He listed thirteen *'great objects'* which were recorded and numbered in the *Poll Book* account—most helpful for the history researcher. They were as follows:

1. *The removal of all restrictions on our Commerce with every country on the globe, and the consequential abolition of the East India and every other Monopoly*
2. *The immediate and entire extinction of Slavery, in every part of the British dominions*
3. *The reduction of Public Expenditure, and the complete revision of the System of Taxation*
4. *The reform of the Church, and the speedy extinction of Tithes*
5. *The repealing of the Corn Bill and the securing [of] Cheap Food*
6. *The reform of the Laws, so as to make Justice speedy and cheap*
7. *The securing [of] Education at the National cost, for all who are too poor to procure it*
8. *The abolition of the punishment of death, and of flogging, and all other corporeal punishments, both in the Army and Navy*
9. *The removal of all existing disabilities on account of religious opinions*
10. *The shortening of Parliaments to three years at most*
11. *The extinction of the suffrage in proportion to the spread of Education*
12. *The Vote by Ballot, as essential to purity and independence of election*
13. *The removal of the burthens that press so heavily on the poor: and generally, the promotion of interests of the many, as of importance than the interests of the few*

Whether he came to the hustings with this entire list or whether he amended or added to it following the other candidates' presentations, James Silk Buckingham covered all bases and such political objectives would not be out of place today.

Indeed, one wonders if the Labour Party adopted object 13 for its current motto: *'For the Many, not the Few'*. Buckingham probably adopted the line from Percy Bysshe Shelley's (1792-1822) poem inspired by the Peterloo massacre on 16 August 1819, *The Masque of Anarchy,* which was published earlier in the year.[359]

---

[359] *The Masque of Anarchy——A Poem By Percy Bysshe Shelley,* Leigh Hunt, 1832, p.47. The line was the final line of the last verse on the ninety-one verse poem

Buckingham concluded by saying that he would form no coalition with any of the other candidates and stressed to the voters that the successful issue of the contest rested entirely with them. Here, he was alluding to the fact that each voter had two votes, one for each of the two MPs.

However, they didn't have to use their two votes and to ensure the election of any particular candidate, that candidate would stand a greater chance of election if just one vote was used; the second vote would, in effect, be a vote against the preferred candidate when totalled up.

The *Poll Book* records that following *'Great Cheering'*, there were several questions put to Buckingham, which were answered satisfactorily; no details of the questions are given. The continued cheering from all quarters of the assembled mass indicated that Buckingham had won the orator's crown, but would he win the election?

James Silk Buckingham
(White House Historical Association)

From the candidates' speeches, we find that there was more policy that they agreed upon than they did not. Indeed, there was little in the way of opposing policy or conflicting ideological views, nothing contentious at all. The hustings appear to have been purely a contest of personalities and oratory skills. There was complete accord on the abolition of slavery and the abolition of tithes.

Only Samuel Bailey failed to mention the Corn Laws and he said nothing in support of further electoral reform, which in itself does not mean he was at odds with his opponents but that he simply failed to offer his views on the issues.

The other three candidates all advocated the review/repeal of the Corn Laws and welcomed electoral reform, promoting further extensions to the franchise and proposing three-year parliaments. However, and perhaps significantly, only Buckingham advocated the provision of universal education paid for by the state; a definite vote winner.

Following the nomination process, Thomas Dunn called for a show of hands in favour of the respective candidates. The *Poll Book* records that John Parker was voted for by *'a considerable number'*; Samuel Bailey *'a trifling majority of hands over the show of Mr Parker'*; *'a show of hands amounting at least to 14,000 or 15,000'* for Thomas Asline Ward; and for James Silk Buckingham *'the show of hands were immense'*.

Thomas Dunn declared that Buckingham and Ward had the most support and were the *'choice of the electors'*. This was received by great cheering but not surprisingly Messrs Bailey and Parker disagreed with this conclusion and demanded an official poll, as most of the hands that went up were not those of qualified electors.

In fairness to Thomas Dunn, and an indication of his dedication to his duty of impartiality, the record of poll shows that he personally voted for both Samuel Bailey and John Parker. To avoid controversy, Thomas Dunn then declared that a poll would be held over the following two days, 13 and 14 December, and that voting would take place in the New Corn Exchange for the Sheffield ward; Healey's Warehouse in the Nursery for the Brightside Bierlow ward; Crookesmoor Workhouse for the Nether and Upper Hallam wards; the School Room in South Street for the Ecclesall Bierlow ward; and the School Room at Attercliffe for the Attercliffe-cum-Darnall ward. Polling would commence at 9:00 am on Thursday, 13 December 1832.

The first return of the poll on 13 December, although not official, indicated that John Parker (1084 votes) and James Silk Buckingham (1060) were in front. Thomas Asline Ward (887) and Samuel Bailey (616), the most popular candidates amongst those without a vote (predominantly, the working classes) faced ultimate defeat.

The poll continued the following day and closed at 4:00 pm on 14 December when upwards of 30,000 people had gathered in the town. There was much bitterness amongst the crowd, the vast majority of which were of the disenfranchised working classes, who would have undoubtedly elected the popular Thomas Asline Ward had they had a vote.

It wasn't long before the murmurings of discontent turned to disorderly protest and by 5:00 pm a crowd of mostly young men and boys had assembled in front of the Tontine Inn in Haymarket, where successful candidate, John Parker, had set up his election committee in the largest room, and they began throwing stones at the windows of the huge coaching house as Parker was addressing his committee.[360]

By 7:00 pm, almost all of the windows in the Tontine's frontage had been smashed and the cry was heard, *On to the Bank—Down with it.* A crowd of between 8,000 and 9,000 moved on to Bank Street where an attack was made on the bank and more windows smashed. From there, they moved on to number 19 Queen Street, the house of solicitor Luke Palfreyman, who was John Parker's agent, and more windows were broken.

Palfreyman, who was at the Town Hall, had been alerted to the situation by his solicitor colleague, Mr Skidmore, who worked from Palfreyman's office at the time. To avoid the mob, he went home via King Street and Angel Street. About fifteen minutes after arriving home, he heard the smashing of glass and on entering his dining room from the kitchen, he found that it was his windows that had been the target of a crowd that had gathered outside his front door.

His wife cowered on the floor to avoid stones as they came through the windows. Palfreyman reached for a pistol and went out to confront the baying throng and begged them to desist saying that his wife was inside in a state of fear. Some called out that they should leave, but others shouted further encouragement to the mob.

Despite being armed Palfreyman was struck by a missile receiving *a severe contusion on the right arm.*[361] Skidmore, also armed with a pistol and who had now joined him, pleaded that Mr Palfreyman was not a well man, hoping in vain, that this would attract some sympathy. The pair then went on the offensive and fired over the heads of the mob, first Palfreyman and then Skidmore.

---

[360] *Sheffield Mercury,* 15 Dec 1832 (courtesy of Chris Hobbs)
[361] Op Cit Poll Book, Companion, p.36

Palfreyman went back for another pistol that he loaded with small nails, having no more balls. He returned to face the mob once more, which had depleted slightly following the first shots, declaring that the next shot would be a fatal one.[362] Skidmore also found another loaded pistol and re-joined him. Before another shot was fired, the police arrived accompanied by a magistrate (also Sheffield's Coroner and a member of John Parker's committee), Thomas Badger, who had just read the Riot Act from a window at the Town Hall.[363]

Thomas Badger read the Riot Act once more and the crowd gradually dispersed. By this time, a dispatch had been sent to Rotherham to call in the regiment of infantry stationed there. A contingency of the town's special constables accompanied by Hugh Parker JP had assembled to face the crowd at the Tontine Inn and the Riot Act was read there.

By 8:00 pm the crowd appeared to have grown and now covered the area of Haymarket, Castle Street and Bank Street, confronting the vastly outnumbered special constables. Scuffles broke out and before long, the Yeomanry were called out and it too joined in the fracas.

The Tontine Inn

---

[362] Op Cit, Vickers, p.96. In the *Poll Book, Companion,* it is recorded that the weapon used by Luke Palfreyman was a blunderbuss. It is likely to have been a blunderbuss style pistol with a flared barrel. The account is from Luke Palfreyman's statement at the Coroner's inquest.
[363] *Sheffield Mercury,* 15 Dec 1832

At a quarter past ten, a detachment of eighty men of the 18th Irish Foot commanded by Captain Graves marched up Waingate and formed a line of 16 to 18 soldiers in the courtyard of the Tontine Inn. The infantrymen had been ordered to load their muskets with ball at Attercliffe Bridge prior to approaching the town;[364] they had marched from Rotherham where they had been sent for the duration of the election.

They were accompanied by Thomas Bosvile JP[365] of Barbot Hall, Ravenfield Park. Bosvile stood with the soldiers and a corporal who formed a front line to face the crowd, which turned its attention and its missiles upon them. Bosvile was hit on the head by a stone at which he shouted *'fire'*, repeating the order three times in panic before Captain Graves gave the fatal order for his men to open fire, all within five minutes of their arrival.

The infantrymen fired in unison and quickly reloaded. No time was given for the crowd to disperse after the first volley. There is some confusion as to whether or not the order was to fire over the heads of the mob but in the event, the infantrymen fired into the crowd and continued to reload and fire until they were brought to a halt by two other magistrates, Hugh Parker and Henry Walker, who had now joined the injured Bosvile.

This account of what took place is recorded in the official *Poll Book* and confirmed by reports in the *Sheffield Register* and evidence given by Thomas Bosvile before the Coroner. Compare this to the account reported by the *Sheffield Mercury:*

> *Mr Bosville, having come out of the Tontine Inn, was in the act of entreating them to go home, when he was dangerously hurt. Several other individuals were also injured. He then, after again and again begging of them to desist, all to no purpose, ordered the soldiers to fire blank cartridge and this was repeated several times, being answered by the multitude with groans, shouts, hisses, and volleys of stones. At*

---

[364] The 18th Irish Regiment of Foot are recorded as being stationed at Sheffield Barracks for part of the time they were in England between 7 March 1832, when it landed at Portsmouth from Corfu, and May 1834 when it embarked at Liverpool for Dublin. See Cannon, Richard, *Historical Record of The Eighteenth or The Royal Irish Regiment of Foot,* Parker, Furnivall & Parker, 1848.

[365] As with Col Athorpe, Bosvile's surname is duplicated and illustrates an idiosyncrasy of the times. Thomas Bosvile is recorded in White's *History and Directory of the Borough of Sheffield, 1833* as sole proprietor of Ravensfield, Lord of the Manor, impropriator and patron of the church.

length, lamentable to relate, it was found absolutely necessary to fire, the soldiers being on duty in the Tontine gateway; and the consequence was that five persons were killed on the spot, and several wounded—one or two dangerously.

At least one newspaper reported that the infantrymen fired *'two, three or four rounds of blank cartridge'* before the order was given to fire ball but this doesn't tally with any other account and would certainly have been stated at the Coroner's inquest had it been the case.

The one thing we can be sure of as being fact from these versions of events, was that five persons were killed on the spot; the rest seems to twist the truth so as to absolve Bosvile of any blame. Captain Graves was known to comment later that had the order been given to charge with bayonets, the consequence would have been ten-times destructive than firing.

The crowd scattered in all directions and once the infantrymen had ceased firing, they were ordered to clear the immediate area and they marched up High Street, along Norfolk Row, Norfolk Street, Market Street and back to the Tontine Inn. Parties of special constables and yeomanry were sent out to clear the wider area of the town.[366]

---

[366] *Independent,* 15 December 1832. See www.voicesofconflict.wordpress.com

FOR CANNONS MILITARY RECORDS.

The 18th Irish Regiment of Foot

Three men and two boys were shot dead and many more were wounded, including two watchmen. A ball that killed one of the boys, passed through his body then through the window of linen draper Frederick Wiley's shop at 16

Market Place, where it continued through seven wooden partitions and shattered a bottle of sherry.[367]

Wiley preserved the hole made by the ball encircling it with the date '1832'.[368] The five who were killed that night were George Grimes, cow keeper of Orchard Street, aged 23; William Howard of Lambert Street, aged 14; James Jackson of Brown Street, aged 40, who had been released from gaol the previous week; David Ogden of Eyre Lane, aged 14; and James Turton of Wheeldon Street, aged 36.

Another young man named Jesse Fretwell of Campo Lane, aged 19, died of his wounds in the General Infirmary on 31 December. The more seriously wounded were taken to the Infirmary with Jesse Fretwell. These were Stephen Clarke, of Hermitage Street, aged 22 (a ball had passed through his thigh); Samuel Martin, a watchman of West Street, aged 47 (fractured shoulder); Charles Eagle, a silversmith of Smithfield, aged 14 (wounded in the stomach).[369]

Samuel Martin was later awarded £20 towards an annuity by the Town Trustees in recognition of him being severely wounded and left disabled in the discharge of his duty.[370] The above account in the *Sheffield Mercury* also suggested that five rioters, described as *'active partisans'* were arrested and taken into custody and that several of the ringleaders were well-known.

However, I have found no reports of anyone being prosecuted for their role in riot. The surgeon who attended the dead and wounded, William Staniforth, told the Coroner at the ensuing inquiry, that Grimes, Howard and Turton were still alive when he went to see them at the Town Hall, where they had been taken.

Grimes, who had been shot in the stomach, the ball passing through him, and Turton, who was wounded in the right side, the ball breaking one of his ribs, both died within minutes of Staniforth's arrival. Howard had been shot in the right side of the neck, shattering the bone. He lingered on, clutching to life for nearly an hour, before he too passed away.

Staniforth returned to his surgery at 2 Castle Street to find that the bodies of Ogden and Jackson had been taken there. Ogden had been shot in the belly, the ball penetrating his intestines, and Jackson in the face, the ball entering at the

---

[367] Op Cit *Poll Book, Companion*, pp.36-37
[368] Op Cit Leader, Robert Eadon (Ed), *Reminiscences*, p.215
[369] Op Cit *Poll Book, Companion*, p.37
[370] Op Cit Leader, John Daniel, p.465

right side of his nose. Jessie Fretwell, who died on New Year's eve, was shot through his thigh and arm by the same ball.

Calm returned to the Sheffield streets on the day after the riot, Saturday 15 December, and the space in front of the Tontine Inn was cleared of people before the official result of the poll was declared:

	Parker	Buckingham	Ward	Bailey
Ecclesall Beirlow	201	185	149	78
Attercliffe-cum-Darnall	69	34	36	33
Nether and Upper Hallam	99	62	44	50
Brightside Beirlow	116	82	82	76
Sheffield	1030	1135	899	576
Total	**1515**	**1498**	**1210**	**813**

John Parker and James Silk Buckingham were duly declared elected to represent Sheffield in parliament. There were no speeches from the victors or any celebrations at the outcome of the poll as such was deemed inappropriate under the circumstances and all efforts were made to ensure there would be no repeat of the previous night's tragic events.

Inquests into the five killed on the night were held at the Town Hall on 17 December before Mr Lee, Coroner of Wakefield, as the Sheffield Coroner, Mr Badger, was a witness to the events. In giving evidence, Thomas B Bosvile confirmed the actions of the military:

> *'A very short space of time indeed occurred, between the arrival of the soldiers at the Tontine and the firing—not so much as five minutes; the soldiers were stoned while drawing up—they entered the yard, and were almost immediately ordered to fire.'*[371]

Robert John Gainsford, a solicitor living at 2 Norfolk Row and a member of John Parker's committee who gave witness evidence at the Coroner's inquiry stated:

> *'The crowd in front of the Tontine was dense and clamorous…There was not time for the people to disperse between each volley…No attempt was made by the yeomanry to disperse the mob before the Infantry fired.'*

---

[371] *Sheffield Local Register*, 1832, p.247

Evidence was taken into a second day and Mr Lee's verdict was declared on 18 December: Justifiable homicide. The same verdict was determined at the later inquest on Jesse Fretwell.

It is ironic that during his opening address to the electors of Sheffield on 12 December, about the reformed parliament that would be elected in the coming days, Thomas Dunn had stated:

> *'The enemies of such a Parliament have asserted that we are not fit to be trusted with the liberty we have obtained; but I feel assured that our love of peace and good order will convince them how much they have dealt in slander, and the close of the present election, in particular, will be an example of peace and good will for all succeeding contests.'* [372]

He couldn't have been more wrong.

The Corn Exchange

It may be of interest to the reader to receive an account of the early representations of Sheffield's first Members of Parliament. The very first action

---

[372] Op Cit *Poll Book, Companion*, p.16

of both members was to jointly make representation to Lord Grey before the first parliamentary session actually sat.

On 28 January 1833, Parker and Buckingham had an interview with the Prime Minister where they expressed their regret that it was not the intention of the Government to introduce a measure for the abolition of slavery. James Silk Buckingham recorded that Lord Grey received them very civilly and favourably and continued to state that,

I am happy to add that the utmost cordiality of sentiment and action existed between Mr Parker and myself in the execution of this mission; and I rejoice exceedingly that our first act as members for Sheffield has been one in which we took so deep and equal an interest in fulfilling our duty to our constituents and pleading the cause of the oppressed. [373]

John Parker was also pleased with his personal performance in the first session of Parliament writing to the *Sheffield and Rotherham Independent* on 28 March 1833, *I have voted on every division, throughout the session.*

However, it was suggested by the editor, Robert Leader, that he did not give universal satisfaction to his constituents.[374] Neither did he give satisfaction to his fellow Sheffield MP. On 8 March 1833, Buckingham presented a petition on behalf of the Sheffield Political Union (SPU) against the introduction of a Bill for the adoption of several measures towards Ireland (Coercion Bill) suggesting that the measures be postponed for three months.

Parker rose to speak against Buckingham's proposal, reflecting the divisions amongst the Sheffield elite on the Irish question at the time; divisions that would lead to the resignations of the SPU leaders on 25 April, including the president and former candidate at the 1832 general election, Thomas Asline Ward, and Ebenezer Elliott, culminating in the demise of the SPU.[375]

An achievement of note of Buckingham in his early parliamentary career, was his innovative publication of parliamentary business—*The Parliamentary Review and Family Magazine*—in which he explained his own voting record.[376] Thus, in giving the public his first-hand accounts of the debates and divisions in the House of Commons, he was the first of many parliamentary correspondents

---

[373] Parker, John, *Chapters in the Political History of Sheffield, 1832-1849,* Leader and Sons, Sheffield, 1884, pp.3-4
[374] Ibid, pp.4-5
[375] Ibid
[376] Ibid, p.4

as the idea was soon after adopted by the provincial daily papers and the role continues to this day.

Despite this achievement, Buckingham's parliamentary career had been a disappointment to the Sheffield Reformers, who shed no tears when he resigned his seat in 1837, following his failure in a long-running compensation claim against the East India Company, and according to the *Sun* newspaper, his general conduct had been such as to *lead to something more than a suspicion that his object was to forward his own personal interests rather than to promote the public good.*[377]

He was succeeded in the Sheffield seat by Henry George Ward. James Silk Buckingham died in London on 30 June 1855 aged 69.

John Parker served the town for twenty years. In 1836, he was appointed a Lord of the Treasury, which necessitated that he be re-elected to his seat. The election took place on 22 August as a near formality; the bogus opposition of a Mr Bell collapsed on the opening of the formal poll.[378] In 1841, he was appointed secretary of the Admiralty, a post he held again between 1849 and 1852. He lost his Sheffield seat to George Hadfield in 1852. John Parker died in 1881 aged 82.

The first parliamentary representatives for Sheffield were both wealthy men and were elected by wealthy men. Whilst they were representing the people of Sheffield, they were not representative of them. However, we can safely say that they fully represented those who elected them. They were not representative of the five men and boys who died on the day of their election; they certainly didn't represent them or their ilk.

---

[377] Ibid, p.16
[378] Ibid

Resurrection Riots

The body-snatchers, they have come
And made a snatch at me
It's very odd that kind of men
Can't let my body be[379].

1835

Prior to the Anatomy Act of 1832, only the bodies of executed felons could be used for dissection in medical science and as rapid progress was made in this field the demand for bodies far exceeded supply. This engendered the macabre practice of employing *'resurrection men'*, also known as *'body-snatchers'* and *'sack-em-up men'*,[380] to source bodies for the medical school dissection tables.

The most notorious perceived body-snatchers were William Burke and William Hare, but they weren't resurrection men at all. Burke and Hare were actually serial murderers who killed at least 16 people in Edinburgh between November 1827 and October 1828 by suffocation, then sold the bodies for dissection. They had decided that murder was an easier task than digging up the bodies but just as profitable, if not more so. There was the added bonus for the Edinburgh anatomy lecturer, Robert Knox, and his medical students in having *'fresh subjects'* to work on.[381]

---

[379] Verse from a contemporary poem by Thomas Hood entitled *Mary's Ghost*. For the full poem see Bailey, Brian, *The Resurrection Men—A History of the Trade in Corpses,* Macdonald & Co (Publishers) Ltd, 1991, pp.173-175
[380] Ibid, p.32
[381] Ibid, pp.101-125

Contemporary sketch of Burke and Hare

Body-snatching was so prevalent in the early 19th century that, in some areas, especially in Scotland, extreme measures were taken by bereaved families to protect the corpses of their dearly-departed. Huge *'resurrection stones'* that could only be lifted by use of a block-and-tackle and an A-frame were dropped into graves over the coffin to prevent access to the body.

Iron mort-safes were constructed to cage-in or rail-off graves. In the New Calton Burial Ground in Edinburgh, a three-storey stone castellated watchtower was built to serve the guarding of fresh graves.[382] A similar construction called the Watch-House can still be seen at Bradfield. In some cases, graves were dug with coffin chambers off-set within the grave to prevent body-snatchers finding the corpse.[383]

It is worth noting that the stealing of a dead body was not a serious crime at this time but classed simply as a misdemeanour. However, stealing a coffin or a shroud was a capital felony under the *'bloody code'*.[384] Consequently, corpses were stripped of their shrouds and carried away in purpose made sacks, hence the term *sack-em-up men*.

Taking the coffin would be too cumbersome a task in any case. It is estimated that in the first decade of the 19th century more than 1,000 bodies a year were

[382] Ibid, pp.xiv-xv
[383] Op Cit Leader, Robert Eadon (Ed), *Reminiscences*, p.350
[384] Op Cit Bailey, *Resurrection Men*, p.21-22.

being *'resurrected'* from burial-grounds in England and Scotland, equating to around three bodies a night.[385]

An example of a mort-safe cage.

The Watch-House at Bradfield (Courtesy of Malcolm Nunn).

[385] Ibid, p.68

Prominent in Sheffield's medical circles and an enthusiast of surgical science was Dr Hall Overend, a surgeon with a practice in Church Street who had established a School of Anatomy and Medicine in Broad Lane in the early 1820s.[386]

Hall Overend was a Quaker and a celebrated medical practitioner in early 19th century Sheffield. He trained two of his sons, John, who died young, and Wilson, who took over his practice in Church Street when he died in May 1831.

Wilson Overend became a prominent surgeon himself and also an infamous Sheffield magistrate.[387] His youngest son, William Overend, became a prominent barrister who chaired two Royal Commissions that sat in Sheffield in the 1860s: the first overseeing the claims made against the Sheffield Waterworks Company following the Great Flood of 1864,[388] the second to investigate the role of Sheffield trade unions in what became known as the *Sheffield Outrages* in 1867.[389]

William Overend also briefly became the Member of Parliament for Pontefract in 1859, after twice, unsuccessfully, contesting a seat in Sheffield and once for East Derbyshire.[390]

---

[386] Op Cit Vickers, p.110
[387] Op Cit Drewry, *Intimidation,* p.65
[388] Op Cit Drewry, *Inundation*, p.134
[389] Op Cit Drewry, *Intimidation,* p.52
[390] Op Cit Leader, Robert Eadon (Ed), *Reminiscences*, p.45

The Reward of Cruelty by William Hogarth (1697-1764) depicts an executed murderer on the dissection table

An official Sheffield Medical School was established in 1829 in Eyre Street, funded by donations from local dignitaries including the Duke of Norfolk and the Earl Fitzwilliam, and was championed by Dr Arnold Knight of the General Infirmary. Fifty pounds was also donated by the Town Trustees.[391]

Dr Hall Overend disagreed with some of the proposals and withdrew from the project but he continued with his own school in Church Street with the assistance of his son, Dr Wilson Overend.

---

[391] Op Cit Leader, John Daniel, p.449

Although Hall Overend did not take an active role in acquiring illegal corpses for his students' dissection table, there was a suspicion that he knew how the cadavers were sourced and that he provided the money to pay the resurrection men. This later proved to be the case. In a conversation between Richard Leonard and a doctor who was one of Overend's students, the latter divulged that:

> 'Mr Overend did not go out, but he knew what was done, and on almost the last occasion when we brought in a body, he happened to be in Church Street, and was in a state of perturbation lest the constables should search the house and find it. I satisfied him at last by showing that the body could not be identified'.[392]

When asked who was employed to do the grave-robbing the doctor replied:

> There were two men employed, but we pupils were active accomplices, planning the operations, keeping watch, giving signals, drawing off the watchers, and carrying away the bodies. When we had got a corpse in the bottom of the gig, or dressed up in a cloak, bonnet and veil, supported between two of us, we were not long in driving to Sheffield.[393]

The resurrection men did not rob the cemeteries in the town but ventured out to other graveyards within a 12 to 14 miles radius of Sheffield to undertake their grisly work. The only exception was, if a corpse of particular interest to Overend was required.

One such case was the body of a deformed woman who had died in childbirth. Overend could not persuade the family to donate the corpse to medical science and, knowing the surgeon's interest, they decided to keep vigil over the grave.

However, Overend's resurrection men managed to steel the corpse between the funeral and nightfall. Thus, the family kept vigil over an empty grave. The skeleton of the woman eventually ended up in the General Infirmary anatomical museum.[394]

---

[392] Op Cit Leader, Robert Eadon (Ed), *Reminiscences*, p.349
[393] Ibid, pp.349-350
[394] Op Cit Bailey, *Resurrection Men*, p.55

The 'Sack-em-up men'

The supply of corpses for dissection remained a problem for the medical schools and on 25 February 1830, members of the Sheffield medical profession presented a petition to parliament, *praying for the removal of impediments which occur in the prosecution of anatomical investigation.*[395]

In the meantime, the medical profession viewed resurrection men as a necessary evil for without them, the teaching of anatomy would be greatly impeded. The Anatomy Act was introduced to remedy the situation by allowing the unclaimed bodies of people dying in the workhouse to be offered to medical schools at the discretion of the overseers, subject to conditions laid out within the Act.

---

[395] *Sheffield Local Register,* 1830, p.215

Sketch of Sheffield Music Hall with the medical School to the right.

On Sunday, 25 January 1835, the intoxicated keeper of the Eyre Street Medical School, who lived on the premises, had an altercation with his wife, also drunk, and shouts of *murder* were heard in the street. The keeper had been joined by an Irishman who he invited into the house, strictly against the rules of the School, and an argument between the three of them resulted in the wife being shoved out into the street.

In her drunken fury, she shouted to her neighbours and passers-by that her husband and his friend were intent on killing her. The police were sent for and the two men were carted off to the Town Hall cells as an inquisitive crowd amassed outside of the school.[396]

It was well-rumoured within the town that the school was associated with the macabre practice of body-snatching and was a receiver of illegally obtained corpses for dissection. The domestic quarrel was broadcast and rumours began that it was related to the gruesome goings-on of the resurrection men and that a woman was being *Burked* in this *house of horrors*.

Some of the gathering crowd broke into the building and on finding partly dissected bodies, went on the rampage, smashing windows and equipment and an attempt was made to set fire to the place. A small case containing the skeleton of a child was taken and nailed to a house opposite to incite further violence.[397]

[396] *Sheffield Iris,* 27 January 1835
[397] Op Cit Leader, Robert Eadon (Ed), *Reminiscences*, p.269

The police soon arrived and managed to contain things, arresting two men, Thomas Staniforth and James Ogden.[398] The police maintained a vigil on the premises overnight but around eight o'clock the following morning, the Medical School was entered by the mob once more, mainly young lads, and the destruction started the night before was resumed with greater intent.

All kinds of furniture, books and equipment were thrown out into the street and set alight. Not content with burning the contents of the school, doors, window frames, staircases, floorboards and panelling were ripped out and added to the bonfire now blazing in the street; the whole building was gutted.

Police turned up much too late to save anything and a fire tender arrived to deal with the fire but the attending firemen were pelted by the mob with stones and slates and were forced to retire. One of the police constables, William Bland, was struck a blow that resulted in severe injury[399] and Thomas Raynor, the Chief Constable, narrowly escaped being stabbed with a scalpel.[400]

Police constables were despatched to Norton to fetch W J Bagshawe and to Treeton for the Rev G Chandler, two magistrates, whilst Thomas Raynor rode off to the barracks for military assistance. At twenty past ten, Thomas Raynor returned with a detachment of the 6th Inniskillen Dragoons, dismounting at the Town Hall leaving the Clerk to the Magistrates, Albert Smith, to lead the Dragoons to Eyre Street.

By this time, the building was also on fire and the firemen returned under the protection of the military. Mr W J Bagshaw arrived and read the Riot Act and fearful of the Dragoons, the mob dispersed. There were cries of *All in a mind for Overend's*, suggesting the mob should continue its mission at Wilson Overend's Church Street surgery.

Although this caused some alarm there was little further damage.[401] The *Iris* reported that windows were broken at the Medical Hall in Surrey Street and at the house of Wilson Overend. Dragoons intervened to prevent this getting out of hand.

Back at Eyre Street, a second detachment of Dragoons arrived around eleven o'clock but all that remained of the Medical School were the walls, and one of

---

[398] Op Cit Drinkall, p.122
[399] *Sheffield Iris,* 27 January 1835
[400] Op Cit Bean, p.111
[401] Op Cit Leader, Robert Eadon (Ed), *Reminiscences*, p.269

them was partly demolished. At half past twelve, the situation was deemed to be under control and the Dragoons returned to the Barracks.

However, before they had had time to unsaddle their horses, they were sent for once more. At half past one, yet another attack was made on what was left of the Medical School and once more the fire was lit. By half past two, the two detachments of Dragoons had returned and were galloping down Eyre Street; the Rev Chandler at the head of one and Mr Bagshaw at the head of the other.

Once more, the rioters fled but one was apprehended and escorted to the Town Hall by a party of Dragoons. Thomas Staniforth and James Ogden were tried on 7 April 1835 on charges of *being concerned in the destruction of the Medical School* but both were acquitted.[402] I have found no account of what became of the other rioter caught on the second day. Nor do we know the fate of the Medical School keeper and his Irish friend.

In concluding the *Iris* article, the writer is critical of the response of the authorities in not doing enough to prevent *such shameful and superstitious destruction of property.* The use of the word 'superstitious' is notable as it infers that this credible belief in the supernatural, in this case of body snatching, was widespread enough amongst the people of Sheffield to incite such a rampage.

Within just three years of the passing of the Anatomy Act, surely everyone was now aware that the activities of the resurrection men had been brought to an end. Clearly, a good number of Sheffield people were not convinced.

1862

Whilst the Anatomy Act was supposed to address the problem of the lack of supply of cadavers for the progress of medical science, it didn't allow for the increase in demand fuelled by its expansion. Even allowing for the use of the unclaimed bodies of paupers dying in the workhouses, demand continued to exceed supply.

So much so that suspicion of the ghoulish activities of resurrection men to meet this demand continued. This suspicion came to a head in Sheffield once more in June 1862 following rumours of the disinterment of recently buried bodies at Wardsend Cemetery, to the north of the town, that were being sold to the Medical School.

---

[402] *Sheffield Local Register,* 1835, p.274

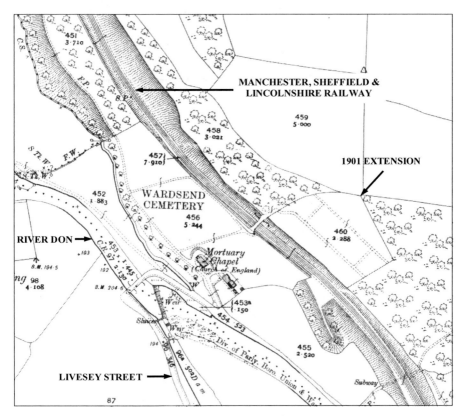

1902 Ordnance Survey map of Wardsend Cemetery.

The Wardsend burial grounds were created as an extension of the cemetery at St Philip's Church, Shalesmoor, as space for burial plots in the churchyard was nearing exhaustion. A 5-acre plot of land between the River Don and the Manchester, Sheffield and Lincolnshire Railway line at Stacey's Spring Wood, near Owlerton, was purchased on 13 June 1857, much of the cost being met by the vicar at St Philip's, the Rev John Livesey.

On 21 June 1857, the churchyard at St Philip's was closed for burials and Wardsend Cemetery was opened. A chapel and a sexton's lodge were later built on the site. Wardsend Cemetery was consecrated by the Archbishop of York, Thomas Musgrove on 5 July 1859.

A further 2-acre plot above the railway line was added to the cemetery in 1901. Although reputed to be the only cemetery in England to be dissected by a railway line, another graveyard had been in the way of a railway line being built in Manchester in 1842 and according to Terry Coleman, the line was driven through it, and another graveyard was disturbed by the Midland Railway at the St Pancras churchyard in 1865.[403]

On 10 March 1862, the body of Joseph Gretorex was taken to the Medical School in Surrey Street from the Sheffield Union Workhouse by the Medical School porter, Moses Walton. This was all above board and within the scope of the Anatomy Act.

Mr Jonathan Barber, surgeon at the Medical School, duly recorded receiving the body with the appropriate paperwork from the Workhouse surgeon, Mr W Skinner, in the School's record book. The body was used in the normal practices of the school and no doubt the students learnt much from its dissection.

The body remained at the Medical School until 12 April when it was put in a box by Moses Walton and 56-year-old Isaac Howard, sexton at St Philip's, then took it away on a wheelbarrow for interment at Wardsend Cemetery. Walton paid Howard five shillings and a further twelve shillings was later paid to Howard by Jonathan Barber for a coffin and for the proper burial, including service, of Joseph Gretorex.

In return, Barber would receive a certificate of interment duly signed by Rev John Livesey. In the meantime, on 24 March, 31-year-old labourer Robert Dixon and his wife, 23-year-old Bethia,[404] moved into the lodge at Wardsend Cemetery following an arrangement with Isaac Howard, who lived about a mile away from the cemetery in Burrowlees.

Not long after moving into the lodge, the Dixons noticed a peculiar smell emanating from the stable, which was locked. Curiosity got the better of Robert Dixon and he knocked out a couple of knots in the wooden boards that formed the ceiling of the stable and the floor of the room above and peering through the resultant holes, was able to see about twenty coffins; small coffins for young children or teenagers, and for infants or babies. None appeared to be coffins for adults.

In one corner, were a number of broken coffins that looked to be made of relatively new timber and in another corner, were a number of used coffin plates. Only Isaac Howard had the key to the stable. Despite this discovery, and no doubt being somewhat concerned about what he had seen, Dixon failed to report his findings to anyone at this time.

---

[403] Op. Cit, Coleman, pp.167-8
[404] Bethia is recorded as Martha in the 1861 census, Bertha in 1871 and Bethia in 1891. See www.chrishobbs.com.

If he confided in his wife, who was obviously aware of the unpleasant smell, she too omitted to tell anyone about the contents of the stable at Wardsend Cemetery. Dixon must have concluded that Howard was disinterring bodies and selling them to the Medical School for Moses Walton was a regular visitor at Wardsend.

On further exploration, Dixon came across a large pit in an unused part of the cemetery grounds, about fifteen feet long by nine feet wide, roughly covered with planks of wood and earth, as if to hide it from view. This too contained coffins and the Dixons observed Howard moving coffins here from the stable.

It is not known whether Dixon confronted Howard about these unseemly activities, or why he didn't immediately report what he had seen to the authorities, or anyone else for that matter. However, things changed when Robert Dixon had a falling-out with Isaac Howard.

Whatever the argument between Dixon and Howard, it clearly engendered enough animosity in Dixon for him to report Howard's activities to his employer, Mr Oxspring, and then on his advice, to the police. A press report of Friday, 6 June 1862 states that on the previous Saturday, Dixon had informed Inspector Crofts of the West Riding Constabulary at Hillsborough that newly-buried bodies were being dug up and sold for dissection.[405]

By the evening of Tuesday, 3 June, Dixon's allegations had hit the rumour-mill of the local populace and a number of them gathered and ascended upon the cemetery to see if there was any truth in the matter. They found the pit containing coffins, some were holding bodies.

In a box on top of the coffins was a body that had clearly been dissected with flesh removed from the bones, it was the body of Joseph Gretorex. This convinced the mob that Isaac Howard was indeed in the *'resurrection business'* and thus, inflamed by their observations, set off for his house. However, they mistakenly went to his previous address,[406] which was now occupied by a clergyman.

Before they realised their mistake, much damage was done to windows, doors and furniture.[407] Now, having been informed that Howard's new abode was at Burrowlees, they set off to vent their wrath there. By this time, Isaac

---

[405] *Birmingham Daily Post*, 6 June 1862. Op Cit www.chrishobbs.com.
[406] The Howards are recorded as living in Freedom Road, Walkley in the 1861 census, suggesting that they had only recently moved to Burrowlees.
[407] Mayhall, John, *The Annals of Yorkshire, Vol. II,* Joseph Johnson, 1865, p.44

Howard had become aware that the game was up and that there was a mob on the rampage seeking his blood.

He fled Burrowlees, leaving his wife to face the mob. A fearful Mary Howard closed the shutters and locked the doors. On arriving at Burrowlees, the mob hesitated for a few minutes at the end of the road leading to Howard's house before advancing on the building, throwing stones at the windows and tearing down the palisades around it.[408]

They eventually broke into the house and turned Mary out before setting about an orgy of destruction, breaking up the furniture, then setting it alight using burning embers from the kitchen fire. After retreating from the blazing house, they stood around armed with stones to deter any intervention to put the fire out. By the time the police arrived, the house was beyond saving. The house and its contents, which were not insured, were utterly destroyed.[409]

News of the rioting reached other parts of the town and early on the following morning an even larger gathering took place at Wardsend Cemetery, including a number of people who had recently buried family members, anxious to find out if their graves had been interfered with.

Many gathered around the pit, holding handkerchiefs or aprons over their faces against the stench emanating from within. Harriet Shearman, the wife of a miller at nearby Philadelphia, arrived a little after mid-day, anxious to know that the body of her infant son had not been disturbed.

Little Edward Charles Shearman, aged two years and one month, had died and been buried at Wardsend on 23 September 1861. Edward Charles was the second child that Harriet and William Shearman had lost in the last three years or so and both were buried at Wardsend in separate graves.[410]

Harriet peered into the pit at the coffins, some with the lids removed. It was in one of these coffins that she recognised the features of her little boy. She had the coffin taken home where, on further examination, she satisfied herself that this was the body of her infant son. Other bodies found in the pit were also identified.

---

[408] Op Cit *Birmingham Daily Post*
[409] Ibid
[410] Infant mortality in Sheffield at this time was around 50% (0–5-year-old). See Drewry, *Intimidation,* p.27

We know of one from the memorial stone that now sits in the Walled Garden in Hillsborough Park as being four months old Louis Bacon who was buried at Wardsend on 12 April 1858. The inscription reads:

…one of the many found in 1862 who had been ruthlessly disinterred. Some people excavated family graves to ensure the contents were intact. In a number of cases, this proved not to be the case, suggesting that the bodies had been taken away and, it was believed, used for dissection.

The police investigation began in earnest that day, Wednesday, 4 June, with the attendance of the Chief Constable, John Jackson, who had the box containing the remains of Joseph Gretorex removed and taken to the stable where it was put into a larger box, then transported to the Town Hall.

On removal of the other coffins in the pit, decomposed body parts were found in a putrefied mess at the bottom of the pit. It is possible that the pit was dug to serve as a charnel house. In the course of their work, grave-diggers often came across parts of previously buried bodies, pieces of coffins and coffin plates, and these would be placed in charnel houses, usually in the crypts of churches, where they would remain for several years.[411]

The chapel at Wardsend did not have a crypt. Whether the pit was created for this purpose, doesn't appear to have been considered by the police, or the mob.

The Sheffield magistrates met on Saturday 7 June to enquire into the reasons for the rioting at Wardsend Cemetery and Burrowlees, taking evidence from John Jackson and a number of witnesses, including Robert and Bethia Dixon, and Harriet Shearman. The mayor, John Brown, chaired the proceedings. After hearing the evidence, the magistrates issued a warrant for Isaac Howard's arrest.

Meanwhile, Isaac Howard had fled to Derbyshire, spending some time in Bakewell and Derby, but he made it known to the police that he intended returning to Sheffield by train on Monday 9 June, hoping that he was now safe from the mob.

Two detectives, named Airey and Richard Brayshaw, went to meet him off the train but he wasn't on it. It transpired that he had got off at Eckington for some reason, and then went to Masborough by a later train.[412] Airey and Brayshaw went to Masborough and searched the public houses, and they found him in the Red Lion.

---

[411] Op Cit Bailey, *Resurrection Men,* p.17
[412] *The Times*, Tuesday, 10 June 1862. Op Cit www.chrishobbs.com.

Howard returned to Sheffield with the officers who had not arrested him at this point and he thought that they were merely escorting him for his protection against any further disorder. The three attended the magistrates' office where Howard made an application to the Bench for compensation for the loss of his house, which was for £500.

Here, detective-officer Richard Brayshaw produced the warrant and applied for Howard's remand on a charge of, *having illegally removed the remains of a child of William Shearman of Philadelphia.*[413]

This took Howard by surprise and acting on his behalf, solicitor Charles Broadbent, applied for bail but this was refused. Albert Smith, Clerk to the Magistrates, commented that bail would be out of the question as,

...at present it was impossible to say what [other] *charges might arise against the prisoner.*[414]

[413] Ibid
[414] Ibid

Rev John Livesey (Courtesy of Friends of Wardsend Cemetery)

Painting of Birley Meadows overlooking Wardsend Cemetery from around the time of the riot. The chapel and lodge are clearly seen. To the right of centre in the distance is the Hillsborough Barracks completed in 1854, replacing the first Barracks built following the Enclosure Riot and completed in 1794. Further to the right can be seen Hillsborough Hall, now Hillsborough Library, built in 1779. The road seen below the Hall is now Penistone Road. Burrowlee is within the area between the Hall and the road; one of the roads off Penistone Road here is called Burrowlee Road where one of the oldest buildings in the area can be found: Burrowlee House, built in 1711. The painting once hung on the office wall at Daniel Doncaster steelworks. Daniel Doncaster took over a forge on Penistone Road in 1898, probably the building seen to the left of centre. For further information about the area see Drewry, Mick (Ed), *The Complete Hillsborough By Her People*, Hillsborough Community Development Trust, 2006. (Image courtesy of Malcolm Nunn)

River Don at Wardsend 1875 by W J Stevenson

On Monday, 23 June, John Livesey appeared before Sheffield magistrates to answer allegations of making false entries in the burial records and for granting false certificates for burials. The curate of St Philip's, Rev W Marshall, produced the burial register, in which was recorded the burial of Joseph Gretorex on 3 April 1862. The entry was signed off by John Livesey.

Moses Walton confirmed that Joseph Gretorex's dissected body did not leave the Medical School until 12 April. Jonathan Barber, surgeon at the Medical School, produced a certificate of interment that he had received in respect of Joseph Gretorex, it too was signed by John Livesey. Barber also confirmed that he had paid the interment fees to Howard. Witnesses were also produced against Isaac Howard.

John Jackson described the pit and its contents, and stated that the box found there containing human remains was taken to the Town Hall. William Skinner, surgeon at the Sheffield Union Workhouse, identified the body as that of Joseph Gretorex.

Jonathan Sutcliffe, a mason of Sylvester Gardens, had previously lived in the lodge at Wardsend Cemetery and used to work on gravestones in the shed there. He brought gasps from the court spectators when he said that he had seen Howard put bodies in the described pit; *brought in a box in a wheelbarrow.* He went on to say, '*I have seen Howard turn remains out of a box and shovel them with a shovel.*'

Joseph Couldwell, who worked for Isaac Howard, stated that he had helped Howard move a box containing the remains of a man from the stable to the pit where it was placed atop the coffins therein. He confirmed that no clergyman was present when the box was taken to the pit, or that the Burial Service was ever given. He then confirmed that the box was the very same box that he had seen at the Town Hall.[415]

There is no clear motive for the disinterment of the children for it appears that Howard made no financial gain. It is suggested that they were relocated to the pit to make room for new burials. If this was the case, there must have been a phenomenal demand for burial plots over the five years that the cemetery had been in use, equating to exhausting an acre of burial ground per year.

However, the pit in which the disinterred bodies were kept was reportedly in an unused part of the cemetery, suggesting that there was still room for new burials, and it would be another 39 years before there was need to extend the cemetery.

John Livesey and Isaac Howard were committed for trial at York Assizes; Livesey was charged with making a false entry of burial and for giving a false certificate; Howard was charged with disinterring bodies. Livesey stated that he would reserve his defence and leave his case entirely to his counsel. The trial took place on 24 July and both were found guilty but the judge accepted that in John Livesey's case, there was no fraudulent intent and a nominal sentence of three-week imprisonment was given.

In August, he was given a free pardon. The road to Wardsend Cemetery from Penistone Road was later named after the Reverend and became Livesey Street. Howard was sentenced to three-months in gaol, the maximum sentence allowed by the Anatomy Act.[416] He would later receive £200 from the county to compensate for the damage to his property in Burrowlees, which he had assessed to be £500.

Whilst the Anatomy Act brought the trade in dead bodies for use in medical science to an end, putting the resurrection men out of business, it failed to resolve the issue of the inadequate supply of cadavers for the dissection tables. In fact,

---

[415] *The Times,* 24 June 1862. Op Cit www.chrishobbs.com.
[416] Three months imprisonment or a fine of £50 was the maximum sentence for any offence covered by the Act. Op Cit Bailey, *Resurrection Men,* p.156

the Act actually reduced the number of available corpses as the lawful use of unclaimed bodies from the workhouses was merely permitted and not compulsory as it was in other countries.[417]

Public sensibilities around the use of human bodies being used at all determined a measure of reluctance within some local authorities. The two cases of resurrection riot in Sheffield came about out of intrinsic suspicion fuelled by unsubstantiated rumour that body-snatching had taken place. But in both cases, this proved to be false rumour, although at Wardsend, there had been contraventions of the Act.

The Anatomy Act had ended the resurrection trade but it did not put an end to the people's sensitivities and suspicions around the procurement of corpses for dissection, despite there now being a legal framework for it and for the teaching of anatomy. Indeed, controversy arose again in Sheffield in January 1882, when the wife of a 36-year-old unemployed draper's assistant, John Wood, who had died of consumption in the workhouse, requested to see the body of her husband before he was buried. She wanted to look upon his face one last time, following a dream urging her that there was something amiss. To satisfy the widow, the coffin lid was unscrewed and lifted to reveal to her horror, the body of a 71-year-old man. John Wood's corpse had been taken to the medical school for dissection and no doubt someone at the workhouse had made a shilling or two.[418]

---

[417] Ibid, p.163
[418] Op Cit Bean, p.20

The 'Resurrection men'.

The Chartist Uprising

Press forward, press forward,
There's nothing to fear,
We will have the Charter,
Be it ever so dear.[419]

1839-40

Born out of a number of political and social campaigns to improve the lives of the working classes throughout the 1830s, Chartism became the foremost and overriding campaign to this end and arguably remains the greatest political mass movement in British history.

Its birth is generally accepted as being on 6 August 1838, when the six points of the *'People's Charter'* were agreed at a great public meeting in Birmingham, although the Charter had been drawn up the previous year by the London Working Men's Association and first published in May 1838,[420] and first proposed in 1777 by the political reformer John Cartwright (1740-1824).[421]

The six points of the Charter were universal male suffrage; no property qualifications for MPs; annual parliaments; equal electoral districts; payment of MPs; and a secret ballot. With the exception of annual parliaments, all the remaining points of the Charter are now enshrined in British law[422] but in these early days of political reform, there was much resistance from the ruling elite and every step towards the democratic political system we know today had to be fought for.

---

[419] Chartist song sung as they marched down Duke Street following a meeting at Skye Edge. Op Cit Leader, Robert Eadon (Ed), *Reminiscences,* p.270

[420] Browne, Harry, *Chartism,* Hodder & Stoughton, 2004, pp.2-3

[421] Op Cit Chase, p.7

[422] The property qualification for MPs was abandoned in 1858; the secret ballot was adopted in 1872; MPs have been paid since 1911; universal male suffrage realised in 1918; a series of reform Acts since 1885 have provided and maintained electoral districts of equal size.

Despite the campaign being generally non-violent, with the Petition to Parliament[423] being its accepted approach of choice, clashes on the streets of the larger towns and cities were inevitable, especially in the industrial towns of the north, which were perceived as political hot-beds.

Indeed, the government took the threat of revolutionary Chartism relatively seriously, being mindful of the European revolutions of 1830[424] and Sir Charles James Napier[425] was appointed commander of the north in 1839 to take charge of the military in response to the threat, despite him being known as a radical sympathiser.[426]

On this move, Napier commented, *Would that I had gone to Australia and been saved this work, produced by Tory injustice and Whig imbecility.*[427] Three regiments were recalled from Ireland to increase the number of troops at his command to 4,700, to cover an area of northern England between the Scottish border and Nottingham.[428]

Napier invited Chartist leaders to an artillery demonstration, to show them what they would be up against should they take the armed revolutionary route to achieve the People's Charter.[429] He wrote of the Nottingham Chartists in 1839,

Poor creatures, their threats of attack are miserable. With half a cartridge, and half a pike, with no money, no discipline, no skilful leaders, they would attack men with leaders, money and discipline, well-armed and having sixty rounds a man.[430]

---

[423] Before universal suffrage petitioning Parliament was the only way to effect political change and unlike the franchise, women were allowed to sign petitions. In all there were three Chartist Petitions to Parliament: 1839, 1842 and 1848. The 1842 petition gathered 3.3 million signatures, representing a third of the adult population. See Loft, Philip, *Power to the People* in *History Today, Vol 69, Issue 5,* pp.13-15

[424] In 1830, there were revolutions in France, Belgium, Poland and Italy.

[425] Sir Charles James Napier (1782-1853), obtained commission and promoted lieutenant 1794; aide-de-camp to Sir James Duff, 1799, and to General Edward Fox, 1803; Captain in Staff Crops, 1805; Major, 1806; severely wounded and taken prisoner at Corunna, 1809; exchanged, 1810; Lieutenant-Colonel, 1811; served against United States, 1813; volunteered on Napoleon's escape from Elba and made CB, 1815; Major-General, 1837; KCB, 1838; Commander of the north, 1839-41; successful campaigns in India, conqueror of Sind, 1841-50; GCB 1843; returned to England 1850.

[426] Op Cit Evans, p.270

[427] Briggs, Asa, *The Age of Improvement 1783-1867,* Longmans, 1964, p.309

[428] Op Cit Chase, p.71

[429] Op Cit Hill, p.166

[430] Op Cit Evans, p.271 also Brown, Richard and Daniels, Christopher, *The Chartists— Documents and Debates,* Macmillan Education, 1987, p.59

Sympathiser or not, Napier was well aware of the futility of an armed Chartist rebellion. Napier's troops were dispersed around the northern towns against his wishes due to the magistrates wanting to protect themselves and their property.

He wanted to concentrate them at either the Leeds or Sheffield barracks. However, this move was blocked by the Home Secretary, Lord Normanby.[431] Charles Napier's brother, Sir William Francis Patrick Napier, quoted the general in his biography of Charles, *Life and Opinions of General Sir Charles Napier,* in 1857:

> *April 9th (1839) The troops are in twenty-six detachments, spread over half England, some two hundred miles from me! The magistrates are divided into Whigs, Tories and personal entities…The town magistrates are liberal from fear of the populace; the country bucks are too old and too far gone. Tories to have hopes of gaining popularity by being Radical; so they labour to get troops near their own houses. Funk is the order of the day, and there is some excuse, for the people seem ferocious enough. But this fear has produced a foolish dispersion of the troops, these magistrates being powerful fellows…[432]*

---

[431] Op Cit Chase, p.70
[432] Op Cit Brown and Daniels, pp. 58-9

Sir Charles James Napier by William Edward Kilburn, 1849.

William Napier further recorded his brother's contempt for the magistrates and the yeomanry, no doubt with the memory of Peterloo in mind:

> *August 15th Napoleon's birthday! All quiet. The magistrates wanted me to call out the yeomanry. No said I no yeomen. If the Chartist want a fight, they can be indulged without yeomen, who are over-zealous for cutting and slashing...*
>
> *December 1st...of all classes the worst are the magistrates. The Tory magistrates are bold, violent, irritating, and uncompromising; the Whig magistrates sneaking and base, always ready to call for troops, and yet truckling to the mob...[433]*

---

[433] Ibid, p.59

It is interesting to note, alongside his derision of the magistrates, Charles Napier's observation that it was Napoleon's birthday, as he recorded his thoughts.

The first major incident of riot in relation to Chartism was a violent attack upon Chartists at Devizes on 22 March 1839, when their Convention delegates' coach was assailed with stones and other missiles, allegedly thrown by a mob led by the county's Under-Sheriff. The delegates and their followers took refuge in a local inn, which was threatened with being set on fire until police and magistrates arrived to restore order.[434]

Several Chartists, including one of its leaders and founder member, William Lovett, who was also largely responsible for drafting the Charter, were arrested in Birmingham on 4 July 1839 following a Chartist Convention there, in what became known as the 'Bull Ring' riot.

Sixty officers of the London Metropolitan Police had been brought in by local magistrates with a remit to arrest any Chartist leader making a speech to the crowd. Three of the officers were seriously injured with stab wounds in the ensuing rampage.[435] Lovett was sentenced to 12 months imprisonment.

Then, on 4 November 1839, 24 Chartists were killed when 7,000 of them, mainly miners and ironworkers, marched into Newport, South Wales, where they stormed the Westgate Inn (the local magistrates had set up an operations base at the inn and a number of Chartists were being held there under arrest), many armed with pikes or muskets.

They were fired upon by soldiers of the 45th Regiment. This loss of civilian lives is the greatest in any insurrection in Britain during the 18th and 19th centuries, more than the, perhaps better-known, Peterloo massacre of 1819 in Manchester when 18 people died and an estimated 700 were injured at the hands of mounted yeomanry.[436]

---

[434] Op. Cit Chase, p.68

[435] Op Cit Chase, p.81

[436] Hibbert, Christopher, *The English——A Social History 1066-1945,* Book Club Associates, 1987, p.495 The Peterloo massacre sparked many demonstrations across the country including one of the largest public meetings seen in Sheffield at Brocco to petition the Prince Regent and parliament to establish an inquiry into the event. Coming together in the Wicker many thousands of members of the clubs and friendly societies in the Sheffield neighbourhood made a procession to the Brocco with banners and flags waving and music played by their respective bands. The meeting heard a number of speakers, including the Earl Fitzwilliam, and after unanimously agreeing the proposals dispersed peaceably. Op Cit Leader, Robert Eadon (Ed), *Reminiscences,* p.209

Twenty-one of the Newport Chartists were charged with high treason and three of the leaders, John Frost, Zephaniah Williams and William Jones, were found guilty and sentenced to death in accordance with that barbaric law: to be hanged, their bodies decapitated and their torso posthumously quartered.[437]

The sentence was later commuted to 17 years transportation and they joined five other Chartists on a prison ship to Australia.

Chartists attack the Westgate Inn, Newport

There was little noticeable Chartist activity in Sheffield in early 1838, which is confirmed in a letter from local solicitor and supporter of Reform Edward Bramley to Sheffield MP Henry George Ward, to which Ward replied,

I rejoice to hear from you that Sheffield continues comparatively free from the contagion'.[438]

---

[437] Prior to the 1814 Treason Act the penalty was even more barbaric in that those found guilty of High Treason were hanged (until near death), drawn (disembowelled alive) and quartered (the body chopped into four pieces). The 1814 Act also permitted the King to authorise beheading as an alternative. This was amended in 1870 by the Forfeiture Act, which changed the penalty for High Treason to hanging, as for murder. The death penalty for High Treason was abolished as late as 1998 by the Crime and Disorder Act. The last person to be executed for High Treason was William Joyce, the British Nazi propagandist nick-named Lord Haw-Haw, in 1946.

[438] Letter to Edward Bramley from Henry George Ward dated 24 November 1838 in Op Cit Parker, p.34

Clearly, Ward was opposed to the Chartists and in the same letter he states, *What they [Chartists] are contending for is unattainable under any conceivable form of human society, and upon this we must take our stand unless we wish to be swept away by the most fearful struggle between mendicancy and property that the world has yet seen.*

However, an active group of Chartists in Sheffield came to public notice in September 1838 when an open meeting in Paradise Square[439] attracted a large crowd. Ebenezer Elliott and Isaac Ironside, described as an able but eccentric politician,[440] were the principal speakers.[441] On 28 January 1839 a number of Chartists attended an Anti-Corn Law[442] meeting at the Town Hall where they made efforts to bring the two forces together in a single cause through amendments to the tabled Anti-Corn Law motion but their proposals were not accepted, being outvoted two to one.[443] The friction between the two movements was prevalent throughout the country and Anti-Corn Law meetings were often disrupted by Chartists who would propose an amendment to the customary motion against the Corn Laws to add and to give priority to universal suffrage. The ensuing arguments often led to meetings ending in disarray. In Sheffield there was much support amongst the working classes for repeal of the Corn Laws but as a body the local Chartists remained hostile.[444] Although there were tentative links between the two movements, the Chartists campaigned for political reform whereas the Anti-Corn Law League's objective was purely one of economics. A further obstacle to them uniting was the issue of social class, the Anti-Corn Law League being predominantly made up of the middle-class whereas the Chartists were working-class, although many of the Chartist leaders

---

[439] Also known as 't' Pot Square' from times when a pot market was held there on market days, Paradise Square was Sheffield's most prominent public meeting place. Before any buildings were erected around the square it was a corn field. The first recorded meeting was when John Wesley preached to one of his largest mid-week congregations on 15 July 1779.

[440] Op Cit Leader, Robert Eadon, p.21 Isaac Ironside had been Thomas Asline Ward's campaign secretary in the 1832 general election

[441] Op Cit Hey, p.138

[442] The Corn Law Acts of 1791 and 1813 restricted the exporting and importing of grain forcing up prices in the interests of landowners. They were eventually repealed in 1846 by Robert Peel due to public pressure following the Irish famine of 1845-46. The Sheffield Anti-Corn Law Society was formed on 8 January 1834, pre-dating the Anti-Corn Law League, established in Manchester, by four years.

[443] Op Cit *Sheffield Local Register,* p.318 See also Op Cit Parker, notes to Letter 43, p.36

[444] Briggs, Asa (Ed), *Chartist Studies,* Macmillan & Co Ltd, 1970, p.361

were from the middle-class. In reality, the Chartists and Anti-Corn Law reformers were frequently at odds with each other; repealing the Corn Laws alone would not improve the social conditions of the working classes, only a voice in Parliament would engender change. Free trade was also seen by some to be a means to lower wages and a distraction from the fundamental struggle for parliamentary reform.[445] Ebenezer Elliott was of both camps having become known for his *Corn-Law Rhymes,* published in 1831, which laid bare his bitter opposition to the *'bread-tax'.*

Delivering the Charter Petition to Parliament, 1842.

On 20 May 1839, simultaneous Chartist meetings took place across the country, including Sheffield, probably at what became their regular meeting room in Fig Tree Lane,[446] where their delegate to the national Chartist

---

[445] Op Cit Briggs *Age of Improvement*, p.319
[446] The Council of the Sheffield Chartists also met in secret at a public house in Lambert Street. This could have been either the Ball or the Birmingham Arms.

Convention that had taken place in London on 4 February, scale-cutter William Gill, is reported to have resigned because *he was resolved not to represent a disunited people.*[447]

The reference here is to the two factions within the Chartist movement: men of *moral force*, such as Ebenezer Elliott and Isaac Ironside, who believed they would win the Charter through rational argument and petition; and men of *physical force*, who were prepared to use violent means to win their objective. The regular Chartist slogan was *Peaceably if we may, forcibly if we must.* Gill was of the physical force persuasion.

Quoted at a meeting of northern Convention delegates on 7 January, Gill considered that *a resort to force would be required to relieve the suffering of the working classes...nothing else than a demonstration of this description would operate upon their hard-hearted relentless tyrants.*[448]

On 15 July, at another mass meeting in Paradise Square, James Wolstenholme[449] was elected to replace William Gill to represent the area, which included Sheffield, Rotherham, Doncaster, Chesterfield and Brampton, at the National Convention. It was also decided at this gathering to hold nightly meetings and special preaching on Sundays.[450]

These regular meetings were received with some alarm amongst certain members of the populace, predominantly non-supportive tradesmen, who made representations to the town's magistrates. On 20 July, the magistrates issued a warning to the people of Sheffield, 16,829 of who had signed the Petition,[451] not to attend Chartist meetings.

Nevertheless, the nightly meetings continued throughout the summer and it was reported that on 27 July, the names of tradesmen who had contributed to the Chartist cause were read out to rapturous cheers; so too were the names of those who refused to contribute, most likely including those who had made

---

[447] Op Cit *Sheffield Local Register*, p.323
[448] Op Cit Chase, p.61
[449] James Wolstenholme was gaoled for 6 months for his involvement in a seditious plot in 1817. See chapter on Pentrich Rising. Wolstenholme and the secretary of the Sheffield Chartists, a man named Chatterton, sailed to the United States in late September 1839. I have not been able to find out whether they went on a mission to promote the campaign or were perhaps anticipating the ascendancy of 'physical force' and avoiding its consequences.
[450] Op Cit *Sheffield Local Register*, p.325
[451] Thompson, Dorothy, *The Chartists—Popular Politics in the Industrial Revolution*, Pantheon Books, New York, 1984, Appendix, p.364

representations to the magistrates, leaving them open to potential boycotting and loss of trade.

Two 19th century views of Paradise Square

On 7 May 1839, the Chartist Convention moved from London to Birmingham, where delegates considered what measures to take to progress the campaign. Up until now, supported actions had been strictly of a non-violent nature, such as boycotting non-supportive traders and withdrawing funds from banks.

At the May Convention, there was a call for a *sacred month* of strike action, in essence a call for a general strike. Whilst on the face of it, this too was a non-violent action, delegates were quick to point out that, within a short time, hungry workers and the agents of government would clash and that violent riots would inevitably ensue.

The proposal was put in abeyance pending the outcome of the Petition to Parliament, due to be submitted on 12 July, but the idea was sent out to the regions for the people to discuss at mass meetings. At a further Convention in July, the *sacred month* was high on the agenda and it was decided to recommend the action should the government reject the Charter. It was during this Convention that the Bull Ring riot (mentioned above) took place.

Back in Sheffield, another mass meeting was held in Paradise Square on 5 August to discuss the *sacred month* proposal. The meeting resolved:

> *That this meeting, while we believe that nothing less than a universal stand can get the Charter, we believe that this town and district are not as yet sufficiently organised for the adoption of the 'sacred month' but, nevertheless, we wait the decision of the General Convention, and*

pledge ourselves to adopt and carry out all measures unconditionally recommended by them for securing the People's Charter.[452]

The Sheffield Chartists clearly recognised that they didn't have the ability to organise a general withdrawal of labour in the district or even in the town. Such a move would be illegal as it would constitute a restraint of trade. Neither did the Chartists have the overall support of the trades' unions, without which such action would have been futile. The trades' unions' position was confirmed at a meeting of delegates from various Sheffield trades' unions on 4 September which resolved:

That they could not, as trades' unions, support the Chartists, or any other political party.[453]

The secretary of the Sheffield Working Men's Association had written earlier, in February:

It is useless for us to attempt to rouse the Working Classes here.[454]

At the height of the call for a general strike to obtain the Charter, its negative reception amongst the Sheffield trade unions was illustrated by no less than seven secretaries of local trade unions writing to the local newspapers to explain that their trades had nothing to do with the Chartist meetings or Chartist resolutions.[455]

Although the Petition to Parliament was rejected, the national Chartist leaders decided against the *sacred month* but recommended three days be devoted to solemn processions proclaimed as a *Grand Moral Demonstration* and on Monday, 12 August there was a watered-down version of the sacred month with a small number of strikes in Sheffield and the Sheffield Chartists holding meetings and processions throughout the morning, in the afternoon and into the evening, resulting in rioting on the streets.

---

[452] Op Cit *Sheffield Local Register*, p.326
[453] Ibid, p.328
[454] Op Cit Chase, p.65
[455] Webb, Sidney and Beatrice, *The History of Trade Unionism,* Longmans, Green and Co, 1896, p.159

In response, on the following day, Sheffield magistrates issued a proclamation forbidding further Chartist meetings. Two of the local Chartist leaders were arrested for their part in the previous day's riots: Peter Foden, a baker, was charged in being concerned with the unlawful proceedings and Charles Fox was charged with seditious language.

Further riots broke out that evening and the police cleared the streets with the help of the military. There were no serious injuries to persons but between 70 and 80 people were arrested and taken into custody. On the following day, Wednesday, 14 August, most of the people taken into custody were unconditionally discharged but three of them were remanded until Friday.

Foden and Fox were further questioned by the magistrates and then bailed to appear at York Assizes charged with conspiracy, sedition and riot. They were remanded to the Wakefield House of Correction until bail was arranged. Bail for Peter Foden was provided by Ebenezer Elliott and James Wolstenholme on 3 September.[456] James Jackson and Isaac Ironside provided bail for Charles Fox on 1 October.[457] There were further disturbances that Wednesday evening and the streets were once more cleared by the police.[458]

On Friday, 16 August the magistrates examined the three remaining prisoners from Tuesday's riots: Moses Farrar, Samuel Nall and John Marsden. Farrar and Nall were committed for trial, which was held on 24 October, and they were found guilty of riot. They were sentenced to 3 months and 1 month imprisonment respectively. Marsden was committed to York. He pleaded guilty of riot on 17 March 1840 and was sentenced to 1 week's imprisonment and to be bound over to keep the peace.[459]

In consideration of the outlawing of their meetings, on Sunday, 18 August the Sheffield Chartists, many of whom were religious men, took their campaign to church with a considerable number of them attending the Parish Church, St. Peter's (now Sheffield Cathedral), where they had requested the vicar, Rev. John Gibson, to preach from a particular text: *James, Chapter 5, verses 1-11:*

---

[456] Op Cit *Sheffield Local Register,* p.328
[457] Ibid, p.330. Charles Fox pleaded guilty on 17 March 1840 and sentenced to 1 week's imprisonment and bound over to keep the peace at a further hearing on 21 March.
[458] Ibid, p.327
[459] Ibid, p.340

Warning to Rich Oppressors

[1] Now listen, you rich people, weep and wail because of the misery that is coming upon you.

[2] Your wealth has rotted, and moths have eaten your clothes.

[3] Your gold and silver are corroded. Their corrosion will testify against you and eat your flesh like fire. You have hoarded wealth in the last days.

[4] Look! The wages you failed to pay the workmen who mowed your fields are crying out against you. The cries of the harvesters have reached the ears of the Lord Almighty.

[5] You have lived on earth in luxury and self-indulgence. You have fattened yourselves in the day of slaughter.

[6] You have condemned and murdered innocent men, who were not opposing you.

Patience in Suffering

[7] Be patient then, brothers, until the Lord's coming. See how the farmer waits for the land to yield its valuable crop and how patient he is for the autumn and spring rains.

[8] You too be patient and stand firm, because the Lord's coming is near.

[9] Don't grumble against each other, brothers, or you will be judged. The Judge is standing at the door!

[10] Brothers, as an example of patience in the face of suffering, take the prophets who spoke in the name of the Lord.

[11] As you know, we consider blessed those who have persevered. You have heard of Job's perseverance and have seen what the Lord finally brought about. The Lord is full of compassion and mercy.

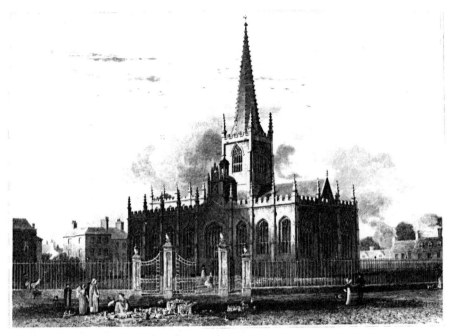

St Peter's Church.

Having already prepared his sermons for the day, the vicar proposed to deliver the text the following week. On the following Sunday, Rev Gibson proved to be good to his word and he preached to the Chartists, who had turned up in greater numbers, from their requested epistle; if only we could hear his address and the response of the congregation.

Even more Chartists attended the Parish Church over the next two Sundays and on 8 September there was a disturbance amongst the congregation when a Chartist tailor called Thomas Mason occupied a pew belonging to a Mr Sorby and was arrested.[460] This upheaval was just too much for the vicar and churchwardens and caused them to bring the incident to the attention of the magistrates and to seek, *the protection of the law against a recurrence of the painful scene* arising from the attendance of the Chartists in church.

On the following Sunday, there were armed police stationed at the churchyard gates.[461] The *Sheffield Iris* reported on 17 September:

It was an extraordinary exhibition, in England, to see a dozen policemen armed with cutlasses surrounding the Church-yard gates on the outside, a posse

---

[460] Roberts, Stephen (Ed.), *The People's Charter——Democratic Agitation in Early Victorian Britain,* The Merlin Press, 2003, p.83
[461] Op Cit *Sheffield Local Register*, pp.328-9

of constables inside, stationed about five or six yards apart around the inside of the railings, admitting only those who had good coats on their backs, and whose respectable external appearance would warrant the conclusion that they were not Chartists. The "Poor Man's Church" now calls in the aid of the civil powers and the military to prevent the poor from contaminating with their presence the cushioned pews and velvet hassocks of the more wealthy and aristocratic sons.[462]

Chartists at Church by H M Page.

This tactic of deploying mass Chartist attendance at church was adopted in various towns where their meetings were outlawed by local magistrates, with the exception of Scotland where no such move took place. There were just three such mass Chartist church attendances in Wales.[463] In Sheffield, the tactic was the most prolonged, with Chartists attending the Parish Church for five consecutive Sundays.[464]

It was during these church gatherings that the future alleged leader of the Sheffield uprising, Samuel Holberry, an imposing figure over six feet tall with

---

[462] Op Cit Roberts, p.84
[463] Op Cit Chase, p.97
[464] Op Cit Roberts, p.78

jet black hair, came to the fore as a leading speaker, both in church and at the Fig Tree Lane meeting house.[465]

Meeting within the sanctuary of the church was a means of lawful assembly but the Chartists could hardly discuss their aims and objectives between the hymns and the sermons. Equally, they could no longer meet in Paradise Square, their usual point of assembly, as the authorities could quickly respond and arrest the leaders.

Of course, that was if the meeting was a Chartist meeting, for the magistrates had by definition, only outlawed the Chartists from holding public meetings. However, the Chartists were able to make a point by holding a *'silent meeting'*, that is a gathering of Chartists but with no speeches or debates to reveal that the meeting was actually a Chartist meeting.

Although not practicable in terms of progressive action, silent meetings were a means of cocking a snook at the authorities and the first such meeting took place on Monday, 9 September at Paradise Square. This first silent gathering appears to have been a peaceful event but at a second meeting at the same venue on the Wednesday, someone fired a pistol and some windows were broken.

On the following night, Thursday, 12 September, silent or not, the meeting in Paradise Square was broken up by the police and the yeomanry (the troops at the Barracks having apparently been called out to Macclesfield); the magistrates weren't standing for the subterfuge. Having fled the police and soldiers, most of the gathering made their way to Doctor's Field[466] and re-assembled there, this time, no doubt, listening to their leaders' oratory.

Before long, the soldiers and constables had caught up with them again and drove them apart. Stones were thrown but there were no serious injuries. Thirty-six Chartists were apprehended and many of them appeared before the magistrates on Saturday at the Town Hall, which was guarded by dragoons and policemen armed with cutlasses.

Six of them were committed to trial at York but allowed bail: Robert Cox, George Gallimore, Joseph Lingard, James Bartholomew, Joshua Crayford and Thomas Powell.[467] A number of the others were required to enter into

---

[465] Op Cit Chase, p.153

[466] Doctor's Field was within the triangle formed by Shoreham Street, Suffolk Road and St. Mary's Road.

[467] The only Thomas Powell recorded in White's Directory of 1837 lived in Glossop Road and was a shoe maker and beer house keeper (Raven). There are three William

194

recognisance[468] and to provide sureties to keep the peace. Also before the magistrates this day, was Thomas Mason[469] who was charged with causing the disturbance in the Parish Church on the previous Sunday.

He was held on bail to appear at the Sheffield Sessions. Those who were not examined on the Saturday came before the magistrates on the following Monday, 16 September. Two of them, William Robinson and Joseph Jowett, were also committed to appear at the Sheffield Sessions. The rest were required to find sureties for their keeping the peace.[470] Robinson and Jowett both appeared at the Sheffield Sessions on 24 October.

Robinson was found guilty of riot and sentenced to one month imprisonment and to find sureties for good behaviour for one year. There was no evidence offered against Jowett.[471] Thomas Mason was also due to appear on 24 October but failed to attend. He was later given up by his sureties and brought before the magistrates again on a bench warrant on 29 October and committed to trial at Doncaster Sessions. His trial was held on 8 January 1840, and he was found guilty of causing the disturbance in the Parish Church and sentenced to two months imprisonment.[472]

Meanwhile, on Wednesday, 11 September, an Irishman named William Martin had been brought before the magistrates charged with sedition following a lecture at the Chartists' meeting room in Fig Tree Lane on the previous Friday. He is reported as having threatened the magistrates by proclaiming:

If any magistrate dares issue a warrant against me or my brothers I will assassinate him, by day or by night. Is there a man amongst you who cannot make a blade that will draw blood?

Well, the magistrates dared and Martin was committed to York Assizes. He was found guilty of using seditious language on 17 March 1840 and sentenced to 12 months imprisonment at the Northallerton House of Correction and bound

---

Robinsons recorded (could be any one of them) but none of the other names mentioned appear.

[468] Recognisance: a bond undertaken before a court or magistrate requiring the observation of a condition, e.g. to appear when summoned

[469] The only Thomas Mason recorded in White's Directory for 1837 lived at 1 Burgess Street and was a tailor.

[470] Op Cit *Sheffield Local Register*, p.329

[471] Ibid, p.331

[472] Ibid, p.337

to keep the peace.[473] Martin would later become a Chartist delegate for Bradford and a Member of Parliament.[474]

Having been dispersed at Paradise Square and at Doctor's Field, the Chartists decided on a meeting venue further afield and on the evening of Monday, 16 September they met outside of the town at Skye Edge, an open and elevated area that gave the advantage of an early warning of any approaching police or soldiers.[475]

This proved to be a good move as the meeting went ahead unhindered but the magistrates were made aware of the gathering after the event and were ready for the next one. However, the intelligence worked both ways and the Chartist leaders learnt that the troops had been issued with ball cartridge in readiness for an attack on their next meeting at Skye Edge planned for the following Wednesday, and it was prudently cancelled.

Other meetings were held outside the town at Hood Hill, near Wentworth, on 22 September, at Attercliffe on 6 October, and at Loxley on 13 October.[476] Between five and ten thousand Chartists were reported to have attended the Hood Hill meeting to see and hear Feargus O'Connor, a principal national leader. Hymns were sung by the assembly—a custom at many of these mass meetings—as was a parody of the National Anthem:

> *'Oh Lord our God arise'*
> *Scatter our enemies,*
> *And make them fall.*[477]

[473] Ibid, p.340

[474] Op Cit Chase, p.184

[475] This advantage was later used by the Sheffield gangs running the illegal tossing-rings in the 1920s

[476] From a pamphlet produced by the Holberry Society entitled *Samuel Holberry (1814-42) Sheffield's Revolutionary Democrat,* c1978

[477] Op Cit Chase, p.141

Feargus O'Connor
(Illustrated London News, April 1848)

Their national convention delegate (James Wolstenholme) having gone to America, the Sheffield Chartists proposed to hold a meeting on 25 November at their Fig Tree Lane meeting room to elect a replacement for a forthcoming convention to be held in Newcastle but the magistrates prevented it from taking place.

On the same day, St Mary's Church on Bramall Lane was fire-bombed, allegedly by Chartists, but I conceive no logical reason for the church being a target for the Chartists.[478] Malcolm Chase suggests that the attack was merely to test the fire-bombs but why a church?[479]

Especially as many Chartists were church-goers. On the following night a torch-lit meeting commenced at Skye Edge where bricklayer James Boardman

---

[478] Op Cit Price, p.45
[479] Op Cit Chase, p.133

was elected the new delegate. The meeting broke up before the magistrates arrived accompanied by troops from the Barracks. Some of the Chartists were pursued and three young men were apprehended in Spital Hill and brought before the magistrates on 29 November, charged with being in attendance of the illegal Chartist meeting.

However, after being questioned, they were discharged. It was at this time that it was reported that Chartists were testing explosives in locations outside of the town.[480]

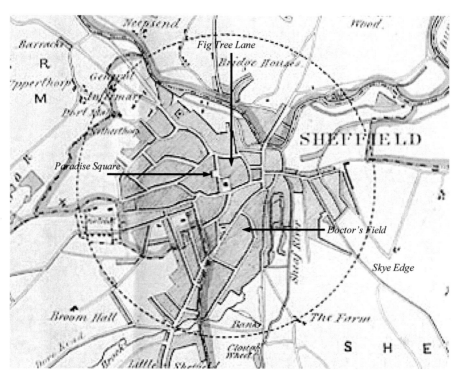

Sheffield 1832 showing Paradise Square, Fig Tree Lane, Doctor's Field and Skye Edge.

On 2 and 3 December, there were lectures at the Town Hall on the Corn Laws delivered by the tutor, lecturer and pamphleteer Canon Sydney Smith (1771-1845). A number of Chartists attended the second lecture and attempted to influence resolutions taken after the talk but as with their previous attempts to align the two causes, they were overwhelmingly outvoted.

---

[480] Op Cit Price, p.45

Undeterred, a number of Chartists attended an Anti-Corn Law meeting on Wednesday, 1 January 1840 at the New Circus,[481] which was attended by the Sheffield Members of Parliament, John Parker and Henry George Ward.

The venue was forced open by the Chartists, led by Peter Foden, before the appointed time and the ensuing uproar caused the meeting to be adjourned to Paradise Square where further attempts by the Chartists to influence resolutions on the repeal of the Corn Laws[482] were again unsuccessful.

Henry George Ward MP

January 1840 saw the culmination of the activities of the *physical force* advocates amongst the Sheffield Chartist movement with a failed plot to take

---

[481] I believe this to be the Circus and Theatre built in 1836-37 across from the cattle market adjoining Blonk Street bridge. It had a 42 ft ring, a 60ft x 40ft stage and stables for 14 horses. See Op Cit White, 1837, p.85

[482] A petition to repeal the Corn Laws was sent from Sheffield on 2 Feb 1839 with 13,000 signatures. The Corn Laws were eventually repealed in 1846

over the town by force. Stirred by the events at Newport, the revolutionaries had by now decided that the Charter would only be realised by force.

There had been rumours of an impending armed uprising in the town for some time, but they had been disregarded as fantasy by the Sheffield authorities. They would have been totally unaware of the unfolding events had it not been for the intelligence gathering of the Chief Constable of Rotherham, John Bland, who saw the *'physical force'* movement as a definite threat to Rotherham and was determined to investigate the rumours.

The Chartists leaders behind the plot consisted of men from the wider area, including Huddersfield, and they had been meeting in secret, mainly at their own houses, and had kept their plans to themselves, keeping the *'moral force'* advocates completely in the dark. Their Achilles heel however, and the instrument of their betrayal, was the Rotherham leader, a man who had wavered between the two groups, James Allen, the landlord at the Station Inn in Westgate and a stove-grate fitter at Messrs Yates, Haywood and Co at Clifton Bank.

Allen was partly aware of the plans, but he had not gained the full confidence of the plotters because of his bouts of reluctance in following the *'physical force'* agenda. However, he knew enough and after being questioned a number of times by John Bland, who no doubt also tried to persuade him of the merits of adhering to the moral ground and to denounce the planned violence, the Chief Constable was able to extract enough from him to be convinced that an armed uprising was being planned.

James Allen was eventually persuaded by the moral argument and became John Bland's spy. He reported back to him on what had been discussed at the secret councils, including one at his own house where the delegates from Huddersfield and other places offered their support for an initial attack on Sheffield where the plan was to seize the Town Hall and the Tontine Inn, where they would establish command headquarters.

From these bases, attacks would be organised to fire the barracks at Philadelphia and the houses and business premises of those who had opposed the Chartists. Magistrates and policemen were also high on their hit-list. Mail coaches were to be stopped; this would signal to other areas that *'all England was up for the Charter'*.

Once he had enough information on the planned uprising Bland took a written statement from James Allen and reported his findings and his concerns personally to Lord Howard, the Earl of Effingham, who was also a West Riding magistrate residing at Barbot Hall, near Rotherham. His Lordship advised that the Sheffield magistrates should be informed as soon as possible. At this, Bland and the clerk to the magistrates, John Oxley, visited Hugh Parker, now the senior Sheffield magistrate, and produced Allen's statement.

Despite all the evidence that the Rotherham Chief Constable presented, Hugh Parker and the Sheffield authorities wouldn't believe a word of it. They couldn't believe that any scheme, *so wild and atrocious could possibly be entertained.*[483]

Contemporary sketch entitled Chartist Row, probably depicting Chartists disrupting an Anti-Corn Law meeting.

The *physical force* Chartists continued to meet secretly on a daily basis, and James Allen continued to report back to John Bland. However, the conspirators were becoming more suspicious of James Allen, who showed a lack of commitment to the proposed violence, and he was kept out of key discussions and denied crucial information such as what arms and ammunition were available and where it was stored; information that John Bland was keen to ascertain.

[483] Op Cit Leader, Robert Eadon (Ed), *Reminiscences,* p.274

All Allen knew was that there were a number of arms depots and that there were plenty of *'cats'*[484] to thwart the cavalry. Nevertheless, he did find out that there would be an offensive in Rotherham and that taking the Court House was its prime objective. From there, attacks would be organised against the local gentry including Lord Howard. Yet still John Bland had nothing to act upon. He couldn't prepare to defend or counter attack without knowing when the plot was to be hatched.

He couldn't raid the arms depots as he didn't know where they were. He could apprehend the leaders but all he had was Allen's testimony which, in itself, wasn't enough to convict them. He simply had to get closer to the plotters and his only conduit was James Allen and the only way Allen was to learn more was to convince the leaders that he was totally committed to the *'physical force'* movement and gain their full confidence.

Bland turned Allen from mere informer into the ultimate *agent provocateur* and by offering 150 men to be made ready for the Chartist offensive in a day or two's notice, Allen was accepted into the inner circle of the plotters.

Allen attended three consecutive council meetings on Wednesday, Thursday and Friday, 8—10 January 1840. At the Friday meeting, it was revealed that the uprising would take place on the following night, Saturday, 11 January. The plan was to start with attacks on targets on the outskirts of the town, firing magistrates houses and bombing the barracks and police office, drawing attention away from the main thrust upon Paradise Square, then the Town Hall and the Tontine Inn.

Eight groups known as *classes,* derived from the Methodist structure, were to rise in Sheffield, supported by other groups in Eckington, Attercliffe and Rotherham, in total around 450 armed men.[485] Any magistrates seen abroad were to be assassinated.[486] However, the precise time of the rebellion and the numerous rendezvous points of the insurrectionists would only be divulged at a final council meeting to be held in Sheffield at three o'clock in the afternoon.

Allen was to attend the meeting and return to Rotherham, as quickly as he could, with the information that John Bland desperately needed: the names of the leading conspirators; the rendezvous points; and the location of the arms depots.

---

[484] Cat: small double tripods of spikes designed so that whichever way they land on the floor there is always a spike sticking up to pierce the horses' hooves. Term comes from them always landing on their feet, as does the proverbial cat.
[485] Op Cit Chase, p.135
[486] Op Cit. Price, p.45

Lord Howard joined John Bland in Rotherham at around three o'clock on Saturday afternoon, and they anxiously awaited James Allen's return from Sheffield. The afternoon passed by and by seven o'clock in the evening, they were beginning to fear that something had gone awry. Had Allen lost his nerve, or worse, had his treachery been exposed?

Before the clock struck eight, James Allen arrived in a state of exhaustion and fright; breathless from his hard ride from Sheffield and now also fearful for his safety once the conspirators realised his treachery. However, for the moment, the Lord and the Chief Constable were more urgently concerned about the information that Allen had brought them.

He reported that the rebel Chartists would meet at their leaders' houses at ten o'clock where they would arm themselves. From there, they would march to their allotted rendezvous points where they would regroup and march to their specific targets, small parties being detailed to raid gun shops on the way. Allen was to command a Rotherham band that would meet up at Brightside at twelve o'clock after raiding local gun shops.

Lord Howard and John Bland deliberated on what they were to now do. It was apparent that for now, Rotherham would be relatively safe as Sheffield was the prime target for tonight's grand uprising and as they saw it, Rotherham would only be threatened should the Chartists succeed in taking Sheffield. They had no jurisdiction over Sheffield, nor were they responsible for the neighbouring town's safety.

They had done their utmost to warn the Sheffield magistrates of the conspiracy and had been derided. However, should the Chartists be successful in taking over the town of Sheffield, Rotherham would undoubtedly be the next target.

Having discovered the plot, they had a moral duty to alert the Sheffield authorities and to provide them with the information that would allow the Sheffield police and military to put a stop to the Chartist uprising. Lord Howard decided that he would take Allen's intelligence to Sheffield and Bland would deal with the Rotherham situation, should anything untoward unfold there.

Lord Howard reached Sheffield a little before ten o'clock to find that the police were already alert to the possibility of a disturbance but was ignorant of any details of the planned uprising. The information that Lord Howard presented engendered a full-scale reaction and the West Yorkshire Yeomanry was immediately called out. The homes of the leaders revealed by Allen were raided and the Chartists were intercepted at their rendezvous points where they scattered in a state of confusion, abandoning their weapons.

One area where weapons were reportedly abandoned was Crookes Moor, another was at the nearby dams.[487] Shots were fired and two or three policemen and a small number of innocent people drawn from their homes by their curiosity or *forced into the street by necessity*[488] were slightly injured but there were no fatalities.

At around midnight, two hours after the uprising was supposed to start, the alleged principal leader, Samuel Holberry,[489] was apprehended at his home at 19 Eyre Street by none other than the Chief Constable, Thomas Raynor, where a considerable quantity of arms and ammunition was found in the attic.[490]

A number of the other alleged leaders were also arrested at their homes, including Thomas Booker, whose house at 2 Bencroft Lane was also raided by Raynor accompanied by a detachment of infantry. Here too, weapons were found, including daggers, hand-grenades, guns and ammunition.[491] Holberry's pregnant wife, Mary, was also arrested.[492]

According to Raynor and James Wilde, one of the other arresting officers (Rotherham Chief Constable John Bland was also in attendance), Holberry was taken whilst in bed, although he was dressed.[493] There is an obvious discrepancy here, as the uprising was to start from Holberry's house at ten o'clock, would he be in bed two hours later?

---

[487] Op Cit Leader, Robert Eadon (Ed), *Reminiscences,* p.277

[488] Ibid

[489] Samuel Holberry was born in Gamston, a village near East Retord, Nottinghamshire in 1814, the youngest of 9 children; enlisted in the army aged 16 and served in the 33rd Regiment of Foot; borrowed £20 from his parents and bought himself out of the army in 1835 then moved to Sheffield working first for a cooper called Mr How, then as a distiller for Messrs Baines and Co; was laid off and briefly went to London before returning to Sheffield where he joined the Sheffield Chartists in 1838; was involved in attempts to raise an uprising in West Yorkshire following the Newport rising; travelled around South Yorkshire and the Midlands to muster Chartist support. Op Cit Price, pp.44-45, also Holberry Society pamphlet

[490] Op Cit Leader, Robert Eadon (Ed), *Reminiscences,* p.277

[491] *Northern Star,* 21 March 1840.

[492] The child, a boy named Samuel after his father, sadly lived for just 18 weeks and died in October 1840. Op Cit Chase, p.156. Mary later married a publican named Charles Pearson and the first of their three children they christened Holberry Pearson. In the 1849 White's Directory they are at the Plumpers' Inn, 51 Duke Street.

[493] Lewis, Catherine, *Samuel Holberry: Chartist Conspirator or Victim of a State Conspiracy?* in SOLON Crimes and Misdemeanours—Vol.3, No.1, March 2009, www.pearl.plymouth.ac.uk, p.119. Also Op Cit Walton, p.176

However, other accounts, including evidence given at Holberry's trial, suggest that the plan was to start at two o'clock. The other Chartists arrested were table knife maker Thomas Booker and his son William, also a table knife maker; Samuel Foxall; John Clayton, an unemployed cutler; John Marshall, table knife maker; Thomas Penthorpe, shoe maker; Joseph Bennison, table knife maker; James Duffy, beer-house keeper; and Samuel Thompson.

The Chartist conspirators appeared before the magistrates on Monday, 13 January where a number of the weapons recovered on the night of the uprising were displayed on a table in court. According to press reports, these included spears, daggers, fire-arms, bomb-shells, hand grenades, ball cartridges and fire-balls,[494] such was confirmed by evidence at the later trial.

The hearing went into the following day and Samuel Holberry and Thomas Booker were committed to York Castle on a charge of High Treason. They were taken to York under military escort. Mary Holberry and Samuel Thompson were discharged.

An eighteen-year-old warehouseman named William Wells appeared to give evidence for the prosecution that was found to be insufficient to implicate Holberry in the planning of the uprising, and he too found himself remanded for being involved in the plot and for misleading the court. The hearing was once more adjourned until Friday, 17 January when Wells and Foxall were further remanded and the hearing further adjourned.

On Monday, 20 January, the Chartists and William Wells were re-examined with Earl Fitzwilliam taking the chair. All, with the exception of Samuel Foxall, who along with Samuel Thompson had turned Queen's evidence against Holberry and were acquitted, were committed to York charged with conspiracy.[495]

Peter Foden, who was to appear at the Spring Assizes to answer charges relating to the riots of the previous August, was also thought to have been involved in the failed uprising and a warrant was issued for his arrest. Foden

[494] Op Cit *Sheffield Local Register,* p.338
[495] Op Cit Lewis, pp.119-120

remained in hiding in Sheffield before moving to Wales where he stayed in various towns. He failed to appear for his trial and Ebenezer Elliott and James Wolstenholme forfeited their bail money.

He came back to Sheffield later in the year and was re-arrested whilst hawking at the Waterloo Tavern and London Oyster Rooms in Watson's Walk on 15 December 1840.

He appeared in court on 20 March 1841 and on the advice of his counsel, he pleaded guilty and was sentenced to two years imprisonment at Wakefield (including the 3 months he had been in custody).[496]

Samuel Holberry, Thomas Booker, William Booker and James Duffy were found guilty of the lesser charge of seditious conspiracy on 16 March 1840; Samuel Thompson was the main prosecution witness. They were sentenced on 21 March: Holberry, four years' imprisonment; Thomas Booker, three years; William Booker, two years, all were gaoled at the Northallerton House of Correction, the Yorkshire gaol that was the farthest away from Sheffield and had a reputation for its prisoners being the worst fed and the hardest worked.

Holberry found himself gaoled alongside William Martin who had been sentenced four days previously. James Duffy was sentenced to three years at the Beverley House of Correction. Also sentenced on the same day were Clayton; Marshall; Penthorpe and Bennison; two years each, and Wells, who had pleaded guilty, twelve months. Charles Fox was also sentenced to one week in gaol for his part in the riots of 12 August 1839 (see above).

George Julian Harney

On 25 August 1841, Thomas and William Booker, Joseph Bennison and Thomas Penthorpe had their sentences remitted and were released.[497] For Samuel Holberry and John Clayton, their terms turned out to be life sentences as they both died in gaol whilst serving their time: Clayton, who had been given hard labour along with three others and spent eight hours a day on the treadmill, died on 1 February 1841, aged 55, at Northallerton, where he was buried; Holberry died of consumption on 21 June 1842, aged 27,

[496] Op Cit Leader, Robert Eadon (Ed), *Reminiscences*, p.278
[497] Op Cit *Sheffield Local Register,* p.358

at York Castle, having been moved from Northallerton *owing to the discipline being too severe.*

According to David Price Holberry spent five weeks on the treadmill and several months in solitary confinement at Northallerton.[498] He and Martin requested to be released from the treadmill and after Home Office approval were instead given nine hours a day oakum picking (unpicking old rope into fibres) with exercise being limited to between thirty minutes and an hour per day.[499]

His health fading, York Chartists campaigned for Holberry's early release on compassionate grounds and on 17 June he was offered release on condition that two sureties of £100 were found. He died four days later.

Samuel Holberry was honoured with a public funeral on 27 June, organised by the national revolutionary Chartist leader and Sheffield organiser, George Julian Harney.[500] Holberry's body had been taken from York to a cottage at Attercliffe, the home of Mary Holberry's parents, from where the funeral procession began. The event was used as a Chartist demonstration and between 20,000 and 50,000 people lined the streets of the town to watch the funeral procession wend its way to the General Cemetery; the population of Sheffield at this time was around 110,000.[501]

Although the alleged conspiracy was uncovered by the Rotherham Chief Constable and his officers, their part in its failure was not publicly recognised and it was their Sheffield counterparts that took the full credit for preventing the armed uprising. John Bland and Lord Howard were quite happy for this to be the case as should their role have been publicised they feared retribution from the

---

[498] Op Cit Price, p.46

[499] Op Cit Chase, p.155

[500] George Julian Harney (1817-97) supported the *physical force* popular revolutionary road to force the Charter into law and believed in the *'sacred right of insurrection'*, often seen wearing a red cap of liberty. Speaking to Derby Chartists in 1839 he advocated that *there is no argument like the sword——and the musket is unanswerable.* He was editor of the *Northern Star* newspaper from 1845 and knew Karl Marx and Friedrich Engels. He stood as a Chartist candidate in the 1847 General Election at Tiverton, the seat of Lord Palmerston, then foreign secretary. He was elected one of three delegates to give a congratulatory address to the new French National Assembly following the February 1848 revolution. He published the *Communist Manifesto* in English in 1850. In 1852, as Chartism declined, he proposed a new political party embracing Chartism, the trade unions and co-operative societies. His proposed socialist party never materialised and Harney withdrew from the political scene.

[501] At the 1841 census the population of Sheffield was 111,000

physical force Chartists still abroad who were a continuing threat to the peace in Rotherham.

Indeed, Lady Howard was so alarmed at the possibility of reprisals that she implored her husband to bind the Chief Constable to a solemn promise not to reveal their part in the failure of the Chartist plot. This he did and John Bland duly obliged His Lordship. To add insult to the injury that Bland must have felt at his part being written out of the public reports, the Sheffield Chief Constable, Thomas Raynor, received a pay rise from 200 guineas to 300 guineas per year, and the Royal Dragoons, the West Riding Yeomanry, the Sheffield police and the Sheffield watchmen were all publicly awarded an official vote of thanks for their services in preventing the rebellion.[502]

Further honours were bestowed on the Royal Dragoons on 7 May 1840 when a piece of silver plate was presented to the commanding officer, Lieutenant-Colonel Marten, *in acknowledgement of the services rendered by himself and his troops during last winter.*[503]

The following entry is from *The Records of the Burgery of Sheffield:*

> 5th May, 1840: *Resolved that the sum of £100 be paid from the funds of this Trust to the Magistrates of the Sheffield Petty Sessions, to be by them appropriated in rewarding extraordinary services rendered by the Constables and Police and others during the outbreak of the Chartists in January last, and in paying the expenses incurred during the time the peace of the Town was interrupted. Resolved that this Trust contribute £10 in aid of the subscription for a piece of plate to be presented to Colonel Martin for his services on the above occasion.*

All that remained for John Bland was to ensure the safety of his spy and *agent provocateur*, James Allen. Despite being a key witness, Allen did not appear in court to give evidence for the prosecution, which incidentally, was undertaken by no less a figure than John Campbell, the Attorney General, who had also prosecuted the Newport Chartists.[504]

However, Allen was soon identified as the Chartists' traitor. He was kept under armed guard whilst moves were made by Earl Fitzwilliam, who made

[502] Op Cit *Sheffield Local Register,* pp.338-9
[503] Ibid, p.341
[504] Op Cit Lewis, p.119

representation on Allen's behalf to the Home Secretary, Lord Normanby, for him to be spirited out of the country and to begin a new life in the colonies.

However, Allen was reluctant to emigrate and alternative arrangements were made for him to move down south and be provided with employment and a new identity. Sometime later, he was recognised by a man who had known him in Rotherham and the government once again provided for his relocation. Nothing is known of his fate thereafter.

John Campbell, Attorney General

The failure of the January uprising virtually put an end to the activities of the *physical force* Chartists in Sheffield but the *moral force* campaign continued and the persistency of their interventions in the Anti-Corn Law League agenda continued at a further series of six lectures in Sheffield, the first being held on 12 October 1840.[505]

---

[505] Op Cit *Sheffield Local Register,* p.346

Contemporary sketch of Chartist riots.

Sheffield was not the only town in Yorkshire where Chartists attempted an armed uprising in January 1840. In the same month, Bradford and Dewsbury also saw violent confrontation with the authorities, although there is no evidence to suggest they were in any way co-ordinated with each other or with the events in Sheffield.

In Barnsley the Chartists, led by William Ashton, were to rise should the Sheffield uprising be successful. Although a large crowd of armed Chartists gathered in Barnsley, it soon dispersed when it was known the West Yorkshire Yeomanry was patrolling and that there had been no news of the Sheffield plot.[506] By the end of March, *physical force* Chartism appears to have fizzled out altogether. Across the country, 543 Chartists were in jail, including many of the national leaders.[507]

The ranks of the Sheffield Chartists diminished and the more orderly conduct of the *moral force* Chartists received less coverage in the local press and from the beginning of 1841, with the exception of the deaths in gaol of John Clayton and Samuel Holberry, there was little significant Chartist activity reported.

Ebenezer Elliott, one of the high-profile supporters, had withdrawn from the Chartists over their disagreements with the Anti-Corn Law campaigners and his rejection of violence. One report tells us that on 11 January 1841, a Chartist

---

[506] Op Cit Chase, p.135
[507] Op Cit Browne, p.134

meeting was held at the Town Hall to petition for the pardon of the leaders of the Newport uprising.[508]

Being held in the Town Hall, the magistrates must have removed the ban on Chartist meetings, an indication that they believed such events no longer threatened the peace in Sheffield. As Chartist meetings in London and Birmingham were being prevented, a further gathering of Sheffield Chartists to discuss the *Plug Plot*[509], in which Chartists in other areas were involved, was held in Paradise Square on 22 August 1842.

In attendance was George Julian Harney who put to the meeting,

Are you ready to fight the soldiers? You may say that this is not the question but I tell you that it would be the question. I do not think you are. I am ready to share your perils but I will not lead you against the soldiers.[510]

The meeting proposed the use of strikes to force the government to accept the Charter and it passed off peaceably. The strikes stopped the mills of Bradford, Halifax and Huddersfield and a miners' strike in Staffordshire developed into a riot but industrial unrest failed to take hold in Sheffield. By the end of the month, the Lancashire and West Yorkshire workers had returned to work and the Chartists' focus returned to the Petition.

Notwithstanding the decline of Chartism nationally, chiefly due to poor leadership, divisions within the movement (*moral* v *physical forces*), the government's continued rejection of the petition and the unprecedented economic boom of the early 1850s that drove the final nail into the Chartism coffin lid, Sheffield maintained its support for the Chartists and elected a number of them to the town council. By the end of 1847, there were eight Chartists on the council and by 1849 they held almost half of the seats.[511]

Just how serious the Chartist uprising in Sheffield was, is open to question. As we have seen, the Sheffield magistrates didn't initially take the threat

---

[508] Op Cit *Sheffield Local Register*, p.349

[509] 'Plug Plot': strikes that started in Lancashire early in August 1842, primarily over pay in a number of industries. The name came about from the actions of strikers knocking the plugs off boilers, thus halting steam-powered production. The strikes spread to the Yorkshire woollen and worsted mills but didn't reach Sheffield. Many of the strike leaders were Chartists and the Lancashire trades unions had expressed support for the Charter. Simultaneous but independent strikes occurred in the Staffordshire Potteries and coal mines, again with links to the Chartists but there is no evidence of any co-ordinated action.

[510] Finn, Joe, *Chartists and Chartism,* Hodder & Stoughton, 1992,p.46

[511] Op Cit Hobsbawm, *The Age Of Revolution*, p.212

seriously and when the critical moment came and the leaders were arrested, where were the supposedly large numbers of armed Chartist rebels? We hear that many abandoned their weapons, but there weren't many facing the magistrates alongside their leaders, as there were following the illegal mass meetings.

If their escape was down to a poor response by the police and the military, how was it that the uprising failed, seemingly with hardly a shot being fired? Although there were some injuries amongst the police, there are no reports of any serious or sustained armed confrontation between them and the Chartists, as there were at Newport and Birmingham, as we would expect, had the uprising been a serious attempt to take the town by force.

There was no substantial evidence given against the Sheffield Chartist insurgents at the trial, only the array of arms found at Holberry's house and the testimony of two Chartists turning Queen's evidence. However serious the uprising was, it is clear that the Sheffield *physical force* contingency was a minority amongst the Chartists and an inconsequential number actually took up arms.

A report in the *Northern Star*,[512] the Chartists own newspaper which had a circulation of over 60,000 (most newspapers at the time had a circulation of around 5,000,[513] the average weekly circulation of the *Sheffield Independent*, the town's most popular newspaper, was 2,326 between January 1839—June 1840[514]) and it would have been read by many more, and read to many more who could not read, called the event, *stark staring mad proceedings of a small knot of fools in Sheffield.*

Also, to consider is the fate of the alleged leaders whose sentences were comparably lenient with those dispensed at Newport. Had there been a serious attempt to take the town, I feel that the sword of justice, as wielded by the State, would have cut more severely. On the other hand, what would have been the outcome had the plot not been betrayed by James Allen? The answer to this question, we shall never know, but by acting in isolation, the Sheffield Chartists were never going to win the day, however serious they were.

The *physical force* element was always a minority amongst the Chartists and it never had the capacity to win the Charter by force against a government ever

---

[512] *Northern Star* first published on 18 November 1837 and edited by Feargus O'Connor, the Irish barrister and Chartists' national leader.
[513] Op Cit Hobsbawm, *The Age Of Revolution,* p.127
[514] Op Cit *Sheffield Register,* p.348

vigilant of the, albeit remote, possibility of revolution. Sir Charles Napier and his army would have had little difficulty in putting down such an uprising in Sheffield if called upon to do so. The fact that they weren't, is highly significant.

My research into the Sheffield Chartists' plot has also left me with questions about the alleged leader, Samuel Holberry. Although he is acknowledged as the prime mover in the Sheffield uprising, he doesn't appear in the story until later on; I didn't come across his name in any of the reports on the illegal meetings and there was no mention of him following the 12 August meeting when Peter Foden and Charles Fox were apprehended.

In fact, I didn't come across his name at all until he was arrested on the night of the planned uprising. Neither, with the exception of Malcolm Chase's extensive book, does he get a mention in books on the general history of Chartism. He wasn't high profile before his arrest, so why has Samuel Holberry come out of this as the Sheffield Chartist martyr, his grave becoming an object of pilgrimage?

He may have been a revolutionary, but he was certainly no Che Guevara but like the renowned Argentine revolutionary he made the mistake of taking up arms to fight for people (Che in Bolivia) who did not totally support him and also like Che Guevara, he was betrayed. Malcolm Chase suggests that the public reaction was more to do with how he was treated in gaol and how this ultimately led to his death, and that the government was implicitly behind it.[515]

We know George Julian Harney organised Holberry's funeral but who amongst the Sheffield Chartists paid for the sculptured bust?[516] The extravagant funeral with oak coffin, which was paid for by the York Chartists along with a death mask, was more about the cause than the man. The group set up in his name, the Holberry Society, wasn't formed until over a century later in January 1978.

It was established by a number of Sheffield trade union leaders with the objective to, *involve the Sheffield Labour movement in an independent investigation of its own history and to re-discover the history that has been hidden or 'withheld' for too long,* when the left-wing of the Sheffield Labour Party was in the ascendancy.[517]

---

[515] Op Cit Chase, p.157
[516] The bust of Samuel Holberry is today in the Weston Park Museum
[517] Op Cit Price, p.154

The president of the Society was Martin Flannery, the Labour MP for Hillsborough. The setting-up of the Holberry Society was more about moulding the political landscape of 1980s Sheffield than celebrating Samuel Holberry or the Sheffield Chartists and the uprising of 1840. The group did, however, persuade the Sheffield Council to commemorate Holberry with a plaque and the *Holberry Cascade* in the Peace Gardens but it has achieved little else.

Catherine Lewis makes the case that Holberry did not in fact plan the Sheffield uprising and that he was a victim of a State conspiracy.[518] Whatever the truth, we owe a debt of gratitude to Samuel Holberry and all of the British Chartists for their part in the progression of democracy in Britain and the perpetual quest for a fair and just society.

For a contemporary picture of life and the politics of the Chartist era, I would refer the reader to Benjamin Disraeli's novel, *Sybil, or The Two Nations,* whose story is set against a backdrop of Chartism.

Left: bust of Samuel Holberry
Right: dedication plaque in Sheffield Peace Gardens

---

[518] Op Cit Lewis, p,110

The Irish Riot

'The misfortune among your Irish people is that men of good character and industrious habits will engage in riots and commit violence, when you ought to be spending your time peaceably at home. This the law will not tolerate.'[519]

1855

On the night of 22 July 1855, there occurred what would have been a relatively insignificant disturbance on West Bar Green by the standards of the time except for one very significant consequence: the death of the first Sheffield policeman to be killed whilst on duty and on his very first day as a watchman for the town.

The Sheffield Town Council took control of the local police force on 4 April 1844 which, becoming the Sheffield Borough Police Force, was ensconced in the Town Hall on Waingate under the supervision of the Watch Committee and the operational leadership of Superintendent Thomas Raynor.

In the 1851 census returns, 22-year-old William Beardshaw is recorded as being a saw and file cutter[520] but in 1855, he successfully applied to join the police force and became a watchman of the town, unaware of just how fatal this career move would prove to be, or how soon.

At around half past eleven on the night of Saturday, 21 July a drunken Irishman, 22-year-old James Burke, entered John Shannon's second-hand clothes shop at 31 West Bar Green. It wasn't clothing that Burke was intent on acquiring but to borrow a shilling off the proprietor. Telling Burke that he was drunk, Shannon bluntly refused his request and pointed him to the door.

---

[519] Judge Baron Martin when sentencing following the trial, *The Sheffield Daily Telegraph,* 13 December 1855
[520] *Kelly's Sheffield Directory 1854* lists a Beardshaw & Son, steel, saw & file manufacturers, 16 & 18 Garden Street. Could William be the son?

In his drunken Irish drawl, Burke threatened, *You buckaroo, if you don't lend me a shilling it's what I do to you*[521]. Shannon pushed him out of the shop where two other men appeared to be waiting for Burke. Also nearby, was a patrolling policeman who ventured over to the commotion that was about to brew.

Police officer John Dickinson managed to persuade James Burke that he should go home and his two companions indicated to the officer that they would see him to his lodgings. This, however, was a ruse and once Dickinson was out of sight the three men returned to the shop and all three entered, one of them, an Irish mason's labourer called William McCormack, grappled Shannon to the floor in front of the counter.

Shannon's son, having heard the commotion, came in and pulled McCormack off his father and the two other men ran out of the shop and disappeared into the night, which was dark due to the street gas-lights not being lit—it transpires that there should have been a good moon that night and it was the policy of the gas company not to light the street lights on a good moon.[522]

On getting to his feet, John Shannon felt for his purse and pocket book and found them missing; the purse, he claimed, contained either £70 or £72, a huge amount of cash equivalent to £5,612.30 at today's value.[523] He shouted out *Welch, I am robbed!*[524] as McCormack ran out of the door. Shannon ran off to the Town Hall where he told Inspector Samuel Linley of the robbery. However, it transpired that the purse and the money had not been taken but had simply fallen out of Shannon's pocket during the struggle. It was later found on the shop floor.

Meanwhile two watchmen, Sampson Bark and John Wood, were attempting to apprehend McCormack, who put up a violent struggle, knocking both officers to the ground before running off in the direction of Queen Street. He was being chased down West Bar Green by Samson Bark when he ran into Police Sergeant James Rogers, who had been patrolling Queen Street.

---

[521] *The Sheffield Daily Telegraph*, 25 July 1855. The word 'buckaroo' is my interpretation of the insult as it is recorded in the report *b-------roo*, suggesting it was too rude to be used in the newspaper. The only other alternative that I can think of is *buggeroo*.
[522] *The Sheffield Daily Telegraph*, 13 December 1855
[523] At the Coroner's Inquest on William Beardshaw, Shannon stated £70, at the later trial he stated £72. Today's value calculated from www.nationalarchives.gov.uk/currency-converter
[524] *The Sheffield Daily Telegraph*, 13 December 1855

The two officers seized him but they found his violent resistance hard to deal with until other officers arrived, then between them, they managed to bundle McCormack into John Thorpe's fish shop at 41 West Bar Green where they double-handcuffed him. Still, the Irishman kicked out at the officers and leg-irons and a cab was sent for from the Town Hall.

Police Inspectors Linley and Sills arrived with the irons and were shortly joined by three more officers: detective Gillott and police officers King and Whaley. McCormack was further restrained with the leg-irons whilst the cab awaited them in Queen Street where the crowd was steadily growing out of curiosity into what the commotion was about.

McCormack was taken out of the back door of the shop by Inspector Sills and Detective Gillott and taken down a passageway onto the street where more policemen and watchmen had arrived at the scene, including William Beardshaw, who had been switched from his own beat in a different area of the town as back-up. They were met by jeering onlookers, many of them the worse for ale, having had their customary Saturday night carouse disturbed by the rumpus on West Bar Green.

Police estimates of the crowd numbered around a thousand and most of them Irish. This was probably an exaggeration but there is little doubt that such a large number of Irishmen were a concern for the officers, fearful of them turning hostile; the sound of windows being smashed had already been heard.[525]

McCormack was quick to sense this anxiety and determined to turn the crowd against the police shouted out, *Are you going to see me taken?* as he continued to thrash about in an attempt to escape the officers' hold on him. A woman threw herself on him giving out what Sergeant Rogers called, *a particular sort of Irish yell for assistance.*

McCormack succeeded in further inciting the crowd and stones and brickbats began to be thrown in the direction of the cab as the officers struggled to push the prisoner inside. Detective Officer Gillott was inside the cab pulling at the Irishman as Sills and other officers tried to push him in. The bombardment of stones and brick-ends increased with many officers being hit, including Beardshaw who received a hit at the side of his head above the right ear.

The cab driver and the horse were hit too and the frightened animal plunged violently dragging the cab forward beyond the control of the driver. McCormack

---

[525] Ibid

was neither in nor out and only Gillott had a hold of him from inside the cab as it lurched forward.

Mindful of McCormack possibly getting entangled in the wheels, after the cab had travelled 30 or 40 yards, he reluctantly released his grip allowing him to escape into the crowd, albeit handicapped by the cuffs and leg-irons.

When the cab driver regained control, Gillott got out of the cab and returned to the scene of the fracas outside of the fish shop to find that the number of rioters had increased and a number of policemen and watchmen were lying injured or walking around stunned from being struck by stones, including William Beardshaw.

Samson Bark had been struck by a file. There then came a cry for assistance from the direction of Paradise Square, and Gillott and Beardshaw went off in response. On arriving at the Square, they found an unconscious John Dickinson being attended to, at John Herbert Walker's surgery at number 12.

Much of the crowd had moved on to Paradise Square, suggesting that McCormack had headed in that direction following his escape. Witnesses later told how police officer Dickinson had been followed by one of the Irish rioters called Robert Smith who gave him a severe beating. Smith continued his attack whilst Dickinson lay unconscious on the floor.

His own daughter was so alarmed at her father's actions that she cried out at him, *Father, for God's sake give over, the man is dead!* Smith's frenzied response was *I'll murder him!*[526] It is likely that Smith was the third man who accompanied Burke and McCormack in the attempted robbery of John Shannon earlier that night, which sparked off the riot, in which case, Dickinson would be able to identify him.

---

[526] Ibid

PC William Blackburn—served with Sheffield Police from August 1831 to March 1867—could well have been involved in the Irish Riot of 1855.[527]

The battle between the mob and the police was still in full flow but Detective Gillott was more intent on finding McCormack and taking Beardshaw with him, he went back to the Town Hall for more men to help search the nearby lodging houses where many of the local Irish community lived.

Gillott, Beardshaw, Inspector Linley and Police Officer Whaley proceeded to search the lodging houses and found McCormack on Broad Lane at around 2:30 am. By this time, he had managed to remove one of the leg shackles and the

[527] BritishPoliceHistory.uk, image Sheffield Local Studies Library: Picture Sheffield s08842

chain between the handcuffs. The four officers took McCormack to the Town Hall and into custody. There were a number of arrests in the night but not all would face trial for the riot.

As night turned to day that Sunday morning, William Beardshaw returned home a little before 7:00 am. His wife, Sarah Ann, was waiting for him and he gave her an account of his first shift on duty, showing her his wound; a real baptism of fire although nothing out of the ordinary according to his colleague Samson Bark who commented to him when he was hit by the stone,

You must not think anything of that in this neighbourhood; it is only breaking you in.[528]

This was no comfort to the rookie officer who, according to his wife, complained all day of the pain in his head. In appearance, the wound looked superficial and there was little bleeding. Despite the constant pain, William Beardshaw, perhaps out of concern for this being only his second day on the job and him not wanting to be seen in a bad light by his employer, went back on duty at 6:00 pm on Sunday evening.

However, a couple of hours into his shift, he became unwell and at around 10:00 pm went to the house of his father-in-law, Mr Roberts, which was much nearer to his beat than his own home; perhaps an indication of just how unwell he actually was. Being much concerned about his son-in-law's condition, Mr Roberts went for the police surgeon, Mr James Farewell Wright of 8 Eyre Street.

Wright listened to Roberts' description of William's condition and gave him some medicine to administer, saying that if he didn't improve, he was to fetch him. At 3:00 am on the Monday morning, Roberts went to fetch Mr Wright. In the meantime, William's wife had been sent for and she arrived at her father's at around the same time finding her husband's condition had gravely deteriorated.

Mr Wright found the patient convulsing when he arrived and only now was he made aware of William's head injury, which he found on inspection to be a slight laceration.

William Beardshaw was now unconscious and the surgeon directed his head to be shaved, cold applications to be made and leeches to be applied to the temple. If he was to regain consciousness, William was to be given the medicine Wright had previously given his father-in-law to administer. The surgeon left a

---

[528] *The Sheffield Daily Telegraph,* 2 August 1855

little after 4:00 am. William Beardshaw never regained consciousness and died a little before 5:00 am.[529]

James Farewell Wright conducted a post-mortem on William Beardshaw assisted by Mr John Herbert Walker and Mr Septimus Arden,[530] the result of which was given by Wright at the Coroner's Inquiry held over two days on Tuesday, 24 July and Wednesday, 1 August:

> *Externally there were no marks of violence excepting the one above the ear. On opening the head, I found several ounces of coagulated blood directly under the outward injury, and corresponding with it. The outward injury resembled in shape a horse shoe. I attribute the cause of death to arise from extravasated blood; the brain was in all other respects healthy, and so was the body. Such an injury as the one deceased had died of would result from a stone being thrown with violence.*[531]

Six Irishmen had been arrested following the alleged robbery at John Shannon's and the riot that followed on the night of Saturday, 21 July as a result of witness evidence given to the police and on being recognised by the police officers caught up in the fracas.

These men had been brought to the Coroner's Inquiry still in custody: James Burke, Cormick Dunlavey, Michael Wallace, Patrick Charleston, William McCormack and William Allen. All six had been charged with having participated in the riot. They were represented by local solicitor Mr George Oxley of 18 Burngreave Terrace, Andover Street.

Throughout the Inquest, the narrative of the previous Saturday night unfolded as various witnesses were called to give evidence. Witnesses included a number of policemen and watchmen but also members of the public. Jane Jubb, wife of William Jubb, a furniture broker of 22 York Street, stated that she saw James Burke throwing stones and bricks at the policemen and watchmen, shouting that he would, *kill the bloody watchman.*

She told how she saw Burke take stones from his pocket and threw them *as though he was in a great passion.* PC 22 Charles Rushton stated that he twice

---

[529] *The Sheffield Daily Telegraph,* 25 July and 2 August 1855
[530] Septimus Arden, surgeon of 26 Surrey Street
[531] *The Sheffield Daily Telegraph,* 25 July 1855. The Coroner was Mr Thomas Badger

saw Cormick Dunlavey, who he knew by sight and had identified amongst ten others in the police yard who had been arrested, throw stones and brick-ends towards the cab. Officer Rushton had been hit twice by stones.

Fourteen-year-old Thomas Chubsey, who lived in Hawley Croft, saw Patrick Charleston, who he had known for about twelve months, kick a policeman in the face whilst he was down on the ground. He also stated that he saw James Burke kick several watchmen but didn't see him throw any stones. He also saw Cormick Dunlavey throw a stone and kick some of the policemen.[532]

Spring knife cutler John Hill, told how he was attacked by Burke whilst he was assisting the police. Burke hit him in the back with an improvised life-preserver using a stone inside a stocking. He also hit him in the right eye with his fist and struck his arm with a penknife. Hill witnessed Burke throw a stone at PC Matthew Greenhough and then run after PC Dickinson, who was later severely beaten by Robert Smith in Paradise Square.

He also verified Jane Jubb's statement that Burke shouted he would kill the watchman. PC Samson Bark stated that he was with William Beardshaw when he was hit by a stone but didn't see who had thrown it due to it being very dark. Inspector Linley stated that he saw all of the prisoners during the riot.

At one o'clock on the second day of the Inquest, Thomas Badger, having received all the evidence, adjourned until two thirty and then presented his summing-up to the jury. There was no evidence against two of the prisoners: William Allen and Michael Wallace. As for the other four prisoners, the jury would have to use its discretion as to the evidence given against them. He went on:

The law threw every protection over police officers in the execution of their duty: to kill one of them is an act of murder, which in other cases would only amount to manslaughter.[533]

The room was then cleared and the jury sent to consider their verdict.

The jury deliberated for one hour and on returning to the re-assembled court pronounced its verdict of 'Wilful Murder' against James Burke and Cormick Dunlavey, despite there being no conclusive evidence that either of them threw the fatal missile. They would face trial at the next York Assizes.

---

[532] It is interesting to note that Thomas Chubsey was in custody himself for something unconnected with the riot when he identified Charleston and Burke in prison
[533] *The Sheffield Daily Telegraph,* 2 August 1855

As for McCormack and Charleston, they remained in custody pending further police investigation into the alleged robbery at John Shannon's clothes shop and their involvement in the riot.

By the time the accused were brought to trial at York in December, Robert Smith and another Irishman named Michael Finnerty had been added to the charge sheet. All were severally charged with rioting and assaulting the police in Paradise Square on 21 July.[534] The trial of James Burke and Cormick Dunlavey was heard by Judge Baron Martin and reported in *The Sheffield Daily Telegraph* on 13 December 1855.

On hearing the opening submissions by the prosecutor, Mr Hardy, in charging the two Irishmen of wilful murder, Baron Martin told the jury that the prosecution must first show that what the prisoners did was with the intent to kill William Beardshaw. On this Hardy turned to the jury and said,

Then gentlemen, I will abandon the charge of murder, and leave it for you to say, as I think you will, that the prisoners were guilty of manslaughter.

As I have pointed out following the Coroner's Inquest, there was no conclusive evidence against either of the two Irishmen to show that it was one of them that threw the fatal stone at Beardshaw, let alone that they did so with the intent to kill him. Evidence was given by all of the witnesses who had attended the Coroner's Inquest and the conclusion was much the same. The jury found Burke and Dunlavey guilty of manslaughter.

It appears from the report that the other four prisoners were tried on the same evidence already presented to the court with the addition of evidence given by Robert Smith and PC John Dickinson. Smith maintained that he had acted in assisting the police, helping the unconscious Dickinson into the surgeon's house, also in picking up a dropped police rattle that he used to summon further help.

John Dickinson, who was so badly injured that he had not yet returned to duty, over four months after the attack, positively identified Robert Smith as his assailant. We must also assume that Michael Finnerty, who didn't feature at the Coroner's Inquest, was subsequently identified as having also taken part in the riot. All four prisoners—William McCormack, Patrick Charleston, Michael Finnerty and Robert Smith—were found guilty as charged.

All six prisoners were brought up together for sentencing. So extraordinary were the sentences doled out by Judge Baron Martin that his address to the

---

[534] *The Sheffield Daily Telegraph,* 13 December 1855

prisoners is worth relating in its entirety as reported in *The Sheffield Daily Telegraph*:

You Burke and Dunlavey, have been found guilty of manslaughter upon evidence which must have been satisfactory to everyone who heard it. You other four have been found guilty of riot; and there is no doubt that the crime in which you engaged was all the same character, nevertheless I shall make a distinction in your punishments. I am sorry that I cannot punish Smith as he ought to be punished. If I had the power I should inflict upon him the same punishment I shall inflict upon Burke, for they were much the worse in this transaction than the other prisoners. Dunlavey has been convicted of manslaughter, but he does not appear to have been so bad as some of the others who have been convicted of riot, and in my opinion, perhaps ought to be punished according to their guilt, and not according to style or title of the crime charged against them. Now you men are all Irishmen. You have lived in Sheffield where you derived the greatest possible advantage of its trade. You came there from a comparatively poor country, and there found the opportunity of earning much better wages that you could have earned at home. But instead of being grateful and thankful for those advantages, you all engaged in a riot because a countryman of yours was taken into custody by a policeman for creating a disturbance. You took part in this riot without any provocation—without any justification; and you thereby exemplified the conduct of people of your country in clanning together when the law righteously arrests one of your countrymen. In this case, so far as I can see, the policeman did no more than his duty—no more than he was bound to do. I shall make an example of you for the purpose of letting it be known that the peace of this country shall be preserved at all risks. As to you Burke I mean to transport you. Your conduct consists in striking a man and using the expression that you would murder him. You struck one person with a stone, and stabbed him with a knife. As to you Smith, you were quite as bad as Burke, but the law will not allow me to punish you as I mean to punish him. You followed Dickinson, beat and punished him in the square when he was lying in a state of insensibility and when your own daughter said to you "Father, for God's sake give over, the man is dead," your answer to your own daughter was, "I'll murder him." Therefore, if I could transport you I most assuredly would.

Here, Dunlavey interrupted the judge:

My lord, I wish to say a few words. It is true I am an Irishman, and that I left my own country to earn a livelihood; but I never was before a magistrate in my life, and can produce many witnesses to prove that I never misbehaved myself. My lord I am not guilty of this charge.

Judge Baron Martin continued:

With the exception of the riot I believe all you say. I believe you could show that up to this time you possessed a good character; but I do not believe that you are innocent of this charge. I am certain you are guilty. The misfortune among you Irish people is, that men of good character and industrious habits will engage in riots and commit violence, when you ought to be spending your time peaceably at home. This the law will not tolerate. But I mean to treat you, Dunlavey, as if you had only been engaged in the riot, because I do believe that was the character of your offence. You, Burke, will be transported for 15 years. In cases of your kind, Smith, I never give more than 18 months' imprisonment; but your conduct was so scandalously bad that I shall sentence you to two years' imprisonment with hard labour. You other men will be imprisoned 12 months each, and kept to hard labour.

It is clear from the judge's remarks that had Smith been charged with manslaughter instead of Dunlavey, he too would have been transported along with Burke. Although charged with the capital offence of murder at the start of the proceedings, then found guilty of the slightly lesser offence of manslaughter, Dunlavey's sentence was no harsher than those simply charged with riot; an extraordinary and favourable outcome for him.

William McCormack, whose initial arrest triggered the 'Irish Riot,' was also fortunate not to have received a harsher sentence. He wasn't charged with robbery or attempted robbery—the initial reason for his arrest—probably due to there not having actually been a robbery as John Shannon's money was later found in the shop. Yet, there was enough evidence to suggest that robbery was his and his two accomplices' intention.

It is also worth noting the judge's comments on the prisoners' nationality in that he infers that Irishmen were inclined towards riot and violence and were troublesome fellows, and that they ought to be thankful of the privileged existence they now enjoyed compared to the pauperism they had escaped in their homeland.

There is no doubt that the Irish immigrants faced not only racial discrimination but also religious prejudice, most of them being Catholics. On a social level, they were lower than the lowest of the British poor and were seen to be dragging the British down to their level as nearly all Irishmen were unskilled and had nothing to offer the employer but their physical graft.

They were more than willing to work for wages that would merely keep them in potatoes and beer, and to pay for the worst form of living accommodation, very often a dark, damp cellar where he and his extended family, and also frequently a pig, would huddle on rags and straw; the embodiment of filth and squalor and a degrading influence on the British workers.[535]

Going barefoot, especially the women and children, was another unwelcome custom introduced by the Irish that was also adopted by the poorer English.[536] The Irish were stereotyped and portrayed as subhuman beings. All of this, the employers used to lower the wages and living standards of all, which engendered an overt aversion towards the Irish amongst the British working classes.

This exacerbated the distrust that the Irish already had of the English and in particular, those in authority and law-enforcement following the oppressive British rule in their homeland that they had fled; in essence a recipe for conflict wherever there were a concentration of Irish immigrants. There was an underlying atmosphere of tension and animosity between the police and the Irish, and the judge's comments confirm this.

From the evidence, it is clear that the greater proportion of the alleged 1,000 rioters were Irish, including at least one woman. People born in Ireland amounted to 3.3% of the population of Sheffield in 1851, numbering in the region of 5,330; the population of Sheffield at this time was around 161,500.[537] This was the result

---

[535] See Op Cit Engels, pp.123-6
[536] Ibid, pp.103-4
[537] Figures based on the 1851 census returns

of a huge increase in the number of Irish immigrants coming to Britain in the wake of the Great Famine of 1846-52.

It is hard to believe that around 20% of Sheffield's Irish community spontaneously rioted on the occasion of one of their member being arrested by officers of the law, not a rare event, later on an exceptionally dark Saturday night. The evidence suggesting that that is just what they did was readily accepted, but I have my doubts.

The repeated figure of 1,000 consistently comes from statements of police officers; perhaps an aspect of consistency from comparing notebooks after the event for their court reports. No estimate is made by any of the other witnesses nor were they asked the question. Numbers certainly increased as the events unfolded as witness Jane Jubb confirmed saying that as she watched the brawl around the cab she saw, *a good many Irishmen come from the direction of Shannon's yard.* [538]

She went on to say that one of the Irishmen gave a whistle at the entrance of another yard and *'many more persons came out, principally Irish.'* The consequence of this evidence was for this particular Sheffield Riot to be called *the Irish Riot.*

Of course, the tragedy of the Irish Riot was the death of watchman William Beardshaw, receiving a fatal injury on his very first shift of duty for the Sheffield Borough Police, perhaps, all for the sake of a shilling. One wonders if John Shannon had lent the drunken Irishman the shilling he wanted, would Burke have returned to the public house with his two companions to continue their carouse as contented Irishmen. Would the alleged attempted robbery not take place for the sake of that shilling? Would the process that continued following that alleged attempted robbery that ultimately led to the death of watchman William Beardshaw not taken place?

As the saying goes, *the outcome of any process is sensitive to its starting point; a small change in starting conditions can lead to vastly different outcomes.* [539] Was it all for the sake of a shilling?

---

[538] *The Sheffield Daily Telegraph,* 25 July 1855
[539] Often termed the 'butterfly effect': *the flap of a butterfly's wings in the Amazon can cause a tornado in Texas.*

A cartoon by Thomas Nast depicting a St Patrick's Day riot in 1867 that appeared in an American newspaper. Note the bestial caricatures of the Irishmen.

The Oldale Riots

'No man is rich enough to buy back his past'[540]

1875

Most of the riots in Sheffield covered in this book are well-documented in numerous contemporary and/or later publications; some more so than others. There were, however, other occurrences of riot that were reported in the local press but not deemed worthy of recording by the local historian. Indeed, there were probably a good number of small incidents that didn't even make the local press; I am sure that there are many in the depths of newspaper archives that are of interest.

One in particular was brought to my attention by Chris Hobbs, who provided me with a copy of a press cutting from 1875. It was about an incident of riot in Sheffield that I had never heard of and the circumstances leading up to it, so discombobulated, that I felt that I must try to unravel it and include it in this book.

In 1782 and again in 1793 Peter Wigfall, a gentleman, made purchases of land that were known as the Grange Ville Estate at Millhouses in Sheffield. These transactions mark the beginning of one of the most bizarre cases of riot in 19th century Sheffield. A widower for a number of years, Peter Wigfall had befriended a surgeon called Thomas Whitehead, who some people thought was a second or third cousin of Wigfall but this was never confirmed.[541]

On 17 May 1812, Wigfall made a will in which legacies of property other than the Millhouses estate where specified but there was no mention of the estate itself. However, in accordance with the will, the residue of both his personal and real estate, which essentially included the land at Millhouses and the houses subsequently built on it, was left to Thomas Whitehead who, along with a Mr Jackson, was also executor of the will.

---

[540] Oscar Wilde on money
[541] *Sheffield and Rotherham Independent,* 22 June 1875, letter from Eddell Charles Penny

One reference to the relationship suggests that Whitehead was possibly living with Wigfall at this time as, sometime during the following year, 1813, according to Wigfall's housekeeper, Mrs Dronfield, the pair had a 'violent quarrel' and Wigfall expelled Whitehead from the house, forbidding him ever to enter it again.[542]

In 1814, Peter Wigfall married Hannah Clark, at which point, the marriage settlement was registered at the Wakefield County Court and the aforementioned will was nullified. In 1828, Peter Wigfall of Highfield died and it is here that the story gets a little complicated.

At the time of Peter Wigfall's death on 11 November 1828, he was living alone, with the exception of his housekeeper, Mrs Dronfield; Hannah, his third wife having died. However, he may have actually divorced Hannah before she died as there is a marriage registered between Hannah Wigfall and Jonathan Oldale, which becomes relevant later in the story.

Immediately after his death, the house and the Millhouses estate was claimed by Thomas Whitehead under the will of 1812. Taking possession of the house, according to Mrs Dronfield, Whitehead burnt any papers that might go against his claim, saying to the housekeeper, *Here I am and here I mean to stick.*[543]

He also laid claim to rent from Joshua Hodgkinson, who had built some houses on part of the Millhouses estate during Wigfall's ownership, but he got short shrift from the property owner who laughed at Whitehead's impudence. Clearly Hodgkinson refused to recognise Whitehead's claim to the estate.

Whitehead's claim to the Millhouses estate, although seemingly dubious, appears not to have been seriously contested until 1837 when a Mr William Speck made a prima-facie claim to the estate as heir-in-law of Peter Wigfall.

However, Speck's claim must have been through a previous marriage and he was not aware of Peter Wigfall's third marriage to Hannah Clark. The marriage between Peter Wigfall and Hannah Clark not only nullified the 1812 will but also any erstwhile claim based on a relationship to Wigfall before he married Hannah Clark.

It is here that the Oldale connection comes to light as Hannah is referred to in the case at York Assizes as being Hannah Oldale, which appears to confirm that the Wigfalls did divorce and Hannah subsequently married Jonathan Oldale. Speck's claim on the Wigfall estate was rejected and he then acknowledged

---

[542] Ibid
[543] Ibid

Hannah and Jonathan's son Joseph Arthur Oldale, a silversmith at Attercliffe, as being the rightful heir-in-law.

Speck defaulted on his costs for this court action and was imprisoned for his debt; the case was a costly speculation on his part. Despite this revelation, for now Whitehead, although having no actual right, remained in possession of the Millhouses estate, possession being in nine points of the law.

Despite the outcome of all this, the tenants on the Millhouses estate continued to refuse to pay Whitehead rent, a situation that continued after his death in 1870 when the estate was inherited by his son George, also a surgeon, practicing at Norfolk Row. It is interesting to note that despite the Whiteheads' demands for rent neither Thomas nor George took proceedings against any of the defaulters. Did they wish to avoid further legal scrutiny of the rightful ownership of the estate?

Joseph Arthur Oldale.

One of the tenants of a house on the estate, Mr Henry Hoole of Hoole, Staniforth & Co, file manufacturers, did pay rent to Thomas Whitehead until around 1850 when Whitehead allegedly went to America. Between Whitehead's leaving and Henry Hoole's death in 1855, no rent was requested or paid.

The circumstances of Whitehead's move to America are interesting as it was at around this time that a Sheffield 'quack' surgeon called Thomas Whitehead was found guilty of manslaughter at York Assizes following the death of George Taylor, who he had been treating for scrofulous ulceration of the arm in diabolical fashion; the description of an eye-witness reported in *The Lancet* conjures up a scene from a mad doctor horror movie.[544]

---

[544] *The Lancet Vol.II,* 1848, p.427

He was sentenced to 12 months imprisonment. I cannot conceive of two surgeons in Sheffield of the same name at this time and I am convinced this quack is the very same Thomas Whitehead of our story. Imprisonment would have explained his absence at this time and if he really did go to America, perhaps, it was to allow the memory of this scandal to fade.

Following his death, Henry Hoole's effects were auctioned off at the house at Millhouses on Thursday, 20 October and what was not sold was carted off to Sheffield, leaving the house empty, and for Joseph Oldale an opportunity to take possession of a piece of that which he was convinced was his inheritance.

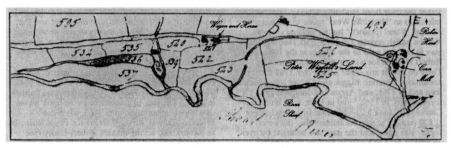

1807 map showing Peter Wigfall's land at Grange Ville Estate, now Millhouses Park

On the afternoon of the auction, Joseph Oldale sent a dozen men to take possession of the house in his name as the rightful owner. This they did without incident. However, by this time, Thomas Whitehead had returned from his absence and on hearing what had happened, sent a number of his own men to take the property back the next day.

There would have been some shouting and threats exchanged but little in the way of physical action and Oldale's troops held their ground and maintained possession of the house for the following week. Perhaps, during this time and previously, Oldale had been in negotiation with Whitehead to press his claim but it is clear there was no movement in resolving the dispute.

With no resolution in sight, Oldale's men prepared themselves for an attack by arming themselves with guns, pistols, daggers, knives, bludgeons, etc.[545] At night the doors were barricaded with large grindlecokes,[546] and bricks, stones and other missiles were stored by the upstairs windows to use against the

[545] *London Morning Chronicle,* Saturday 29 October 1855
[546] Grindlecokes: worn out grinding stones

expected attack, which came at around 2 o'clock in the morning of Friday, 28 October.

Around twenty burly men, mainly armed with heavy sticks stormed the house, attacking doors and windows through which they could gain entrance. It appears that the defenders were not only taken unawares but many were the worse for drink having had a bit of a session the previous evening; the delay in the attack had lulled them into a false sense of security.

First, the attackers smashed the shutter of one of the windows and forced out the frame and its iron stanchion, thus giving them a way inside. Some of the men within were so drunk that they slept on, oblivious of what was going on, despite the racket of smashing glass and cracking window frames.

What followed was a noisy battle of hand-to-hand fighting interspersed with the odd crack of gunfire. One of the besiegers called Jowett was severely wounded when he was hit on the head with a teapot thrown from an upstairs window. One of the defenders received a similar wound and bled profusely. It is a wonder nobody was killed in the mêlée.

The uproar eventually woke the drunken defenders and on realising the peril they were in, set fire to the straw they had slept on so as to create a distraction to aid their flight. One retreated into a side room and up a ladder escaping through a skylight in the roof and over an adjoining house. Oldale's men managed to get away, abandoning the house whilst Whitehead's men turned their attention to extinguishing the fire.

During the morning, the conquerors raised a flag over the house to celebrate their victory. The building was reinforced in the following days by what the *London Morning Chronicle* described as, a party of forty to fifty as rough and reckless fellows as can be, found in Sheffield. Sentinels were posted on the road and a guard was posted at each door, and in military fashion, a password was required from all who were allowed to enter the house.

Six police constables were belatedly sent to prevent a breach of the peace. Oldale probably abandoned this initiative as I have found no further reports of trouble following this encounter. Whitehead did, however, take proceedings against Oldale with the local magistrates but the case was dismissed.[547]

Having decided that the physical approach to claiming his inheritance wasn't going to work, he turned to the courts and on 24 March 1857, Joseph Oldale recovered possession of the Millhouses estate at the Court of Exchequer of Pleas

---

[547] *Sheffield and Rotherham Independent,* 22 June 1875, letter from Eddell Charles Penny

at Westminster despite an appeal made by George Whitehead on a legal technicality, which was dismissed.

However, this turned out to be a Pyrrhic victory as Oldale couldn't afford the costs accrued in making his claim to the Court, which amounted to £118-12s-6d (equivalent to £7,014.20p at today's value), an amount it would take a skilled tradesman like Joseph Oldale 593 days to earn.[548]

He tried to avoid arrest for this debt but was eventually accosted and taken to York Castle where he was imprisoned for two years and, according to his accountant, Eddell Charles Penny, he was the first bankrupt discharged from York under the 1861 Bankruptcy Act,[549] which suggests that Oldale was gaoled in 1859; he was released on 14 November 1861.[550]

However, his release changed nothing in relation to his claim as until he discharged his bankruptcy, he would be unable to recover the property. It is likely that Oldale was unable to find the necessary finance as he made no attempt to do this for the next eleven years but it appears that he did make at least one attempt at claiming property as an action was taken against him for *illegally distraining some goods* and was ordered to pay £15 damages.

According to Penny, this judgement was given due to poor legal representation on Oldale's behalf and on the later production of the Exchequer of Pleas judgement, the same judge overturned his initial decision, adding that Oldale *had a right to send the bailiffs* and awarding costs against the plaintiff.[551]

It is at this time that the story takes another twist as a report in the press in March 1858 tells of Joseph Oldale being accused of the forgery of an entry of marriage in the Parish Registry.[552] The marriage in question was that between Peter Wigfall and Sarah Housley, dated August 1740; Housley was Oldale's wife Hannah's maiden name.

It is alleged that Oldale forged this entry to aid his claim to the Millhouses estate and it was George Whitehead, the son of Thomas, who took out the warrant against Oldale. There is little doubt from the evidence uncovered that the entry of marriage was a forgery, and a crude one at that, but this only came to light following Oldale's request for a copy of the Register for evidence to be submitted at his trial at York; on examining the Register before taking a copy the sexton

---

[548] www.nationalarchives.gov.uk/currency-converter
[549] *Sheffield and Rotherham Independent,* 22 June 1875, letter from Eddell Charles Penny
[550] *London Gazette,* 6 December 1872, p.6194
[551] *Sheffield and Rotherham Independent,* 22 June 1875, letter from Eddell Charles Penny
[552] *London Morning Chronicle,* 27 March 1858

spotted the discrepancy and reported it to the vicar of Sheffield, Rev Thomas Sale.

The Parish Register was compared to the duplicate at the Archbishop's Court at York and the forgery was confirmed. The sexton and clerk both confirmed that Oldale had had access to the Register a number of times over the last four or five years (since around 1853/54) but insisted that he was never left alone with the books as that would have contravened Church policy.

It also emerged at the hearing that Oldale had engaged a searcher of records and genealogist, Mr J E Ross, between 1852 and 1856. Ross gave evidence at the hearing that simply confirmed Oldale's guilt. Oldale was remanded in custody for a week. The date of the forgery case, it being prior to the bankruptcy hearing at York, suggests that Oldale evaded arrest for around twelve months.

At the time of writing, I have been unable to ascertain whether Oldale was convicted of the forgery, which seems likely, or whether he was gaoled purely for the debt and bankruptcy.

Rev Thomas Sale

In 1868, Joseph Oldale applied once more to the courts to recover one of the properties on the Millhouses estate; a cottage tenanted by Mr Thomas Gregory. Using the Exchequer of Pleas judgement, Oldale pursued his claim at the Sheffield County Court to evict Thomas Gregory and to gain possession of the cottage.

If Oldale thought his bankruptcy had been forgotten, he was sorely mistaken and the judge told him that until the bankruptcy was removed from his file, he would be unable to recover the property in his own name.[553]

Joseph Oldale finally paid his creditors the full 20s in the pound, having his first meeting with them on 18 December 1872,[554] and applied for the annulment of his bankruptcy in 1873. The process took nine months to obtain the order due to what Penny calls, *a number of frivolous objections.* Joseph Oldale's bankruptcy was finally annulled on 12 June 1874.[555]

By now Thomas Whitehead, had passed away in the summer of 1870 and Penny states that his will was read on 2 August of that year, his sons George and John inheriting his estate and the mantle of alleged interlopers. Now fully armed with the Exchequer of Pleas judgement and without the impediment of bankruptcy, Oldale once more staked his claim to the Millhouses estate.

However, he was faced once more with excessive legal costs, the security of which was demanded by the then owners, which now included William Wentworth-Fitzwilliam, the Earl Fitzwilliam, as the Whiteheads had sold parts of the estate to now third parties in this dispute. Frustrated once more in being unable to take the legally recognised means to claiming the estate, he once more resorted to the direct route and the conflict of 1855 returned with a vengeance.

On 25 May 1875, Thomas Godson, the head of the Sheffield branch of the Magna Charta Association[556] and agent acting for Joseph Oldale, sent notice to some of the tenants of properties belonging to the Earl Fitzwilliam, including the Robin Hood public house, that henceforth their rents should be paid to him on behalf of Joseph Oldale. Not surprisingly, these notices were ignored.

---

[553] *Sheffield and Rotherham Independent,* 22 June 1875, letter from Eddell Charles Penny
[554] *London Gazette,* 6 December 1872, p.6194
[555] *London Gazette,* 19 June 1874, p.3140
[556] There is a suggestion in contemporary press reports that this association was supportive of Oldale's claim but I'm more inclined to believe that Godson was acting in an individual capacity as his agent. There is no plausible reason for this short-lived Sheffield branch of the organisation to have an interest in his claim.

One of these properties was a house being prepared as a public house pending issue of a licence occupied by brewers Thomas Berry & Co but had subsequently been bought by the Wesleyan Methodists to convert into a chapel. Godson took twenty men and broke into the house and, having changed all the locks, left half a dozen men to defend it.

He then went to a field behind the Robin Hood where a post with a notice advertising the field to be let for building development was taken down and the access gate chained and padlocked. Other fields nearby were similarly claimed.

Later that evening, having learnt of Godson taking possession of the house, Thomas Berry gathered together twenty of his draymen and set off with them in three cabs to Millhouses to reclaim it, which they did with little difficulty, outnumbering Godson's men over three-to-one.

Godson's padlocks on the gate were also removed and replaced. Following this episode, there was a lull in proceedings but more confrontation took place, and things came to a head a month or so later.

The Robin Hood, Millhouses (Picture Sheffield y02421).

Thomas Berry (Picture Sheffield s08779)

Stables and dray yard at Thomas Berry's Brewery, Moorhead (Picture Sheffield s10054).

On Monday, 21 June Joseph's two sons, John and Henry Oldale, Thomas Godson, Eddell Charles Penny and a number of other men arrived at Millhouses in a wagonette. They entered one of the claimed fields being rented from Earl Fitzwilliam by farmer and corn miller Charles Speight of the Ecclesall Corn Mill and proceeded to take scythes to the grass.

They toiled until sunset, harvesting what was an excellent crop and hauled it away to Sheffield in a regular relay of carts that had been organised for the job. Charles Speight protested but could only look on in awe at the theft of his crop. On the following day, in anticipation of a repeat of Monday's events, Speight barricaded the gate to the field and organised a number of his labourers to stand guard.

The magistrates must have also been informed of the previous day's incident as a number of police constables had also arrived to ensure there was no breach of the peace. As expected Oldale's men, whose numbers had increased, returned, only to find their entry to the field blocked but not to be outdone they attempted to gain entry by wheeling a cart into the goit surrounding the field that fed the corn mill dam so that the floor of the cart would act as a bridge over the hedge.

On entering the field in this way, they were immediately set upon by some of Speight's men wielding sticks and were successfully repelled. The arrival of more policemen prevented an escalation of the skirmish. Again, determined to get into the field to continue their harvest, the cart was dragged from the ditch by Oldale's men and used as a battering ram against the gate, which was smashed to pieces on its first impact.

One of Speight's men was almost crushed between the gate and the cart, a near-miss that could have been serious or even fatal. At this point, Thomas Godson made a speech to the onlookers who had turned out to witness the spectacle out of curiosity, or for entertainment, to explain that what they were doing was, *not strange or extreme at all, but was perfectly regular, perfectly in obedience with authority, and to her Majesty.*

Despite, or perhaps because of the police attendance, Oldale's men continued to cut the grass without further interference.[557]

---

[557] *Leeds Mercury,* Saturday, 26 June 1875

Sketch of Charles Speight's Corn Mill (Picture Sheffield s09626).

The spectacle of these events created much interest locally and news of what had taken place at Millhouses over the two days had reached the town and attracted the interest of a growing audience and on the next day, Wednesday, 23 June, a crowd of around 2,000 spectators were not disappointed.

As they had anticipated, Oldale's men returned at around nine o'clock to continue their reaping but overnight Charles Speight had once again organised the barricading of the gate to his field, this time, with a stout piece of wood and a tree trunk which was much more of a barrier than the original gate.

To reinforce Speight's band of men, the Earl Fitzwilliam had sent a contingency of thirty of his gamekeepers who took up position behind the barricade. Oldale's men were unable to storm this fortification and turned their attack towards a small bridge that also gave access to the fields but here they were again turned back by the defenders.

Undeterred, Oldale's men, to the cheering and banter from the excited crowd, unharnessed some horses from their carts and roped them to the wood and tree trunk, which they effortlessly dragged away. John Oldale had brought with him a saw for which he had determined a particular purpose. On entering the field, as the rest of his men, now accompanied by many of the crowd, for who being spectators wasn't enough entertainment, skirmished with their opponents, John

Oldale took the saw to the fence that divided Speight's field from that of his neighbour's, William Smith, who was also landlord at the nearby Wagon and Horses public house.

Evidently, they intended continuing their harvesting in Smith's field once they had cleared Speight's. There was a large police presence but officers didn't get involved in the fighting and once the fracas had subsided, Oldale's men, seemingly aided by many from the crowd who had joined in, continued with the cutting and carting away of the grass.

And, according to a *Leeds Mercury* account, they threatened to remove tiles from the houses of the tenants who wouldn't recognise Oldale's claim, and to pull up the rails of the Midland Railway Company whose line from Sheffield to London ran through the estate, although the railway line ran along the other side of the river, which was probably the boundary of the estate.[558]

Earl Fitzwilliam, by now, tired of this troublesome interruption of his noble existence, decided that very day to put an end to it by arranging an application to the magistrates and summonses for riot and assault at Millhouses to be issued on Joseph Oldale and his chief followers: Thomas Godson, Eddell Charles Penny, John Oldale, John Fisher and Thomas Allen.

In yet another twist in this veritable saga, on the following day, Thursday, 24 June, a good number of Oldale's men returned to the fields at Millhouses, apparently intent on continuing the work of possession and, on completion of these fields, were to move on to other fields on the estate.

However, there was discontent among the men as only a few had been paid the previous night and it was rumoured that not only was there no money to pay the rest, payment of any future wages was in doubt. It appears that the number of men unpaid was in the hundreds and they decided not to undertake any further work until wages were forthcoming. In an instance of irony, they barricaded the entrance to the fields to keep the carts and the cut grass from being taken out.

[558] Ibid

The Wagon and Horses, Millhouses (Picture Sheffield s07065).

All six of the accused appeared at the Leeds Assizes on Friday, 13 August where they was also charged with unlawfully and maliciously committing damage to a certain field to the amount of £30 by cutting and carrying away the grass growing upon said field.[559]

All expressed their regret at having done what they did and were bound over to appear at the next Assizes for judgement unless they were to reimburse Charles Speight and William Smith for their losses and to abstain from any further annoyance towards them.

In the event they failed to meet with these conditions and appeared at the March Assizes 1876 for sentencing: Joseph Oldale was gaoled for 6 months; Thomas Godson, 4 months; Eddell Charles Penny and John Oldale, 3 months. It was felt that the other two defendants, John Fisher and Thomas Allen, had simply done the work they were ordered to do as any employee might do and under this understanding were entered into their own recognisance in £10 each to keep the peace for 12 months and to then be discharged.

Although for the purpose of their involvement in this case, they were considered and recorded as being labourers, Fisher was actually a Millhouses farmer and scythe maker living at nearby Pingle Head, and Allen a beer-house keeper at 57 New George Street.[560]

[559] *Birmingham Daily Post,* Monday, August 16 1875, issue 5333
[560] White's *History and Directory of the Borough of Sheffield*, 1871-2

Thus ended the Oldale Riots for nothing further is recorded as occurring in this vein but the disputed claim remains in Chancery to this day. Joseph Oldale died on Christmas Day 1888 having failed to realise his inheritance and Earl Fitzwilliam continued to add to his wealth from the rents and sales of land and property. In an obituary in the *London Guardian* it is inferred that:

> *Had he allowed his supposed rights to remain dormant, he would in his old age have been possessed of some means. He preferred, however, to spend his money in asserting a claim which he, at any rate, believed to be just and legal, but which, founded or unfounded, only led, as such claims too often do, to financial loss.*[561]

Yet, the disputed Oldale entitlement was not forgotten by his family who, as late as 1945 met to discuss the options in pursuance of the claim. By this time, the estate belonged to Sheffield City Council, it having been bequeathed by the 7th Earl Fitzwilliam in 1907; Grange Ville Estate was now part of Millhouses Park.[562]

However, as Joseph found when he originally went to law to claim the inheritance, the family decided that they simply couldn't afford the potential legal costs that such a move would entail; as ever is the case, justice applies for those who can better afford to obtain it. I wonder how many people playing and watching cricket at Millhouses today are aware of the drama that unfolded on the wicket a century and a half ago.

---

[561] *London Guardian*, 2 January 1889
[562] www.millhousespark.co.uk

William Wentworth Fitzwilliam—6th Earl Fitzwilliam and his shield of arms

In a final aside to this obscure saga, I found that Oldale's accountant and agent, Eddell Charles Penny, following his 3 months in gaol, seems to have gotten into financial difficulties himself, probably due to the impact upon his reputation following his involvement with Joseph Oldale and now having a criminal record.

It appears that he was in partnership with Richard Henry Penny, probably his brother, in a Public Accountants and Auctioneers business at Bacup, Lancashire. Whether this partnership was in existence during our period isn't known, but on 23 September 1864, the partnership was dissolved and Richard Henry Penny continued the business alone, paying and receiving all debts owing from and to the said partnership.[563]

---

[563] *London Gazette,* 27 September 1864

Sheffield 1858

Salvation Army Riot

'People fashion their God after their own understanding.
They make their God first and worship him afterwards.'[564]

1882

Perhaps, the most astonishing of all the disturbances that have occurred in Sheffield over the years took place in 1882 when the recipients of the wrath of the Sheffield mob were the relatively innocuous Salvation Army. However, put into context of the Victorian era, the early Salvationist movement vigorously challenged social norms that we would consider totally unacceptable today: low age of consent;[565] child prostitution; excessive drinking and a high level of drunkenness.[566]

Created as the East London Christian Mission in 1865 by the Methodist Reform Church minister William Booth and his wife Catherine in London's East End, where they found, *A population sodden with drink, steeped in vice, eaten up by every social malady,*[567] the Salvation Army was, and remains, a Christian mission and charity that aims to lift people out of poverty and destitution through religion and education, offering friendship, practical help and support for all people in need.[568]

In 1878, William Booth restructured the mission on army lines and self-styled himself The Salvation Army's first *general*. Its members became *soldiers* led by ministers who were the *officers* of *God's Army*. Catherine Booth was known affectionately by the Salvationists as the *Mother of The Salvation Army*.

---

[564] Oscar Wilde on religion
[565] Sexual intercourse with girls under 12 years of age was illegal up until 1875 when the age of consent was raised to 13. In 1881, a Lords' Committee was informed of a pregnant 9-year-old girl in London. In 1885, the age of consent was raised to 16 and the promotion of child prostitution was made illegal. See Chesney, Kellow, *The Victorian Underworld,* Maurice Temple Smith, 1970, footnote p.325
[566] I am grateful to Claire Anderson of The Salvation Army for this input.
[567] Op Cit Hunt, pp.385-386
[568] Op Cit Claire Anderson

The Salvation Army had its own uniforms, its own colours (flag or gonfalon—a banner hung from a crossbar) and its own bands that led its recruiting parades. The Salvation Army bands are not so conspicuous today but I remember very well one parading up Bradfield Road, where I lived as a lad, with colours unfurled regularly on a Sunday morning; an unimaginable event today.[569]

General Booth took his army on the road and membership of the Salvation Army spread rapidly as it extended its work amongst the growing industrial towns and cities, attracting wide-spread interest for the first time in 1881.[570] Although it attracted many members up and down the country, it also generated much opposition amongst the people that it aimed to help, principally due to its hostility towards drinking, smoking and gambling, the very pastimes that, although exacerbating their base status, were also a brief distraction from the poor people's miserable lives.

Not surprisingly, chief amongst the dissenters were the publicans whose trade the Salvation Army was undermining. Pub density in Sheffield was one of the highest of the large industrial towns and cities in England. A survey of 1896 showed there was a pub per 176 persons in Sheffield compared to 215 in Birmingham; 279 in Liverpool; 345 in Leeds; 393 in London. Only Manchester had a slightly higher pub density than Sheffield with a pub per 168 persons.[571]

The pub culture was, perhaps, the only culture embraced by the whole of the working classes and despite the efforts of the Salvation Army, the temperance movement, teetotalism and Victorian legislation designed to suppress it, such as the introduction of licences for beer-houses as well as public houses, and statutory closing times in the 1872 Licensing Act, which caused riots in Liverpool and troops to be required to dispel protesting crowds in Ashton and Maidstone,[572] it survives to this day, albeit at a continuingly diminishing rate, as the number of public houses decline due to high revenue on alcoholic drinks, ever-increasing pub prices, cheap supermarket beer and the consequential changes to social habits.

---

[569] Organised Salvation Army parades still take place but one would not be practicable on Bradfield Road with the level of today's traffic
[570] Op Cit Gretton, p.66
[571] Dyos, H.J. and Wolff, Michael (Eds), *The Victorian City-Images and Realities Volume 1,* Routledge & Kegan Paul, 1976, p.162
[572] Op Cit Thompson, F.M.L., p.306 and pp.316-317

The consumption of alcohol per head in Britain increased throughout our period and peaked in 1900 when it then began to fall. By the 1950s, it had fallen to less than half of what it was in 1900.[573]

In some areas, there was organised opposition to the Salvation Army and parades and meetings were disrupted by hecklers and missile-throwers, and a number of its members were assaulted. The situation got so bad that in 1881 a question was raised in Parliament to which the Home Secretary, Sir William Harcourt, replied that, *if the Salvation Army complained of attacks, it was fair to remind the Army that its methods where somewhat provocative.*[574]

He issued advice to magistrates that although Salvation Army processions were not illegal and could not be legally prevented, where there is likely to be a breach of the peace, *magistrates should, by every means in their power, endeavour to prevent them.* It would appear that such organised hostility towards the Salvation Army occurred in Sheffield when General William Booth and his wife brought their *Council of War* to the town in January 1882.

Salvation Army parade disrupted by hecklers and missile throwers.

---

[573] Hoggart, Richard, *The Uses of Literacy,* Penguin Books, 1962, p.353
[574] Op Cit Gretton, p.66

In Sheffield, the Salvation Army had established two meeting places: the Salvation Army Meeting House in Spital Street and the Salvation Army Gospel Hall in Thomas Street, the latter being known as the *Barracks*. Meetings and processions, collectively called a *Council of War*, were planned for the weekend, the first being a *Hosannah Meeting* held on the night of Saturday, 14 January.

This appears to have attracted little attention and went off without a hitch. At 6:30 am the following morning, Sunday, 15 January, a further meeting was held at the Thomas Street *Barracks*, followed by a *Baptism of Fire* service at 10:30 am. In the afternoon, there was a procession from Thomas Street to the Albert Hall[575] at Barker's Pool, on the corner with Burgess Street, where a *Grand Council* was to be addressed by General Booth and his wife.

As the Salvationists marched through the town, they were threatened by a hostile crowd but the abuse was predominantly verbal and the parade managed to reach the hall unharmed. However, the crowd remained outside the hall as the *Grand Council* took place and mud and stones were thrown at the Salvationists as they left.

There was a police presence in the town, including the Chief Constable, John Jackson, who considered the event to be a minor commotion and foresaw no problem with the parade planned for the following day. He could not have been more wrong.

On Monday afternoon, at around 1:30 pm, about 700 Salvationists set off from the Thomas Street Barracks in a procession led by *Lieutenant* Emmerson Davison, a converted Northumbrian wrestler who now lived in Leeds, on a white horse, dressed in a scarlet uniform, complete with polished helmet.

Davison was also sporting cut lips from a stone that hit him the previous night. The parade, marshalled by a *Major* Cadman, included three carriages carrying the officers of the Salvation Army, including General Booth and his wife, and a brass band. The band, conducted by a *Captain* Fry and consisting of twelve players had its own uncovered carriage drawn by four horses. There were just two police officers in the area to oversee the *Triumphant March*.

---

[575] The Albert Hall was a concert hall that opened in 1873. It was built at a cost of £20,000 and could hold up to 2,500 people. It became a cinema after the First World War but also continued to host stage shows. It was damaged by fire in 1937 and later demolished to be replaced by what is now (2017) the John Lewis store. See Op Cit Vickers, pp.237-9, also Kelly's Directory 1881, p.1016

The Chief Constable of Sheffield, John Jackson.
(Courtesy of the National Emergency Services Museum)

Davison led the procession along a route down Thomas Street to Broomhall Street, then along Fitzwilliam Street and Regent Street as a crowd gathered to heckle and spit at them once more, and again mud, stones and other brickbats began to fly. And once more, Emmerson Davison was a highly visible and easy target for the missile throwers, which included a number of women.

The former wrestler bore the brunt of the confrontation and his bright red tunic soon turned a mud-spattered russet and his helmet was knocked from his head. Attempts were made by some in the crowd to wrest the Salvation Army banners from the troop but they were fought off and the colours were saved. Tension grew, as did the crowd of roughs, and in an effort to diffuse the growing menace the procession split into two strands with Davison leading one group, which included William and Catherine Booth's carriage and that of the band, which had abandoned its playing, down St Philip's Road and on to West Bar.

The other section, including the third carriage, went by a more direct route to the Albert Hall. Reports on the number of roughs described by *The Illustrated Police Gazette* as *having had its home in the slums*,[576] ranged from 1,000 to 4,000.

---

[576] *The Illustrated Police Gazette* 18 January 1882

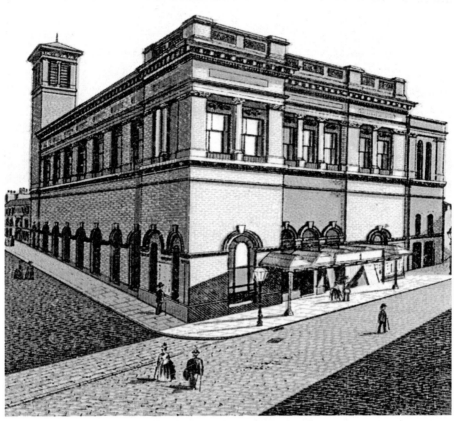

The Albert Hall, Barker's Pool.

As the section led by Davison reached the bottom of Snig Hill, the ex-wrestler was hit on the head by a stick of wood thrown by a young man called Arthur Henry Woollen, which rendered him stunned to the extent that he almost fell from his horse, which also suffered injury.

Two of his *soldiers* had to support him and lead the horse the rest of the way to the Albert Hall where more of the mob were waiting with another salvo of missiles. Many local shopkeepers had closed and shuttered their shops for the afternoon in anticipation of trouble.

On reaching the hall, the Booths, their fellow officers and band members scurried from the carriages, many bruised and bleeding from head wounds, all covered in mud, and quickly made their way into the building. Major Cadman was also injured.

A doctor was sent for to administer to Davison, who was concussed and had to be carried into the hall. The doctor also attended a female trumpeter from the band who had fainted. Emmerson Davison was later taken to hospital where he remained in a critical condition for a number of days.

Undaunted, the Salvationists cleaned themselves up and proceeded with their *Holiness Convention*, staying in the hall for their tea and then prepared for a further meeting in the evening. It was reported that William Booth prayed for Davison's recovery and for others injured in the melee. He also led a prayer for forgiveness of the *Sheffield Roughs*.

Studio portrait of a Sheffield Salvationist.[577]

Arthur Henry Woollen, a cutler by trade, was arrested on Friday morning and charged with assaulting Emmerson Davison; witnesses had come forward

[577] This early photograph was taken at James Syrus Tulley & Co of 24-30 Division Street. James Tulley can be found in local trade directories from 1862 to 1901

identifying him as the man who had thrown the stick. Two other men were also arrested as being the ring-leaders of the riot, suggesting that the attack had been organised in advance.

Although one of the worst incidents of anti-Salvation Army riots, there is no evidence to suggest that opposition to the Salvation Army in Sheffield was as well-organised as in some areas where specific groups were set up calling themselves *The Skeleton Army*, and who arranged their own parades to intimidate the Salvationists and attack their buildings.

First founded at Exeter and Weston-Super-Mare, the Skeleton Army set up branches throughout the south of England. Substantial anti-Salvation Army riots also occurred in Arbroath and Forfar in Scotland, and at Bath, Guildford and Plymouth. In 1883, there were regular battles on Sundays between the two Armies outside the Eagle Tavern, City Road, in London.[578] Dragoons had to be called out to quell the fighting between the two Armies at Worthing in 1885 and in the same year *savage riots* occurred in Derby where stones were thrown and band instruments were used as weapons.[579]

In a period of twelve months, 669 Salvationists were reported to have been *brutally assaulted*, including 251 women; 56 Salvation Army buildings were wrecked and 86 Salvationists, 15 of them women, were arrested and imprisoned.[580]

---

[578] Op Cit Gretton, p.110
[579] Ibid, p.167
[580] See Church History Review website: https://lexloiz.wordpress.com/2017/10/23/the-skeleton-army/

THE SKELETON RIOT AT WORTHING

Skeleton Army attacks a Salvation Army building at Worthing 1885.[581]

The Skeleton Army hound the Salvationists.[582]

---

[581] Ibid
[582] Sketch from the *War Cry,* 26 December 1891

On Wednesday, 18 January, a deputation led by Mr H J Wilson JP, met with the mayor, Michael Hunter Jnr., to protest at the inadequate policing of the weekend's events. Others in attendance were Rev. Samuel Chorlton of Christ Church, Pitsmoor; Mr J H Barber; the Town Clerk, Mr J Yeomans; and the Chair of the School Board.[583]

The Chief Constable was also present and the mayor expressed the view that the police were not to blame for the scandalous behaviour of the roughs. He also said that the Salvation Army had a right to have a procession but also he had hoped they would be careful not to arouse opposition. It is clear that opposition needed little arousing and that short of cancelling their parade, the Salvation Army could not have prevented the riot.

Whilst John Jackson was exonerated by the mayor, having witnessed the trouble on Sunday, he clearly misjudged the situation and was not prepared for the confrontation that took place on Monday, leaving the Salvationists totally defenceless against the mob. He would also have been well aware of other disturbances engendered by opposition to the Salvation Army up and down the country, and of the advice on the subject disseminated by the Home Secretary.

The earliest photograph of Sheffield Salvationists from 1890 *(Courtesy of The Salvation Army).*

---

[583] Possibly Skelton Cole Esq. who was the first chair of the new Sheffield School Board that was formed on 4 December 1879

The whole affair scandalised the town and there were widespread reports in the press from Leeds to Cornwall,[584] but in fairness to the wider Sheffield population, there were a good number of what the police termed *the more respectable portion of the populace* who were sympathetic to the Salvation Army's plight and shouted *shame* at the attackers.[585]

Indeed, a good number of the 700 Salvationists on parade were Sheffield people and there were a contingent of them amongst the notables; a Mrs *Major* Corbidge and a *Private* Hamilton were two Sheffield people who rode with the General and Mrs Booth in their carriage. However, there was not enough of the more respectable portion of the populace to prevent the shameful attacks.

Nor, it would seem, were there enough police to stop them. The reading of the Riot Act didn't apply as there were no assembled crowd but a mob on the move that followed the procession, and bringing out the militia would only have exacerbated the situation; one army on the march was one too many.

Catherine Booth (The Mother of The Salvation Army) and 'General' William Booth (insets). Main sketch from *The Illustrated Police Gazette*, 18 January 1882, depicting the attack on the Salvation Army outside of the Albert Hall

---

[584] See www.chrishobbs.com
[585] Op Cit *The Illustrated Police Gazette*

Nationally, persecution of the Salvation Army continued for another ten years and its work came to the unfavourable attention of trade organisations when it attempted to address the problems of the unemployed by way of a scheme to provide relief work. In 1890, William Booth published a book on poverty and deprivation called *In Darkest England* as an appeal to the country for money to fund a scheme that would provide relief work, refuges, night shelters and other institutions.[586]

Twelve months later, the *Darkest England* scheme came under some scrutiny over the £17,000 that had been spent on it and on how the work had been regulated. This was at a time when the Salvation Army experienced some of its most violent opposition in Eastbourne where the local authorities used a local Improvement Act to ban their street processions.[587]

Booth established a committee to investigate the administration of the scheme, which reported in 1892, that the financial accounts had been adequately kept but the committee also found that the relief work was undermining the labour market and had created as much destitution as it relieved.[588]

It was in 1892 that the Act of Parliament used by the Eastbourne authorities to inhibit the Salvation Army's activities was repealed and also in this year the violence against it petered out.

---

[586] Op Cit Gretton, p.281
[587] Ibid, p.304
[588] Ibid, p.321

Anti-Mormon Riot

God is a concept
By which we measure
Our pain.[589]

1884

Religion and religious intolerance have been the cause of many a conflict throughout history and religion has arguably been the catalyst for most of the wars around the world. In England, the Civil Wars of the 17th century were predominantly about king Charles I insisting that he ruled by *divine right,* and the perpetual conflict between Protestantism and Catholicism; the French historian and statesman Francois Guizot described the English Civil War as a *Puritan Revolution.*[590]

Oliver Cromwell provided his armies with a *Souldier's Pocket Bible* in 1642 to help them fight *God's Battles.*[591] Whatever the cause of war, most armies would consider that God was on their side; the motto on the belt buckle of the German army in the Second World War was *GOTT MIT UNS*—'God with us'.

Conflict often arises out of the desire for domination by one religion over all others and probably, just as often out of differing interpretations of a single religion. Such a conflict, albeit a small isolated incident, occurred in Sheffield in December 1884.

A self-styled ex-Mormon priest by the name of Mr W Jarman had been addressing meetings in Sheffield lambasting the Latter-Day Saints following his experience of the Mormon sect when previously living in Utah. He had embarked on a crusade against the Church of Jesus Christ of Latter-Day Saints, a relatively

---

[589] The opening line of the song *God* by John Lennon on his first solo studio album *John Lennon/Plastic Ono Band*, 1970
[590] Op Cit Hunt, p.139
[591] Champion, Justin, *The Real Information Revolution*—a review of *The Gutenberg Bible* in *History Today Vol 68, Issue 10,* October 2018, p.94

new evangelical religious sect founded by Joseph Smith in West Missouri in 1830 following *divine revelations*.

Any new religious movement will generate suspicion and opposition, often violent opposition, as did the early Wesleyan Methodists in Sheffield (see chapter on Anti-Methodist Riots) whose first chapel in Cheney Square and subsequent chapels in Pinstone Street were attacked and demolished by rioters in 1743, partly destroyed in 1744, and totally destroyed in 1746 respectively.[592]

Following Joseph Smith's death by assassination whilst in prison on charges of riot and treason in 1844,[593] the Mormon sect transferred to Salt Lake City under the leadership of Brigham Young. As with most religious movements the Mormons set out to preach their interpretation of God's Will to the world and to recruit converts.

Perhaps, the most repugnant aspect of the Mormon sect was their predilection for polygamy, provoking a natural culture clash with British morals that stirred inherent resistance towards them. The Mormons also posed a possible threat to the ruling classes as the sect had created a theocracy in their native Utah, the Mormon Commonwealth, in the 1840s.[594]

It is in the 1840s that I found the earliest reference to the Mormons in Sheffield, where one of their very first meeting houses in England was located, with conferences of the Sheffield branch being held at the Hall of Science in Rockingham Street on 23 December 1849 and on 19 May 1850.

The first Mormon mission to England took place in 1840 seeking converts for emigration to North America. The offer of not only a new religion but the prospects of a new and a better life was irresistible to many people of the industrial towns and cities of England.

By 1850, the Mormon Church had 30,747 members in England compared to 21,092 in North America, and many of those were from England: almost 100,000 people emigrated to Utah in the 19th century and several hundreds of them were from Sheffield.[595]

The Report from the 1849 conferences makes reference to there being twelve branches in and around Sheffield in 1846 including Rotherham, Doncaster,

[592] Op Cit *Sheffield Local Register*, p.42
[593] See www.bbc.co.uk/legacies/immig_emig/england/south_yorkshire/article_3.shtml
[594] Hobsbawm, Eric, *The Age Of Empire 1875-1914*, Weidenfeld & Nicolson, 1995, p.95
[595] www.bbc.co.uk/legacies/immig_emig/england/south_yorkshire/article_3.shtml

Chesterfield and Nottingham with a membership of 610 Mormons; Sheffield had the largest membership with 357.

In 1849, there were twenty-six branches with a membership of 1,789. By May 1850, membership had risen to 1,903. The President of the Sheffield Branch was Elder J V Long and for the whole of the British Isles, Elder Orson Pratt. The national office of the Latter-Day Saints was in Liverpool.

I have found no reports of opposition to the Mormons in Sheffield during these early years but their presence attracted some organised hostility in 1884 instigated by the crusading Jarman whose own message from God and his experience of the controlling Elders in Utah inspired him to oppose this mission with equal zeal and he recruited a number of followers in Sheffield, forming a committee to organise resistance.

NAMES OF BRANCHES	NAMES OF PRESIDENTS.	Elders.	Priests.	Teachers.	Deacons.	Removed by Letter.	Received by Letter.	Cut off	Dead.	Emigrated.	Baptised.	Total.	Owing the Offi. e.	Amount donated to El Dunn.	Amount done of to El Roger
Sheffield	El. J. V. Long	9	17	13	3	2	4	0	4	18	10	337	0 0 0	3 13 7½	1 15 8
Attercliff	" H. Roper	1	2	3	1	2	0	0	0	5	0	34	0 0 0	0 2 6	0 3 6
Deepcar	" G. Butler	0	1	1	0	0	0	0	0	0	7	14	0 0 0	0 7 0	0 0 0
Pilley	" Wadsworth	2	4	4	1	0	0	2	0	1	0	57	0 0 0	0 2 0	0 0 0
Stambro'	" Palfreyman	3	3	1	1	0	0	2	0	0	0	18	0 4 14	0 2 9	0 1 0
Woodhouse	" Harly	6	3	2	1	0	0	2	0	0	0	60	0 0 0	0 5 8	0 4 8
Rotherham	" G. N. Tingle	3	9	4	3	1	0	0	0	2	8	123	9 14 2½	0 10 2½	0 10 0
Schols & Thorp	Priest Hall	0	0	0	3	0	0	0	0	0	0	14	0 0 0	0 0 0	0 0 0
Doncaster	El. G. Yeardley	4	5	3	2	0	0	0	0	4	0	34	1 16 11	0 0 0	0 0 0
Skellow	" Wright	1	5	1	1	0	0	0	0	0	4	34	0 0 0	0 0 0	0 0 0
Mattersey	" J. Haigh	1	3	1	1	0	0	0	0	0	1	39	0 0 0	0 0 0	0 1 10
Misson	" Nickelson	1	2	1	1	1	0	2	0	6	4	34	0 0 0	0 3 8	0 0 0
Grinley	" Walker	0	0	0	0	0	0	0	0	0	0	11	0 0 0	0 0 0	0 0 0
Calver	" Buckley	0	3	1	0	0	0	0	0	0	0	32	0 9 7½	0 0 0	0 0 0
Chesterfield	" Allen	2	6	5	3	13	3	2	1	2	10	201	4 14 0	0 9 5	0 0 0
Bolsover	" Crich	2	3	5	3	0	0	0	0	7	8	46	0 13 7	0 5 0	0 0 0
Clay Cross	" Spooner	1	2	1	1	0	0	1	0	0	2	24	0 13 7½	0 0 0	0 0 0
Staveley	" Shepard	1	4	3	1	2	7	1	0	0	4	22	0 5 0	0 2 6	0 2 6
New Brinsley	" Birch	1	6	3	0	0	1	4	0	0	1	14	0 0 0	0 5 6	0 5 0
Eastwood	" J. Stones	1	2	2	1	2	1	2	1	0	3	51	0 6 9	0 8 0	0 8 6
Heanor	" W. Stones	5	9	4	3	2	3	6	0	0	10	27	0 0 0	0 4 6	0 4 0
Nottingham	" J. Wigley	1	2	1	0	0	1	3	1	0	36	212	6 3 7	1 16 0	0 16 0
Arnold	" H. Kirk	1	2	0	0	0	1	3	1	0	23	66	0 0 10	0 0 0	0 0 0
Calverton	" Hazzeldine	2	4	2	4	3	1	6	0	0	7	49	0 4 4	0 0 0	0 0 0
Mansfield	" M. Slack	0	1	1	1	2	7	1	0	0	16	135	4 0 0	0 15 6½	1 10 0
Sutton	Priest Wilson	0	0	0	0	7	1	0	0	10	38	0 0 0	0 4 1½	0 0 0
Scattered		0	0	0	0	0	0	0	0	0	0	21	0 0 0	0 0 0	0 0 0
Total		53	101	65	34	34	29	38	9	54	164	1789	29 9 4½	9 17 10	6 1 2

List of Sheffield area branches from the 23 December 1849 Conference Report.

The president of the Mormon's European mission, described as one of the twelve apostles, was Elder John Henry Smith. Accompanied by a number of other elders, Smith organised a conference at the Ellesmere Temperance Hall at Townhead Street[596] on Sunday, 7 December 1884 where he was to give an address. News of the conference gave Jarman the opportunity to go on the

---

[596] Ellesmere Temperance Hall was built by the Sheffield Temperance Association in 1867 at a cost of £2,500. Its large meeting room had a capacity of 2000

offensive and he arranged for around 500 of his supporters to disrupt the proceedings.

On gathering, Jarman led his supporters on a march through the town to the Temperance Hall where they invaded the meeting as Elder Smith rose to speak. Pandemonium broke loose as Jarman and his followers attempted to clear and take over the platform. They were met with resistance from the elders who were described in the press as, *all muscular men of unusual height and strength.*[597]

Two policemen in attendance attempted to put a stop to the fracas but reinforcements were required. Within a short time, a further contingency of Sheffield police arrived under Inspector Samuel Smith and Jarman's protestors were ejected through the front door and the platform was regained by the Mormon Elders.

Almost immediately the invaders returned through an unguarded side door and once more attacked the platform, this time from behind. A number of people were injured, including one of the Elders and a policeman who suffered *a nasty kick on the kneecap.*[598] After a prolonged struggle, Jarman's mob was driven out once more but the police failed to disperse them. They remained en masse and continued to shout their protests until a second conference was about to begin inside the Hall at around 6 o'clock in the evening.

Jarman's anti-Mormons once again attacked the Hall, this time in larger numbers whereupon Smith and the other Elders decided to abandon the event and were escorted to safety by the police. Following their success the anti-Mormons held a further mass gathering to celebrate their victory but there was no further trouble.

Following this incident, Elder John Henry Smith applied to the Chief Constable, John Jackson, for police protection of the Elders at any future Mormon meeting. In reply, John Jackson informed Smith that as the Temperance Hall was not licensed as a church or chapel he could not interfere unless there were further disturbances of the peace. It would appear that, for the moment, the Mormon elders gave up on Sheffield as later that same day, they left for their national base in Liverpool.[599]

---

[597] *The Times,* 8 December 1884. See also www.chrishobbs.com
[598] Ibid
[599] *Birmingham Daily Post,* Tuesday, 9 December 1884. See also www.chrishobbs.com

Conclusion

The notion of Sheffield in the 18th and 19th centuries being a hotbed of Radicalism is debatable. The evidence to support the argument is at best circumstantial, despite the propensity to riot. Whilst the governments of the day feared a repetition of the European political revolutions and in particular that which occurred in France in 1789, their fears of a British revolution were unfounded and the notion that Sheffield could be a seat of national insurrection was absurdly conceived.

Just how real this threat was considered by the State is also debatable but it did take what it considered appropriate precautions to respond should trouble arise; the building of military barracks in the provinces, as at Sheffield, was not for the protection of the people against external foes but for the protection of the State against internal insurrectionists, as were the use of spies and *agent provocateurs* to infiltrate them.

This was also reflected at the local level where magistrates acted on behalf of the State and enforced law and order with the same misconceived fears in their minds when people took to the streets in protest and rioted, perhaps with the exception of the anti-Methodist riots of the 1740s, when local magistrates appear to have turned a blind eye and at least one of their agents, the army captain, had actually joined the ranks of the mob, and the anti-Salvation Army and anti-Mormon riots of the 1880s, that clearly had no conceivable connection to conflict with the State but were reactions to religious interference in social norms, particularly with their approach to drinking, for many people a temporary release from a miserable existence and for some, the pub landlords and beer-house keepers, the means of a sustainable living.

However, the overthrow of the government and/or the abolition of the monarchy were never the prime motives behind any of the Sheffield riots during this period. The belief in some quarters of a Jacobin connection to the Methodists was also misconceived but undoubtedly there were Jacobins amongst them.

The nearest that any Sheffield people came to being revolutionary were the small number of plotters who shared the aspirations of the Pentrich rebels in 1817 and the physical force Chartists taking up arms in 1840, neither of whom had any conceivable chance of success.

In all of the occurrences of riot in Sheffield during this period, the causal factors were deprivation, injustice, inequality or unfairness, both real and perceived. Yet, in all except the anti-religion riots there was a political context. The coal riots and enclosure riots targeted the most powerful and influential of Sheffield men: the Dukes of Norfolk and, in the case of the Enclosure riots, also the magistrate and Vicar of Sheffield, Reverend James Wilkinson.

The Enclosure Acts that enlarged the estates of the rich and greatly affected, and were understandably resented by, the dispossessed poor, were legislated by successive national governments. The move came at a time of pent-up anger and resentment engendered by the recent injustices of the Establishment.

The same can be said to a degree of the Irish Riot of 1855 where recent oppression and famine in their homeland, from where they had fled, was an underlying factor behind the Irishmen's savage attack on the police. The election riot of 1832 was about the still grossly inequitable electoral system despite this (limited) political reform giving Sheffield its first MPs.

It also demonstrated the class division that the Act defined and fuelled the rise in Chartism; a precursor for the Chartist rising of 1840, which was about the struggle for further political reform and extending democracy. The recurring episodes of the lack of provisions and inflated food prices were also perceived to be at the hands of the ruling classes who, with the odd exception, didn't care about their impact on the necessitous poor.

The fact that the government consisted almost exclusively of large agricultural land-owners and country gentlemen who enacted laws to protect themselves was not lost on the common people, who had to bear the consequences. Even the resurrection riots had an indirect political dimension, in that those who ran the Medical School and the Workhouse which provided the bodies for its anatomy lessons were of the ruling class and represented the Establishment.

One overriding aspect of all of these riots and uprisings is that the protests had a class dimension: the poor/working classes on the one side, the wealthy, and especially the ruling elite, on the other. This is constant throughout our period and perhaps the clearest example was the Oldale riots, albeit a personal dispute over an inheritance, that ostensibly ended as a battle of the classes; the humble silversmith against the noble Earl. The latter was always going to be the winner.

Also, the wealthy, be they land-owners or, increasingly as we near the end of our period, industrial capitalists, invariably passed on their power and influence through the generations, thus preserving the ruling dynasties. This too wasn't lost on the townsfolk as we discern from the anonymous leaflet published in 1825 describing the administration of the town as a *Family Compact* or *Holy Alliance* of six to eight respectable families.

When we consider today's society, little has changed in this regard. The tendency to riot in modern Sheffield may have diminished but the people's inclination to protest and demonstrate is ever-present, including the odd occurrence of civil disobedience, which, as ever, is met with the law-enforcing arm of the State.

Epilogue

During my research for this book, particularly on the social and economic conditions of the period covered, it soon occurred to me that there are distinct parallels with the social and economic conditions of 18th century and 19th century Britain and the Britain of today (2020) and that relatively speaking little has changed in the social order.

Despite the establishment of a Labour political party that has governed the country during five parliaments (1924, 1945-51, 1964-70, 1974-9 and 1997-2010), and its creation of the welfare state following the Second World War, the fact that some people, many who are in work, are reliant on the charity of food-banks in 21st century Britain, acknowledged as the fifth most wealthy country in the world, is an indictment on the British political-economic system; food-banks are the equivalent of the 18th century poor relief and soup kitchens.

The present Tory government's claim of record numbers of people in work does not hide the fact that wages have stagnated and that the labour market is blighted with job-insecurity due to the pace of change in consumer markets in what has been termed the digital economy, and the growth of zero-hour contracts in the labour market.

And there are still over one million people registered unemployed and claiming benefits. Just as the industrial revolution impacted upon social conditions in the 18th and early 19th centuries, the digital revolution has adversely impacted upon those at the bottom of the economic ladder whilst bringing untold wealth to a few at the top. The government itself is made up of multi-millionaires who live on a different planet to the greater part of the population.

Capitalism is an economic system based on exploitation; the exploitation of labour and resources by the capitalist, be they industrial, commercial or digital. There is another distinct parallel with the industrial revolution of the late 18th and early 19th centuries and the digital revolution of the late 20th century continuing into the 21st century as the chief beneficiaries of both were/are the capitalists.

I remember well my first trade union conference in 1979, when I was a delegate to the biennial delegates' conference of the Transport & General Workers Union held in Scarborough. The debates on the UK economy centred on the then developing computerised information technology in industry and commerce.

Computerised systems would, it was argued, lead to considerable social benefits. Workers would benefit from higher pay, shorter working hours, long weekends, more holidays, better pensions and earlier retirement. Such aspirations were not to be realised. In reality, the gains made by this new technology were creamed off and continue to be creamed off by the capitalists and many workers are today relatively worse off than they were in 1979.

Unregulated capitalism engenders unregulated and extreme exploitation and we see the results of that in Britain today despite regulatory quangos that oversee some aspects of the free-market economy; an economy tainted by corporate and individual greed. We see the results daily on our digital TV screens and internet media.

Former publicly-owned industries and services that are essential to life and social well-being, such as water, gas, electricity, public transport, railways, post office and telecommunications, are now in the hands of the private sector and owned by companies, many of them foreign, with multi-millionaire owners squeezing ever more profit out of the service-users with inflated prices (e.g., utilities) and reduced services (e.g. public transport).

The National Health Service is being privatised by stealth as more private companies take over non-clinical services and private medical companies compete for the wealthy patients wishing to avoid waiting lists for treatment and operations. Meanwhile, the number of food-banks grows, real wages are driven down, homelessness and levels of personal debt grows and the void between the rich and the poor escalates to obscene levels.

The last time I visited the centre of Sheffield, I saw this reflected in the number of rough-sleepers sheltering in the doorways of vacant shops and offices. A recent survey reported that there are 320,000 homeless people in the UK, 6,000 of them in Yorkshire.

In 2018, 627 homeless people died on the streets with an average age of 44 for men and 42 for women; fifteen of them in Sheffield. Other recent surveys suggest that some 4 million workers are living in poverty, 1.5 million people are destitute and that one in three children live in poverty as the Tory government continues its social-economic policies of austerity and welfare reforms whilst offering tax-breaks to huge multinational companies whose sole objective is to amass even greater profits.

And even still, centuries later, indifference to the plight of the poor by the government, and contempt shown by a number of the ruling class who still believe they have a given right to rule, is evident; as in previous centuries there is a glaring disconnect between the government and the governed. Even a United Nations report on the level of poverty in Britain today stated that the British government was in denial of the adverse effects of their policies.

The workhouse may no longer be with us today, but there are a growing number of people who would be resorting to it if it was still around. However, poverty-linked ailments and diseases that were rife in the 19th century, such as scarlet fever and whooping cough are being increasingly treated today and hospital admissions for malnutrition have increased by 54% since 2010; the link between poverty and poor health is well documented.

Thankfully, today there are other ways to register our discontent than to riot and our right to peacefully protest is protected by law, although large-scale riots have continued to occur in British towns and cities in recent times, the most violent in the 1980s in the inner-city areas of Liverpool, Bristol and London, and in 1990 against the Tory Government's Poll Tax.

A further, race-related riot occurred in Brixton in 1995 and then there were the student-led riots in 2010. The last Mayor of London, now Tory Prime Minister Boris Johnson, thought it necessary to buy a number of water cannons to use against protestors; he clearly recognised that government policy was likely to provoke riot and he was equally prepared to subject the insurgents to physical injury to disperse them.

The people of Sheffield today are not slow to exercise their right to protest as we have seen recently with the opposition to the Sheffield City Council's policy to fell perfectly healthy mature trees to reduce highways maintenance costs. Yet, just as in earlier times, the powers that be, have seen fit to have some of the protestors arrested and brought before the courts. Little has changed. [600]

---

[600] Written before the Covid-19 pandemic of 2020

Appendix

Norfolk Street Riots
Joseph Mather

Corruption tells me homicide
Is wilful murder justified,
A striking precedent was tried
In August, 'ninety-five,
When arm'd assassins dressed in blue
Most wantonly their townsmen slew,
And magistrates and juries too
At murder did connive.

I saw the tragic scene commence;
A madman drank, without offence
Drew out his sword in false pretence,
And wounded some more wise;
Defenceless boys he chased about,
The timid cried, the bold did shout,
Which brought the curious no doubt
To see what meant the noise.

The gazing crowd stagnated stood
To see a wretch that should know good,
Insatiate thirst for human blood
Like one sent from beneath;
This gave me well to understand
A sword pat in a madman's hand,
Especially a villian grand,
Must terminate in death.

'Twas manifest in the event

That what the bloody tyrant meant
Was murder without precedent.
Though by injustice screened,
The 'Courant' may her columns swell,
Designing men may falsehoods tell,
Not all the powers of earth and hell
Can justify the fiend.

This arm'd banditti, filled with spleen,
At his command, like bloodhounds' keen,
In fine, to crown the horrid scene.
A shower of bullets fired.
The consequence was deep distress,
More widows, and more fatherless,
The devil blushed and did confess
'Twas more than *he* required.

Corruption cried for this exploit
"His worship shall be made a knight,
I hold his conduct just and right.
And think him all divine."
Oppression need not fear alarms,
Since tyranny has got such swarms,
Of gallant heroes bearing arms,
To butcher grunting swine.

The stones besmeared with blood and brains,
Was the result of Robin's pains,
Surviving friends wept o'er the stains,
When dying victims bled;
As Abel's blood aloud did call
To Him whose power created all,
Eternal vengeance sure must fall
Upon his guilty head.

Ye wanton coxcombs, fops, and fools,

Aristocratic dupes and tools,
Subject yourselves to better rules,
And cast away that badge.
Remember on a future day
Corruption must be done away,
Then what will you presume to say
When truth shall be your judge? [601]

---

[601] The song is included in a volume of Mather's Ballads and other contemporary songs that was published by John Wilson in July 1862. This has been re-published by Steven Kay and Jack Windle, in a book entitled *Seditious Things—The Songs of Joseph Mather—Sheffield's Georgian Punk Poet,* 1889 books, 2017. A CD of the same title that includes eight of Mather's songs, including *Norfolk Street Riots,* performed by Ray Hearne is also available from www.1889books.co.uk

Bibliography

Addy, John, *A Coal and Iron Community in the Industrial Revolution,* Longman, 1969

Addy, John, *The Agrarian Revolution,* Longmans, 1967

Addy, Sidney Oldall, *A Glossary of Words used in the Neighbourhood of Sheffield,* Trubner & Co, 1888

Bailey, Brian, *The Luddite Rebellion,* Sutton Publishing, 1998

Bailey, Brian, *The Resurrection Men—A History of the Trade in Corpses,* Macdonald & Co (Publishers) Ltd, 1991

Baines, Edward, *History, Directory & Gazetteer of the County of York,* published by Edward Baines at the Leeds Mercury Office, 1822

Baines, Thomas, *Yorkshire Past and Present Vol 1, Part 1 and Part 2,* William Mackenzie, 1870

Bean, J P, *The Sheffield Chronicles,* D&D Publications, 2008

Bentley, David, *The Sheffield Hanged 1750-1864*, ALD Design & Print, 2002

Bradbury, Frederick, *A History of Old Sheffield Plate,* Macmillan and Co Limited, 1912

Briggs, Asa (Ed), *Chartist Studies,* Macmillan & Co Ltd, 1970

Briggs, Asa, *The Age of Improvement 1783-1867,* Longmans, 1964

Briggs, Asa, *Victorian Cities,* Penguin Books, 1975

Brown, Richard and Daniels, Christopher, *The Chartists—Documents and Debates,* Macmillan Education, 1987

Browne, Harry, *Chartism,* Hodder & Stoughton, 2004

Bryant, Arthur, *The Years of Endurance 1793-1802,* The Reprint Society, 1944

Bryant, Arthur, *Years of Victory 1802-1812,* The Reprint Society, 1945

Bunyan, Tony, *The Political Police in Britain,* Julian Friedmann Publishers, 1976

Cannon, Richard, *Historical Record of The Eighteenth or The Royal Irish Regiment of Foot,* Parker, Furnivall & Parker, 1848

Chase, Malcolm, *Chartism—A New History,* Manchester University Press, 2007

Chesney, Kellow, *The Victorian Underworld,* Maurice Temple Smith, 1970

Clarke, Stephen Reynolds, *The New Yorkshire Gazetteer or Topographical Dictionary,* Henry Teesdale & Co, 1828

Coleman, Terry, *The Railway Navvies,* Penguin Books, 1976

Court, WHB, *A Concise Economic History of Britain—From 1750 To Recent Times,* Cambridge At The University Press, 1958

Crossley, David (Ed) with Cass, Jean; Flavell, Neville; and Turner, Colin, *Water Power on the Sheffield Rivers,* Sheffield Trades Historical Society and University of Sheffield, Division of Continuing Education joint publication, 1989

Davison Ingledew, CJ, *The Ballads and Songs of Yorkshire,* Bell and Daldy, 1860

Derry, John, *The Story of Sheffield*, S R Publishers Ltd, London, 1981

Disraeli, Benjamin, *Sybil, or The Two Nations,* Wordsworth Editions Limited, 1995

Drewry, Mick, *Intimidation—The History, The Times And The People Of The Sheffield Outrages,* Austin Macauley Publishers, 2017

Drewry, Mick, *Inundation—The History, the Times and the People of the Great Sheffield Flood of 1864,* Youbooks.co.uk, 2014

Drewry, Mick (Ed), *The Complete Hillsborough By Her People,* Hillsborough Community Development Trust, 2006

Drinkall, Margaret, *Sheffield Workhouse,* The History Press, 2011

Dyos, HJ and Wolff, Michael (Eds), *The Victorian City-Images and Realities Volume. 1,* Routledge & Kegan Paul, 1976

Dyos, HJ, and Wolff, Michael (Eds), *The Victorian City-Images and Realities Volume 2,* Routledge & Kegan Paul, 1973

Engels, Friedrich, *The Condition Of The Working Class In England,* Penguin Books, 1987

Evans, Eric J, *The Forging of the Modern State—Early Industrial Britain 1783-1870,* Longman, 1996

Finn, Joe, *Chartists and Chartism,* Hodder & Stoughton, 1992

Fletcher, J.S., *The Making of Modern Yorkshire 1750-1914,* George Allen & Unwin Ltd, 1917

Fraser, Antonia, *Perilous Question—Reform or Revolution? Britain on the Brink, 1832,* Public Affairs, 2013

Grainge, William, *Yorkshire Longevity,* Thomas Thorpe, 1864

Gretton, RH, *A Modern History of the English People 1880-1898,* Grant Richards Ltd, 1913

Hall, T Walter, *A Catalogue of the Ancient Charters,* J W Northend, 1913

Hammond, J.L. and Hammond, Barbara, *The Skilled Labourer 1760-1832,* Alan Sutton Publishing Limited, 1995

Hammond, JL and Hammond, Barbara, *The Town Labourer 1760-1832—The New Civilisation,* Alan Sutton Publishing Limited, 1995

Harvie, Christopher, Martin, Graham and Scharf, Aaron (Eds), *Industrialisation & Culture 1830-1914,* The Open University Press, 1970

Hibbert, Christopher, *The English—A Social History 1066-1945,* Book Club Associates, 1987

Hill, C P, *British Economic and Social History 1700-1975,* Edward Arnold, 1981

Hobsbawm, EJ, *Industry and Empire,* Penguin Books, 1975

Hobsbawm, Eric, *The Age Of Revolution 1789-1848,* Weidenfeld & Nicolson, 1995

Hobsbawm, Eric, *The Age Of Capital 1848-1875,* Weidenfeld & Nicolson, 1995

Hobsbawm, Eric, *The Age Of Empire 1875-1914,* Weidenfeld & Nicolson, 1995

Hoggart, Richard, *The Uses of Literacy,* Penguin Books, 1962

Hunt, Tristram, *Building Jerusalem—The Rise and Fall of the Victorian City,* Phoenix, 2005

Hunter, Joseph, *Hallamshire—The History and topography of the Parish of Sheffield,* Lackington, Hughes, Harding, Mavor and Jones, 1819

Howard, John, *State of the Prisons,* 1777

Jones, Melvyn (Ed.), *Aspects of Sheffield 2,* Wharncliffe Publishing Limited, 1999

Kay, Steven, and Windle, Jack, *Seditious Things—The Songs of Joseph Mather—Sheffield's Georgian Punk Poet,* 1889books, 2017

Knipe, William, *Criminal Chronology of York Castle,* C.L. Burdekin, 1867

Leader, John Daniel, *Records of the Burgery of Sheffield,* Sheffield Independent Press Limited, 1897

Leader, Robert Eadon (Ed), *Reminiscences of Old Sheffield, its Streets and its People,* Leader and Sons Independent Office, 1876

Leader, Robert Eadon, *Sheffield in the Eighteenth Century,* The Sheffield Independent Press, 1901

Lecky, William Edward Hartpole, *England in the Eighteenth Century, Vol III,* Longmans Green and Co, 1892

Lee, Andrew, *The Red Flag of Anarchy—A History of Socialism & Anarchism in Sheffield 1874-1900,* Pirate Press Sheffield, 2017

Machan, Peter, *Sheffield's Time Trail: True Tales From The Norfolk Heritage Trail,* Green Estate Ltd, 2004

Mayhall, John, *The Annals of Yorkshire Vol. 1 and Vol. II,* Joseph Johnson, 1865

O'Grada, Carmac, *Ireland—A New Economic History 1780-1939,* Clarendon Press, 1995

Parker, John, *Chapters in the Political History of Sheffield, 1832-1849,* Leader and Sons, Sheffield, 1884

Paulus, Carolus, *Some Forgotten Facts in the History of Sheffield and District,* Sheffield Independent Press, 1907

Price, David, *Sheffield Troublemakers—Rebels and Radicals in Sheffield History,* Phillimore & Co Ltd, 2012

Redford, Arthur, *The Economic History of England 1760-1860,* Longmans, 1960

Roberts, Stephen (Ed.), *The People's Charter—Democratic Agitation in Early Victorian Britain,* The Merlin Press, 2003

Seed, Rev. T Alexander, *Norfolk Street Wesleyan Chapel, Sheffield,* Jarrold & Sons, 1907

Skelley, Jeffrey (Ed), *The General Strike, 1926,* Lawrence and Wishart, 1976

Smith, William (Ed), *Old Yorkshire—Vol. 5,* Longmans, Green & Co, 1884

Stevens, John, *England's Last Revolution—Pentrich 1817,* Moorland Publishing Company, 1977

Stokes, John, *The History of the Cholera Epidemic of 1832 in Sheffield,* J W Northend Ltd, 1921

Taylor, John (Ed), *The Illustrated Guide to Sheffield,* Pawson and Brailsford, Sheffield, 1879

Taylor, Rev. R.V., *Yorkshire Anecdotes,* Whittaker & Co, 1883

The Local Register and Chronological Account of Occurrences and Facts Connected with the Town and Neighbourhood of Sheffield, Robert Leader at the Office of the Sheffield Independent, 1830 (Continued to 1857)

Thompson, Dorothy, *The Chartists—Popular Politics in the Industrial Revolution,* Pantheon Books, New York, 1984

Thompson, E.P., *The Making of the English Working Class,* Pelican Books, 1968

Thompson, F.M.L., *The Rise of Respectable Society—A Social History of Victorian Britain, 1830-1900,* Fontana Press, 1988

Vickers, J Edward, *A Popular History of Sheffield,* Applebaum, 1987

Walton, Mary, *Sheffield—Its Story and its Achievements*, The Sheffield Telegraph & Star Limited, 1948

Watson, J Steven, *The Reign of George III 1760-1815,* Oxford at the Clarendon Press, 1992

Webb, Sidney and Beatrice, *The History of Trade Unionism,* Longmans, Green and Co, 1896

White, William, *History, Gazetteer and Directory of the West-Riding of Yorkshire Vol. I,* Robert Leader, Independent Office, Sheffield, 1837

Woodward, Sir Llewellyn, *The Oxford History of England—The Age of Reform 1815-1870,* Oxford University Press, 1962

Other Publications:

Birmingham Daily Post, 6 June 1862 and 16 August 1875

Criminal Chronology of York Castle, published by C L Burdekin, 1867

History Today, Vol.68, Issue 8. August 2018; *Issue 9,* September 2018; *Issue 10,* October 2018; *Vol.69, Issue 1,* January 2019 and *Issue 5,* May 2019

Independent, 15 December 1832

Leeds Mercury, April 1812, 26 June 1875

London Gazette, 27 September 1864, 6 December 1872 and 19 June 1874

London Morning Chronicle, Saturday 29 October 1855 and 27 March 1858

London Guardian, 2 January 1889

www.millhousespark.co.uk

www.nationalarchives.gov.uk/currency-converter

Northern Star, 21 March 1840

www.parliament.uk/livingheritage

Railway World Special: The Woodhead Route, 1986

Reading Mercury, 17 August 1795, Vol. XXXIV, issue 1752

Report of the Sheffield Conference of the Church of Jesus Christ of Latter-Day Saints, 23 December 1849, and *Sheffield Quarterly Conference,* 19 May 1850

Robson's Birmingham and Sheffield Directory, 1839

Samuel Holberry (1814-42) Sheffield's Revolutionary Democrat, pamphlet produced by the Holberry Society, c1978

Sheffield Mercury, 15 Dec 1832

The Concise Dictionary of National Biography—Vol. I A-F, Vol. II G-M and Vol. III N-Z, Oxford University Press, 1994

The Courant, 22 August 1795

The Illustrated Police Gazette, 18 January 1882

The Lancet Vol.II, 1848

The Masque of Anarchy—A Poem By Percy Bysshe Shelley, Leigh Hunt, 1832

The Poll Book of the Borough of Sheffield, December 13 and 14 1832, A Whitaker and Co, Iris Office, 1833

The Sheffield Daily Telegraph, 25 July 1855, 2 August 1855 and 13 December 1855

The Times, 10 and 24 June 1862

Transactions of The Hunter Archaeological Society Vol. IX, 1967

White's *History and Directory of the Borough of Sheffield,* 1833 and 1871-2

War Cry, 26 December 1891

Other Sources:

www.bbc.co.uk/legacies/immig_emig/england/south_yorkshire/article_3.shtml

BritishPoliceHistory.uk

Church History Review website: https://lexloiz.wordpress.com/2017/10/23/the-skeleton-army/

www.chrishobbs.com

Priories Historical Society website

Lewis, Catherine, *Samuel Holberry: Chartist Conspirator or Victim of a State Conspiracy?,* in SOLON Crimes and Misdemeanours—Vol.3, No.1, March 2009, www.pearl.plymouth.ac.uk

The Victorian Web

www.voicesofconflict.wordpress.com

www.wardsendcemetery.wordpress.com